Real Scientists
Real Faith

Edited by R. J. Berry

MONARCH
BOOKS

Oxford, UK & Grand Rapids, Michigan, USA

First published in the UK in 2009 by Monarch Books
(a publishing imprint of Lion Hudson plc),
Wilkinson House, Jordan Hill Road, Oxford OX2 8DR.
Tel: +44 (0)1865 302750 Fax: +44 (0)1865 302757
Email: monarch@lionhudson.com
www.lionhudson.com

ISBN: 978-1-85424-884-8 (UK)
ISBN: 978-0-8254-6289-4 (USA)

Distributed by:
UK: Marston Book Services Ltd, PO Box 269, Abingdon, Oxon OX14 4YN;
USA: Kregel Publications, PO Box 2607, Grand Rapids, Michigan 49501

Unless otherwise stated, Scripture quotations are taken from the Holy Bible, New International Version, © 1973, 1978, 1984 by the International Bible Society. Used by permission of Hodder & Stoughton Ltd. All rights reserved.

This book has been printed on paper and board independently certified as having come from sustainable forests.

British Library Cataloguing Data
A catalogue record for this book is available from the British Library.

Printed and bound in England by CPI Cox & Wyman.

Contents

Foreword

I Believe in God, Maker of Heaven and Earth

R. J. Berry

R. J. (Sam) Berry, born 1934. Educated at Kirkham Grammar
School, Shrewsbury School, Cambridge University and
University College London. Fellow of the Royal Society of
Edinburgh and the Institute of Biology. Professor of Genetics
at University College London, (1978–2000). President of the
Linnean Society (1982–85), the British Ecological Society
(1987–89), the European Ecological Federation (1990–92), the
Mammal Society (1995–97), Christians in Science (1993–95).
Author of *Adam and the Ape* (1975), *Inheritance and Natural
History* (1977), *God and the Biologist* (1996), *Science, Life and
Christian Belief* (1998, with Malcolm Jeeves), *God's Book of Works*
(2003), *Natural History of Islands* (2009); editor of *Real Science,
Real Faith* (1991), *Environmental Dilemmas* (1993), *The Care of
Creation* (2000), *Environmental Stewardship* (2006), *When Enough
Is Enough* (2007); etc.

Sometime in the late 1980s, a Christian publisher asked me to
write a textbook on science and religion. I replied that I did not
know enough to give a rounded view of the subject, but that I
knew quite a number of scientists who were Christians and I
could ask them to write down their stories. The result was *Real
Science, Real Faith*, published in 1991, with sixteen contributions
from scientists from a range of disciplines. The book was well
received; it was reprinted and is now available electronically.
Clearly, many people found the experiences of Christians who

had succeeded in science both encouraging and stimulating, and it has seemed worthwhile to produce another collection along the same lines. The Christian publisher who approached me more than twenty years ago was Tony Collins. I am grateful to him and to Monarch for their support for both the original and this second offering.

The criterion for invitations to contribute in this volume was the same as in the earlier book: senior scientists from a variety of disciplines with a firm Christian faith. The reason for confining the contributions to senior scientists was because they can uniquely illustrate some of the problems and dilemmas – both intellectual and moral – experienced during a lifetime's career. Most of the authors are from Britain; Joan Centrella, Francis Collins, David Myers and Cal DeWitt are from the United States; and Gareth Jones is from New Zealand. Emphases may be different in different parts of the world, but the challenges are essentially the same everywhere – science knows neither political nor language boundaries. Women are grossly under-represented – but women are, sadly, few in the higher reaches of science.

No one declined my invitation to write. The only instruction I gave was to ask each contributor to write how their faith affected their science and how their science affected their faith. Each was free to describe their personal experiences, the ways they have dealt with problems, or to reflect on their life as Christians in a scientific world. Many of the writers describe how they had to face up to reinterpreting their understanding of God or the Bible; none of them have had to compromise their beliefs because of their science. All the chapters have been written specially for this book, with the exception of Donald MacKay's, which was originally delivered as a Riddell Lecture at the University of Newcastle, and is reprinted with permission. Francis Collins's contribution is an edited and revised version of an interview with Denis Alexander (author of Chapter 2) published in the June 2008 number of the magazine *Third Way*.

Because the remit I gave to the contributors was very broad, their responses are very different, but all agree without reservation that any conflict between science and faith can be resolved if one is prepared to examine the roots of the conflict and is honest and courageous enough to change any understanding that is faulty. Francis Collins makes this point explicitly. Embarrassed by a patient who asked him what he believed, he 'was forced to accept that outside a few little dabblings here and there, I'd never really tried to understand what was the foundation upon which believers rest their faith.' Andy Gosler, brought up as a Jew, was forced to examine the philosophical roots of his faith as a reaction to the utilitarianism of Richard Dawkins. Alister McGrath began exploring through realizing that there are limits to scientific explanation. Wilson Poon was forced out of an entrenched creationism through reflecting on how science actually progresses – which is not through rejecting a theoretical framework at the first sign of difficulties. Joan Centrella writes about 'science and faith being stridently proclaimed as antagonists by people on all sides', although conflicts of another kind were more important to her: she renounced her faith because of her church's attitude to women and only returned after fifteen years because of problems in her personal life that she could not handle on her own.

In terms of their religious backgrounds and denominational allegiances, the eighteen contributors to this book are probably as diverse as any group of Christians in the sort of places where science is practised, but all claim to have examined the reasons to believe in the Christian faith and have decided both that belief is intellectually superior to non-belief and also that it is important – it works in real life. As the title has it, here are *real scientists* who have a *real faith*. Are they odd? Soon after the original *Real Science, Real Faith* was published, another collection of essays (*Can Scientists Believe?*) appeared, edited by Nevill Mott, a Nobel Prize-winner. He wrote to me that he found *Real Science, Real Faith* 'rather depressing' because of its inference that 'a Christian is necessarily one who looks to the Bible'. I found this an interesting but surprising response, because a scientist (almost by definition) is a person who seeks to use *all* the relevant evidence in his or her reasoning – and has to be ruthless in assessing the evidence. I suspect a similar attitude to the Bible may be true of the authors in this volume. Notwithstanding, we need to recognize this is a secondary issue: the important thing – as a number of contributors herein make explicit – is not Bible belief *sensu stricto*, but one's reaction to Jesus as the Christ. Such commitment to the Christ has implications in many areas of life, but our attitude to the Bible is subsidiary and subordinate to acknowledging Jesus as Lord and Saviour.

This acknowledgment is, of course, the core of Christianity. The tragedy is that some people make additional beliefs a requirement for salvation – most obviously, in the context of science and faith, a denial that evolution has happened – or ignore the implications of the fact that God is Creator as well as Redeemer. This God calls us to study and rejoice in his work (as Andrew Briggs reminds us, 'Great are the works of the Lord, studied by all who delight in them' – the research scientists' text, Psalm 111:2). There is a long-standing tradition in Christianity that God wrote a Book of Works (Creation) as well as a Book of Words (the Bible). The two Books are clearly distinguished in Psalm 19, verses 1–6 and 7–13. On the title page of the *Origin of Species*, Darwin quoted (presumably with approval) from Francis Bacon's *Advancement of Learning* (1605): 'Let no man think or maintain that anyone can search too far or be too well studied in the book of God's words or in the book of God's works; rather let all endeavour an endless progress or proficience in both.' We ignore either book at our peril. As Derek Kidner pointed out in his Tyndale Commentary on Genesis, 'It was Galileo's telescope that conclusively refuted the interpretation of Psalm 96:10 ['The world is fixed immovably'] as a proof-text against the earth's rotation.'

The media loves conflict. It makes for good reading or viewing. But we must not get carried away. Time after time the infamous debate between the Bishop of Oxford, Samuel Wilberforce, and Thomas Huxley at the 1860 meeting of the British Association for the Advancement of Science is recycled to show that faith and science cannot co-exist. But the 1860 debate was not really about evolution *versus* creation or even science *versus* religion. On the Bishop's side it was about the danger of legitimizing change in an age when he believed it was having dangerous social and theological effects; Huxley's aim was the secularization of society – to establish the legitimacy of science against what he regarded as the improper influence of church leaders. Wilberforce reportedly went away happy that he had given Huxley a bloody nose, while Joseph Hooker (who spoke after Huxley) told Darwin that Huxley had been largely inaudible. As far as the audience was concerned, many scored it as an entertaining draw (Brooke, 2001). The tragedy has been a regularly stoked legacy of inevitable conflict between science and faith, encouraged by Huxley himself and fuelled by two much-read manifestos by John William Draper (*History of the Conflict between Religion and Science*, 1875) and Andrew Dickson White (*A History of the Warfare of Science with Theology in Christendom*, 1886).

Once we get away from the obsession with an inevitable conflict in the faith–science area, we begin to realize that thinking sensibly about the issue can contribute positively to maturity by enabling the development of a mutually supportive framework of both faith and science, producing a robust theology of nature[1] as opposed to raking over the coals of old disagreements. Such a theology involves:

- An unapologetic and unyielding acceptance of a God who is outside creation and yet who has created and in some way oversees his work (Psalm 104:27–30; Colossians 1:17; Hebrews 1:3) – 'Even the wind and the sea obey him' (Matthew 8:27). God is both transcendent and immanent.

- A belief that the natural (or scientific) and the religious accounts of the world are incapable of conflicting; any apparent differences may result from imperfect scientific understanding or wrong exegesis.

- As full as possible understanding of the world. Scientific interpretations may be provisional, but they are based on the way things are. It is distorting and ultimately self-defeating to try to temper scientific knowledge because of theological or philosophical doctrine.

- A sense of awe and wonder. Creation is God's work, but at

the same time we must remember that Adam was placed in a garden 'to till it and look after it', not to preserve it in a pristine condition.

We are told that God saw all that he had made and declared it to be 'very good' (Genesis 1:31). It would be misleading to equate this state with perfection. God judged his creation as fit for his purposes, a fitness which allowed for change. We have to acknowledge that change is an inevitable part of God's plan for our history and destiny: we began in a garden, we are headed for a city; the Israelites moved from a wilderness into a Promised Land; the first Adam has been replaced by a more glorious second Adam. The world is not the same as it was at its beginning: there were once dinosaurs, now there are none; for most of the earth's history, there have been no humans. The study of the natural world is science. All science is provisional. Interpretations change. Some of the science represented in the following pages will fade into history; some will be a building-block for future advances.

I disagree with a number of the authors in this book on some issues they discuss. I may be wrong; they may be wrong. We must never assume that science is giving us a final picture. Always we must test our interpretations against new discoveries and new hypotheses. Only God is unchanging. He has given us his word – Christ the living Word, and the Bible, the written word. And we must take care not to assume that our understanding of the word is the same as its reality. As Gareth Jones says of Donald MacKay (p. 62):

> He rejected loose thinking to bolster viewpoints put forward as Christian ones. From time to time this got him into trouble with those who felt he was rejecting enshrined Christian truths. For MacKay this could never be the case, since his love of the truth shone through in everything he said and wrote. But he was not prepared to accept positions simply because they were put forward as being Christian. For him, if anything truly was Christian it could be argued

for and supported from Scripture. He also cautioned about arguing too strongly from the silence of Scripture. But this was part of his incisiveness, and of his longing to be true to what Scripture has to say, rather than to what we think it should be saying.

The following chapters are all written by leading scientists. Try to understand their struggles and the ways they resolved their dilemmas. Disagree if you like, but seek to discover the mind of Christ in the debates. This may mean 'thinking outside the box'.

In my student days, I had pinned above my desk the concluding words of the book of Ecclesiastes: 'Of making many books there is no end; much study is a weariness of the flesh.' I suspect many students feel the same. It was only much later that I realized that the author of Ecclesiastes (expositors call him – or her – Qoheleth) was an experimental scientist (many centuries before the word 'scientist' was invented). Ecclesiastes can (and perhaps should) be read as a sort of laboratory record of a series of investigations. Where a mathematician writes 'QED' at the end of a proof, Qoheleth wrote 'futility' or 'vanity'. For him, 'God is utterly present and at the same time utterly absent. God is "present" in every event and yet no event is a "place of encounter" with God, since humans do not understand what his will is' (Murphy, 1992: lxix). The Christian can – and should – have a similar attitude. To know the mechanism behind an event does not exclude God as the ultimate agent. It is a philosophical bloomer of the first water to assume that only one explanation is possible.

In an orgy of experimenting with different attitudes and behaviours, Qoheleth travelled a long way to his version of the last things. His experimenting matured his thinking. It was only then that he could write, 'Fear God and obey his commandments; this sums up the whole duty of mankind' (Ecclesiastes 12:13). Our challenge is to journey to the same place.

NOTE

1. Distinguish the 'theology of nature' from 'natural theology'. The latter seeks to argue from natural phenomena to God – see Alister McGrath, 2008, *The Open Secret. A New Vision for Natural Theology*, Oxford: Blackwell.

CHAPTER 1

Science, Faith and Making Sense of Things

Alister McGrath

Alister McGrath was born in Belfast and was a convinced atheist until going to university. He read Chemistry at the University of Oxford and earned a DPhil in Biochemistry before switching to theology and subsequently the award of a Doctorate in Divinity. From 1995 to 2005, he was Principal of Wycliffe Hall in the University of Oxford; in 2008 he moved from a Chair in Historical Theology in the University of Oxford to a Professorship in Theology, Ministry and Education at King's College London. He has written widely on the relationship between science and the Christian faith, including two widely read critiques of the ideas of Richard Dawkins (*Dawkins' God*, 2005 and *The Dawkins Delusion*, 2007); his most recent book is *The Open Secret: a New Vision for Natural Theology*, (2008).

'Real scientists do not believe in God!' This soundbite will be depressingly familiar to those who have struggled through the endless digressions, exaggerations and misunderstandings found in Richard Dawkins' *God Delusion* (2006). It is a viewpoint that can only be sustained by the relentless use of selective attention and turbocharged shock-and-awe rhetoric, rather than evidence-based argument. Yet it is a view that many in Western culture seem prepared to accept as the wisdom of our age. As Karl Marx once pointed out, the constant repetition of something that is fundamentally untrue creates the impression that it is trustworthy and reliable.

Dawkins seems to regard the intrinsic atheism of the natural sciences as self-evidently true to all except those who are congenital idiots, or whose minds have been warped and infested by the debilitating notion that there exists a God who might be interested in us and our well-being. Perhaps this may help us understand his anger, intolerance and arrogance at the persistence – some would say resurgence – of belief in God, when the secularizing prophets of the late 1960s and early 1970s foretold its inevitable death.

Dawkins is modest in the provision of autobiographical detail. However, if I have understood his account of his own conversion to atheism, the pivotal element of the process was a growing belief that Darwinism offered a far superior account of the nature of the world than anything based on an appeal to God. Dawkins' discovery of Darwinism began during his time as a student at Oundle School, and was consolidated during his study of zoology at Oxford University. The natural sciences thus acted as a catalyst for his deconversion from what appears to have been a somewhat anaemic form of nominal Anglicanism.

Now, all of us are prone to see our own personal histories as somehow disclosing a broader pattern of things, or the deep structure of reality. Beliefs that we personally find to be compelling must be so for all. Unsurprisingly, those who don't fit the pattern are seen as dangerous. They tend to get dismissed as oddballs, idiots, or psychotics. Why? Precisely because they are a threat to the credibility of the simplistic creed they refuse to accept. For what Dawkins regards as a universal, normative pattern is nothing more than one possible intellectual option among several, each of which have found their supporters over the years. In this essay, I shall tell my own story, and leave it for my readers to decide whether it has wider significance.

My love affair with the natural sciences began when I was nine or ten. I was overwhelmed with the beauty of the night sky, and longed to explore it further. I ransacked my school library for books on astronomy, and even managed to build myself a small telescope to enable me to observe the moons of Jupiter. Around the same time, a great-uncle who had headed up the pathology department at the Royal Victoria Hospital, Belfast, gave me an old German microscope, which allowed me to explore another new world. It still sits on my study desk, a reminder of the power of nature to enthral, intrigue, and provoke questions.

One of those questions troubled me greatly. While in my teens, I had absorbed an uncritical atheism from writers such as Bertrand Russell. Atheism was, I believed, the natural resting-place for a scientifically informed person, such as myself. The natural sciences had expanded to inhabit the intellectual space once occupied by the derelict idea of God. There was no need to propose, let alone take seriously, such an outmoded idea. God was a baleful relic of the past, revealed as a delusion by scientific advance.

So what was life all about? What was its meaning? As I reflected on the scope and power of the sciences, I gradually came to the view that there was no meaning to life. I was the accidental by-product of blind cosmic forces, the inhabitant of a universe in which one could speak only of direction but not purpose. It was not a particularly appealing idea, but I found solace in the idea that its bleakness and austerity were certain indications of its truth. It was so unattractive that it just had to be right. I must confess to a certain degree of smugness at this point, and a feeling of intellectual superiority over those who found solace and satisfaction in their belief in God.

Yet questions remained. As I continued to examine the night sky, I found its silence disturbing. I used to enjoy looking through my small telescope at M31, a famous nebula in the constellation of Andromeda which is bright enough to be seen by the naked eye. I knew that it was so distant that the light now leaving the nebula would take 2 million years to reach earth. By that time, I would have died. The night sky thus became a sombre symbol of the troubling brevity of human life. What was the point of it? Tennyson's lines from 'The Brook' seemed to sum up the human situation:

> For men may come and men may go,
> But I go on for ever.

However, I remained obstinately convinced that the severity and dreariness of this position were confirmations of its truth. It was axiomatic that science demanded atheism, and I was willing to be led wherever science took me.

And so I continued working at mathematics, physics and chemistry, eventually winning a scholarship to Oxford University to study chemistry. At that stage, most people gained admission to Oxford in the seventh term of the sixth form. I learned that I had won a scholarship to Oxford in December 1970, but was not due to begin my studies until October 1971. What was I to do in between? Most of my friends left school in order to travel or earn some money. I decided to stay on, and use the time to learn German and Russian, both of which would be useful for my scientific studies. Having specialized in the physical sciences, I was also aware of the need to deepen my knowledge of biology. I therefore settled down to begin an extended period of reading and reflection.

After a month or so of intensive reading in the school science library, having exhausted the works on biology, I came across a section that I had never noticed before. It was labelled 'The History and Philosophy of Science', and was heavy with dust. I had little time for this sort of stuff, tending to regard it as uninformed criticism of the certainties and simplicities of the natural sciences by those who felt threatened by them. Philosophy, like theology, was just pointless speculation about issues that could be solved through a few decent experiments. What was the point? Yet by the time I had finished reading the somewhat meagre holdings of the school in this field, I realized that I needed to do some very serious rethinking. Far from being half-witted obscurantism that placed unnecessary obstacles in the relentless pace of scientific advance, the history and philosophy of science asked all the right questions about the reliability and limits of scientific knowledge. And they were questions that I had not faced thus far. The under-determination of theory by data, radical theory change in the history of science, the difficulties in devising a 'crucial experiment', and the enormously complex issues associated with devising what was the 'best explanation' of a given set of observations – questions such as these crowded in on me, muddying what I had taken to be the clear, still, and above all *simple* waters of scientific truth.

Things turned out to be rather more complicated than I had realized. My eyes had been opened, and I knew there was no going back to the simplistic take on the sciences I had once known and enjoyed. I had enjoyed the beauty and innocence of a childlike attitude to the sciences, and secretly wished to remain in that secure place. Indeed, I think that part of me deeply wished that I had never picked up that book, never asked those awkward questions, and never questioned the simplicities of my scientific youth. But there was no going back. I had stepped through a door, and could not escape the new world I now inhabited.

By the time I arrived in Oxford in October 1971, I had realized that I had a lot of rethinking to do. Up to that point, I had assumed that, when science could not answer a question, there was no answer to be had. I now began to realize that there might be limits to the scientific method, and that vast expanses of intellectual, aesthetic and moral territory might lie beyond its compass. I would later find this idea expressed by Peter Medawar, in his excellent *Limits of Science* (1984). Emphasizing that 'science is incomparably the most successful enterprise human beings have ever engaged upon', Medawar distinguished between what he termed 'transcendent' questions, which are better left to religion and metaphysics, and scientific questions about the organization and structure of the material universe. With regard to these latter, he argued, there are no limits to the possibilities of scientific achievement. So what about the question of God? Or of whether there is purpose within the universe? Medawar was clear: science cannot answer such questions, even though there may be answers to be found:

> That there is indeed a limit upon science is made very likely by the existence of questions that science cannot answer, and that no conceivable advance of science would empower it to answer... I have in mind such questions as:
> How did everything begin?
> What are we all here for?
> What is the point of living?'

I could no longer hold on to what I now realize was a somewhat naïve scientific positivism; it became clear to me that a whole series of questions that I had dismissed as meaningless or pointless had to be examined again – including the God-question.

Having set to one side my rather dogmatic belief that science necessarily entailed atheism, I began to realize that the natural world is conceptually malleable. Nature can be interpreted, without any loss of intellectual integrity, in a number of different ways. Some 'read' or 'interpret' nature in an atheistic way. Others 'read' it in a deistic way, seeing it as pointing to a creator divinity, who is no longer involved in its affairs. God winds up the clock, then leaves it to work on its own. Others take a more specifically Christian view, believing in a God who both creates and sustains. One can be a 'real' scientist without being committed to any specific religious, spiritual or anti-religious view of the world. This, I may add, is the view of most scientists I speak to, including those who self-define as atheists. Unlike their more dogmatic atheist colleagues, they can understand perfectly well why some of their colleagues adopt a Christian view of the world. They may not agree with that approach, but they're prepared to respect it.

Stephen Jay Gould – whose sad death from cancer in 2002 robbed Harvard University of one of its most stimulating teachers, and a popular scientific readership of one of its most accessible writers – was absolutely clear on this point (Gould, 1999). The natural sciences – including evolutionary theory – were consistent with both atheism and conventional religious belief. Unless half his scientific colleagues were total fools – a presumption that Gould rightly dismissed as nonsense, whichever half it is applied to – there could be no other responsible way of making sense of the varied responses to reality on the part of the intelligent, informed, people that he knew.

The real problem is that, since the scientific method clearly does not entail atheism, those who wish to use science in defence of atheism are obliged to smuggle in a series of non-empirical metaphysical ideas to their accounts of science, and hope that nobody notices this intellectual sleight of hand. Dawkins is a master of this art. In his superb recent study *The Music of Life* (2006), the Oxford systems biologist Denis Noble took a passage from Dawkins's *The Selfish Gene* (1976), and rewrote it, retaining what was empirically verifiable, and inverting Dawkins' somewhat questionable metaphysical assumptions. The result dramatically illustrates the ease with which non-empirical assumptions can be imported into scientific thinking.

First, consider Dawkins' original passage, which sets out a gene-centred approach to evolutionary biology, which was then gaining the ascendancy. Note how agency is attributed to genes, which are portrayed as actively controlling their destiny. I have italicized what is empirically verifiable:

> [Genes] swarm in huge colonies, safe inside gigantic lumbering robots, sealed off from the outside world, communicating with it by tortuous indirect routes, manipulating it by remote control. *They are in you and me*; they created us, body and mind; and their preservation is the ultimate rationale for our existence.

In rewriting this, Noble moves away from any idea that genes can be thought of as active agents. Once more, I have italicized what is empirically verifiable:

> [Genes] are trapped in huge colonies, locked inside highly intelligent beings, moulded by the outside world, communicating with it by complex processes, through which, blindly, as if by magic, function emerges. *They are in you and me*; we are the system that allows their code to be read; and their preservation is totally dependent on the joy that we experience in reproducing ourselves. We are the ultimate rationale for their existence.

Dawkins and Noble see things in completely different ways. (I recommend reading both statements slowly and carefully to appreciate their differences.) They both cannot be right. Both smuggle in a series of quite different values and beliefs. Yet their statements are 'empirically equivalent'. In other words, they both have equally good grounding in observation and experimental evidence. So which is right? Which is the more scientific? How could we decide which is to be preferred on scientific grounds? As Noble observes – and Dawkins concurs – 'no-one seems to be able to think of an experiment that would detect an empirical difference between them.'

Let me return to explaining my own change of mind on the relation of science and faith. Having realized that a love of science allowed much greater freedom of interpretation of reality than I had been led to believe, I began to explore alternative ways of looking at it. While I had been severely critical of Christianity as a young man, I had never extended that same critical evaluation to atheism, tending to assume that it was self-evidently correct, and was hence exempt from being assessed in this way. During October and November 1971, I began to discover that the intellectual case for atheism was rather less substantial than I had supposed. Far from being self-evidently true, it seemed to rest on rather shaky foundations. Christianity, on the other hand, turned out to be far more robust intellectually than I had supposed.

My doubts about the intellectual foundations of atheism began to coalesce into a realization that atheism was actually a belief system, whereas I had somewhat naively and uncritically assumed that it was a factual statement about reality. I also discovered that I knew far less about Christianity than I had assumed. It gradually became clear to me that I had rejected a religious stereotype. I had some major rethinking to do. By the end of November 1971, I had made my decision: I turned my back on one faith, and embraced another.

It did not take me long to begin to appreciate the intellectual capaciousness of the Christian faith. Not merely was it well grounded; it was also intellectually enabling and enriching. Here was a lens, which enabled reality to be brought into sharp focus. The Christian faith both made sense in itself, and made sense of things as a whole. 'I believe in Christianity as I believe that the sun has risen, not only because I see it, but because by it I see everything else' (C. S. Lewis). I suddenly found that the entire scientific enterprise made a lot more sense than I had ever appreciated. It was as if an intellectual sun had risen and illuminated the scientific landscape, allowing me to see details and interconnections that I would otherwise have missed altogether.

In September 1974, I joined the research group of Professor Sir George Radda, based in Oxford University's Department of Biochemistry. Radda was then developing a series of physical methods for investigating complex biological systems, including magnetic resonance approaches. My particular interest was developing innovative physical methods for studying the behaviour of biological membranes, which eventually extended to include techniques as different as the use of fluorescent probes and antimatter decay to study temperature-dependent transitions in biological systems.

But my real interest was shifting elsewhere. I never lost my fascination with the natural world. I just found something else rising, initially to rival it, and then to complement it. What I had once assumed to be the open warfare of science and religion increasingly seemed to me to represent a critical yet constructive synergy, with immense potential for intellectual enrichment. How, I found myself wondering, might the working methods and assumptions of the natural sciences be used to develop an intellectually robust Christian theology? And what should I do to explore this possibility properly?

In the event, I decided that I could best achieve this goal by ceasing active scientific research, and becoming a theologian. I was, however, determined that I would be a theologian who was up to date in his reading of the scientific literature, especially in the field of evolutionary biology, and who actively sought to relate my science and my faith. I had no time for the 'God of the Gaps' approach, which sought to defend the existence of God by an appeal to gaps in scientific explanation. While an undergraduate at Wadham College, I had come to know Charles Coulson (1910–74), Oxford University's first professor of theoretical chemistry, who was a vigorous critic of this approach. For Coulson, reality as a whole demanded explanation. 'Either God is in the whole of Nature, with no gaps, or He's not there at all.'

I increasingly came to the view that the explicability of nature was itself astonishing, and required explanation. As Albert Einstein pointed out in 1936, 'the eternal mystery of the world is its comprehensibility.' For Einstein, explicability itself clearly requires explanation. The most incomprehensible thing about the universe is that it is comprehensible. The intelligibility of the natural world, demonstrated by the natural sciences, raises the fundamental question as to why there is such a fundamental resonance between human minds and the structures of the universe.

As I reflected on the cognitive implications of the Christian faith, I came to see that it offered a 'big picture' account of things, which allowed us to make sense of what we observed in everyday life, and especially in scientific explanation. 'Religious faith', wrote William James (1842–1910) with his characteristic insight, is basically 'faith in the existence of an unseen order of some kind in which the riddles of the natural order may be found and explained.' Human beings long to make sense of things – to identify patterns in the rich fabric of nature, to offer explanations for what happens around them, and to reflect on the meaning of their lives. It is as if our intellectual antennae are tuned to discern clues to purpose and meaning around us, built into the structure of the world. 'The pursuit of discovery,' the chemist-turned-philosopher Michael Polanyi (1891–1976) noted, is 'guided by sensing the presence of a hidden reality toward which our clues are pointing.'

This led me to take a second step, moving away from the idea that one can 'prove' the existence of God from the natural world. Rather, I came to see that the key point is that there is a high degree of intellectual resonance between the Christian vision of reality and what we actually observe. The Christian faith offers an 'empirical fit' with the real world. This notion of 'empirical fit' was explored theologically by the Oxford mathematician and philosopher of religion Ian T. Ramsey (1915–72), who stated it as follows:

The theological model works more like the fitting of a boot or a shoe than like the 'yes' or 'no' of a roll call. In other words, we have a particular doctrine which, like a preferred and selected shoe, starts by appearing to meet our empirical needs. But on closer fitting to the phenomena the shoe may pinch. When tested against future slush and rain it may be proven to be not altogether water-tight or it may be comfortable – yet it must not be too comfortable. In this way, the test of a shoe is measured by its ability to match a wide range of phenomena, by its overall success in meeting a variety of needs. Here is what I might call the method of empirical fit which is displayed by theological theorizing.

This is a fundamentally empirical notion, originating within the natural sciences, which Ramsey believed – rightly, in my view – had considerable theological potential.

This led me to consider the apologetic possibilities of the natural sciences. I became interested in the field of natural theology, which I understood, not as an attempt to deduce the existence of God from a cold, detached observation of nature, but rather as the enterprise of seeing nature from the standpoint of faith, so that it is viewed, interpreted and appreciated with Christian spectacles. Events and entities within nature are thus not held to 'prove', but to be consonant with, the existence of God. What is observed within the natural order resonates with the core themes of the Christian vision of God.

An example is provided by the doctrine of creation set out in the writings of Augustine of Hippo (354–430), unquestionably the most respected and widely cited theologian in Western Christianity. Augustine does not translate his theological principles into explicit scientific statements, even though at times his statements reflect the prevailing consensus of his era. Rather, Augustine bequeathed to his successors a set of theological principles concerning the Christian doctrine of creation that are capable of provisional correlation with the scientific worldview of our own day.

Augustine interweaves biblical interpretation, an appeal

to 'right reason', and a knowledge of contemporary science in his theological reflections concerning creation, which can be summarized as follows:

1. God brought everything into being at a specific moment.

2. Part of that created order takes the form of embedded causalities which emerge or evolve at a later stage.

3. This process of development takes place within the context of God's providential direction, which is integrally connected to a right understanding of the concept of creation.

4. The image of a dormant seed is an appropriate, but not exact, analogy for these embedded causalities.

5. The process of generation of these dormant seeds results in the fixity of biological forms.

The first of these points is significant. God, Augustine insists, could not be considered to have brought the creation into being at a certain definite moment in time, as if 'time' itself existed prior to creation, or as if creation took place at a definite moment in a chronological continuum. For Augustine, time itself must be seen as an aspect of the created order, to be contrasted with the timelessness which he held to be the essential feature of eternity. Augustine thus speaks of the creation of time (or 'creation *with* time'), rather than envisaging the act of creation as taking place in time. Time is a constituent characteristic of the domain of the created, which remains dependent upon its creator. 'We speak of "before" and "after" in the relationship of creatures, although everything in the creative act of God is simultaneous.' There is no concept of a period intervening before creation, nor an infinitely extended period which corresponds to 'eternity'. Eternity is timeless; time is an aspect of the created order. This fits remarkably well with contemporary cosmological theory, which insists that time and space both came into being in the primordial cosmic event usually referred to as the 'big bang'.

The first four of these points are all derived from Augustine's reading of Scripture; the fifth is what seemed to be a self-evident truth to Augustine, in the light of his personal experience and the contemporary scientific consensus. Augustine's espousal of the fixity of species is best seen as a provisional judgment of experience, not a fixed statement of theological interpretation. As Augustine himself constantly and consistently emphasized, there is a danger of making biblical interpretation dependent on contemporary scientific opinion, leaving its outcome vulnerable when today's consensus is replaced with tomorrow's.

My point is that, rather than suggesting that God offers an explanation of what the natural sciences are currently unable to explain, we ought to emphasize the importance of belief in God in explaining the 'big picture' – that is to say, the overall patterns of ordering which are discerned within the universe. The British philosopher of religion Richard Swinburne insists that the explanatory aspects of theism are not limited to the fine details of reality, but extend far beyond these to embrace the great questions of life – those things that are either 'too big' or 'too odd' for science to explain. The reliability of such explanations is, of course, open to challenge; there is, however, no doubt that such explanations are being offered, and are seen as important.

An obvious example of 'big' and 'odd' things about the universe that seem to demand an explanation are what are now widely described as 'phenomena'. The language of 'fine-tuning' has increasingly been found appropriate to express the idea that the universe appears to have possessed certain qualities from the moment of its inception for the production of intelligent life on Earth at this point in cosmic history, capable of reflecting on the implications of its existence. Nature's fundamental constants turn out to possess reassuringly life-friendly values. The existence of carbon-based life on Earth depends upon a delicate balance of physical and cosmological forces and parameters, which are such that were any one of these quantities to be slightly altered, the balance would be destroyed and life would not exist. While these phenomena do not represent a 'proof' of the existence of a creator God, they are clearly consistent with the view of

God encountered and practised within the Christian faith. The observation of anthropic phenomena thus resonates with the core themes of the Christian vision of reality.

Yet my deepest intuition about the relation of science and faith is that theology has much to learn from the working methods and assumptions of the natural sciences. In a major three-volumed work entitled *A Scientific Theology* (2001–3), I set out a vision of how Christian theology could benefit from the intellectual rigour of the sciences. Throughout the centuries, Christian theology has engaged with a series of conversation partners, ranging from Platonism to existentialism. The slightly condescending phrase *ancilla theologiae* ('handmaid of theology') is sometimes used to refer to this process of intellectual engagement and enrichment. In my view, the natural sciences have a key role to play in catalysing the development of Christian theology, and I hope to be able to play a small part in encouraging this development.

I myself owe an enormous amount to scientists who, like Charles Coulson, set out to integrate their faith and work. There is huge potential for intellectual synergy. It is my hope that many active scientists will catch something of this vision, and come to appreciate the importance of their faith for informing and energizing their work – and passing on this vision to their students and colleagues.

CHAPTER 2

A Different Drum-Beat
Denis R. Alexander

Denis Alexander read biochemistry at Oxford University and then went on to a PhD in neurochemistry at the Institute of Psychiatry in London. Following this, he spent fifteen years in academic positions in the Middle East, in Turkey (1971–80) and as Associate Professor of Biochemistry at the American University of Beirut, Lebanon (1981–86). Since 1989 he has been at The Babraham Institute, Cambridge, for many years as Chairman of the Molecular Immunology Department. He is a Fellow of St Edmund's College, Cambridge and Director of the Faraday Institute for Science and Religion, based at the College. His first book on science and faith was *Beyond Science* (1972). More recently he has written the critically acclaimed *Rebuilding the Matrix – Science and Faith in the 21st Century* (2001) and co-authored *Beyond Belief – Science, Faith and Ethical Challenges* (2004). His most recent book is *Creation or Evolution – Do We Have to Choose?* (2008). Dr Alexander is Editor of the journal *Science & Christian Belief*.

My lab assistant carried on calmly with her experiment, set up temporarily in the corridor, while the explosions of incoming shells boomed from just up the street. Having a lab at the American University Hospital in West Beirut with windows facing toward the opposing side during the civil war of the early 1980s was not, I sometimes reflected, a smart move. There are not many parts of the world where scientists have to move their experiments into the corridor to avoid shrapnel.

This was not really what I had in mind when I embarked on a career in biochemistry. The influences that tipped my interests in the direction of the biological sciences were a mother who had been one of the rare women to read physiology at Oxford in the late 1920s; a GP grandfather whom I never met because he died in the closing days of the First World War, but whose inherited microscope opened my young eyes to the fascination of all things creepy-crawly; and a brilliant biology teacher at school who made the subject interesting. But history was an attractive alternative. It was an era when my historian uncle, the late A. J. P. Taylor, was delivering popular TV history lectures (without notes) at a time when the idea was quite novel. History looked cool. Writing was an early passion and my eldest brother had chosen to study history. But as my mother wisely advised, one can read history as a hobby, whereas science as a part-time interest is more difficult, not least because the specialized language makes it less accessible. Her argument tipped the balance: I chose science, later finding that her advice was entirely correct.

The central importance of the Christian faith was as much a part of my upbringing as an appreciation for the arts and the sciences. Faith and science were always together, never pitted against each other. Darwinian evolution was simply assumed as background knowledge for any budding biologist. Creationism had not yet been invented or, if it had, remained unknown and unmentioned. When, at the age of thirteen, I put my personal trust in Christ as Saviour and Lord and became a Christian, it was a natural maturing of a faith already nurtured by example. I have always thought that the deepest influence on any growing child is not their parents' overt exhortations and teaching, but the implicit understanding of what, deep down, really matters most to them.

By the time I went on a gap-year to Canada before taking up my place as an open scholar at Oxford to read biochemistry, a standard type of academic research career seemed to lie ahead. A conveniently placed uncle, at that time General Manager of Schweppes, arranged by a piece of pure nepotism that I should work in a factory that made Welch's grape-juice, and there I laboured in the early months of 1964. We were told that we could drink as much grape-juice as we liked. It was very refreshing for the first week, but the attraction soon palled. The time in the factory was followed by some months of travelling in the USA and Canada.

Periods away from home during one's formative years can provide opportunity for reflection. I was not expecting that my gap-year would radically affect my life's direction, but it was then that I gained the clear conviction that God wanted me overseas in a cross-cultural context, using my science in the service of others. Some words of Jesus spoke to me very powerfully during this time: 'From everyone who has been given much, much will be demanded; and from the one who has been entrusted with much, much more will be asked' (Luke 12:48). I had been given much: the benefits of a secure, loving Christian home; financial security; a good education; the fruits of science; the prospects of an Oxford degree. What was I going to give in return? At the time I had no idea what this might involve.

Oxford and London

I was at Oxford from 1964 to 1968. My tutor at St Peter's College was Arthur Peacocke, later to gain a high profile in the area of science and religion, but at that time known principally for his work on the structure of DNA. Weekly tutorials with Arthur and one other undergraduate were always stretching. My grasp of irreversible thermodynamics, a topic dear to Arthur's heart, was never strong, and discussing the topic with a world expert must have been tedious for the expert on occasion. But Arthur was very focused, arriving in a whirl of papers and departing in a cloud of dust for the next appointment. His output was prodigious; by the end of his academic career he had published 12 books and more than 200 papers.

During this period, Arthur organized a College group with the aim of introducing students to systematic theology. Every week we discussed a chapter of *Christian Doctrine* by J. S. Whale, but science was never far from theology in our discussions. Arthur provided a role model, someone who regarded science and theology with equal seriousness, combining both worlds in one career.

There were plenty of other role models around for those who knew where to look. I became involved with the Oxford Inter-Collegiate Christian Union (OICCU), later to become its President, and it was a time when the OICCU often invited scientists as speakers. One of these whose influence was perhaps the greatest on my own thinking was Professor Donald MacKay, at that time Professor of Communications at Keele University, a Chair not of IT, as the title might suggest, but of cognitive science – the way the brain interprets and perceives the world around us. Donald MacKay was without doubt one of the major pioneers in building an effective dialogue between science and faith during the latter half of the twentieth century. There have not been many scientists in recent times who have published, as MacKay did, papers on philosophy in the journal *Mind* in parallel with his neuroscience papers in *Nature*.

I listened to Professor MacKay several times in my student years, but one occasion stands out above all the others. He had been invited to give a seminar to the Humanist Society, at that time the biggest society in the university and aggressively anti-Christian. Professor MacKay had laryngitis and could only speak in a whisper; we had to strain to hear what he was saying. As was his wont, MacKay gave a very clear and accessible account of how to relate scientific and religious types of explanation, showing how they provided complementary rather than rival accounts of the same reality. Both accounts were needed to do justice to the world around us. After the talk was over I was chatting with the student Secretary of the Society. 'If I ever become a Christian, it will be because of that man,' he said, pointing to Professor MacKay. I don't know if he ever did, but I do know that the Treasurer of the Humanist Society around that period became a Christian a year after leaving Oxford, later to write a book critiquing atheism.

One of the many stimulating aspects of the 1960s was the intellectual, political and social turmoil that swept across the campuses of the Western world during that period. Fuelled by the anti-Vietnam war movement, radical left-wing groups proliferated. I well remember a lecture-room full of Oxford undergraduates waving their 'little red books' of the thoughts of Mao in the air. I doubt many had actually read it, but this was an era of left-wing icons and sloganeering. There were protests about almost everything. At the same time there were sea-changes going on in music and the arts. For all its extremes and its posing, the sixties post-War-bulge generation was destined to make a lasting impact on the cultural milieu of this country.

Into this heady mix came Francis Schaeffer, at first sight an unlikely candidate as a commentator on the 1960s counter-culture. He had been pastor of a rather conservative church in the USA, but a series of events brought him to Europe to set up a centre in Switzerland called l'Abri where people could stay and investigate the intellectual case for Christianity. Schaeffer encouraged Christians to leave their cultural ghettoes and engage with secular culture, immersing themselves in books, art and films. His printed and taped messages spread across the Christian world of the time, encouraging us to grapple with our faith and its intellectual underpinning. It was through Schaeffer that I learnt how people's world-views are shaped by a few key underlying presuppositions. Though not himself strong in the sciences, it was Schaeffer who got us narrowly focused scientists into reading Sartre and Camus, and to take a greater interest in the arts.

The main intellectual challenges thrown at the Christian faith in 1960s Oxford were moral and political. Christianity was on the side of the bourgeoisie, not the masses. Religion supported the *status quo*; it was the opium of the people. On the other hand, I don't think Christians reading science were in any doubt that religion and science were harmonious first cousins. Occasionally humanists might try to attack Christian faith using varying forms of naïve reductionism, but there was nothing of the concerted attempt to hijack the prestige of science to promote atheism of the kind popularized by Richard Dawkins in later decades. Out of the many OICCU meetings that I attended during those four years, I cannot remember a single one where evolution was discussed as a topic that might be of concern to Christians. The background assumption was simply that evolution was God's chosen method for bringing biological diversity into being. Of creationism there was no sign.

I was a voracious reader as a student, but the only book that gave me any pause for thought as far as the roots of my own faith were concerned, was *Battle for the Mind – a Physiology of Conversion and Brainwashing* by William Sargant. In the book Sargant argued that the ways in which POWs are forced to confess and people are religiously converted are pretty much the same. I remember wondering whether I had simply been 'brainwashed' into faith by my family upbringing? Journalistically it would be of more interest if I could recount some 'crisis of faith' that arose from this new insight but, boringly, I simply chewed on the problem when I had time, and it gradually dissolved for what now seem very obvious reasons.

For a start, most religious conversions, certainly the ones I knew about (including mine), were simply nothing like the dramatic brainwashing episodes that Sargant recounted in his book, but were instead very ho-hum, mundane affairs. Second, the whole point about the brainwashing techniques recounted by Sargant is that they don't work in the long run. For sure, the POW confesses under duress, but at home after the war he reverts to his previous beliefs. The very term 'brainwashing' is a misnomer because long-term memory is remarkably resistant to change, whatever short-term changes may be effected by psychological manipulation. Third, in any case, all beliefs have to be justified rationally by appeals to evidence, so the fact of having been raised either with or without a certain belief provided no support *per se* for or against its truth status. Fourth (a related reflection), had I been brought up in Saudi Arabia, it was much less likely that I would have become a biochemist; nevertheless, I would still be able to give grounds for believing that biochemistry was a well-justified way of spending one's time, despite the fact that my environmental and cultural milieu had clearly been influential in guiding me towards such a belief. In the end there has to be, by definition, a psychological account for the holding of any or all beliefs, but this insight, important as it is, does little to tell you whether those beliefs are well-justified beliefs.

London and the Institute of Psychiatry

A fascination with the workings of the brain led to a PhD in neurochemistry. There were several reasons for this choice of research area. Since the resolution of the structure of DNA had provided a mechanistic basis for genetics, the last great frontiers of ignorance seemed to be in the neurosciences. Nearer home, my eldest brother, nearly a decade my senior, had been an open scholar at Trinity College, but had there suffered a mental breakdown, diagnosed as manic-depressive psychosis. I think the knowledge of that fact at a young age, coupled with the ensuing realization that so little was known about the causes of such pathology, was a significant influence in choosing the path of the neurosciences.

When I think of the efforts nowadays to select the most promising PhD students, the way my own PhD place was secured seems remarkably casual. My tutor wrote to an acquaintance of his running a neurochemistry laboratory at the Institute of Psychiatry in Camberwell Green, London. A letter came back saying, 'Fine, I've got two MRC [Medical Research Council] bursaries next academic year. He can have one of them' – which is how I came to do my PhD studies with Dick Rodnight, later to become Professor of Neurochemistry. The MRC bursary paid about £500 a year, plenty enough to live on in the London of the late 1960s.

After Finals at Oxford, I went travelling, then showed up at the Institute of Psychiatry at roughly the right time. It turned out that the holder of the other MRC bursary had arrived a week earlier, so had the opportunity of first pick on the two research projects on offer. He had chosen what seemed at the time a much more interesting project: the electrical stimulation of brain slices to investigate the turnover of protein phosphorylation, the addition of phosphate groups to proteins being a key modifier of their function. I was left with what seemed a less interesting goal: to work out how the sodium-potassium pump works at the biochemical level. This is the vital pump found in the membranes of all nerve cells that 'recharges' the electrical difference across the membrane, thereby making possible the next nerve impulse. In the event the other person's project turned out to be technically challenging and it took him four years, whereas my project was relatively easy, and took only two years (plus a few months to write up). There are sometimes unexpected benefits that result from being late for things.

My research involved scraping the cerebral cortex off frozen ox brains and using it to make purified synaptic plasma membranes, rich in my precious sodium-potassium pump. Obtaining ox brains was a non-trivial exercise. They needed to be undamaged, so I collected them from a Jewish slaughterhouse in east London where the animals were killed by cutting the throat rather than by the more normal method of a steel bolt into the brain. Since, unlike most nationalities, the British do not fancy brain salad, it was then just a question of tipping the worker ten bob (50p in 'new' money) to carefully cut out the brain. Double-wrapped in plastic bags, the brains were quick-frozen in dry-ice and transported back to the lab strapped to my Honda 49cc motorbike. Although I did come off my Honda twice during my sojourn in London (once in the middle of Trafalgar Square), my real concern was having an accident when the brains were on board. Fortunately this never happened; people rushing to help might have become somewhat alarmed.

I mention all this to illustrate the fact that PhD projects in biological subjects might sound straightforward at first, but are rarely that simple in practice. But we neurochemists certainly considered ourselves a cut above the less reductionist work carried out on the floor below. There we volunteered for the researchers working with Hans Eysenck, the Professor of Psychology. It was all great fun and involved performing fairground-type games, like moving a coil along a wire without touching it, at the same time being blasted (or not) with loud noises through earphones, all the time being watched through mirrors, supposedly secretly. The real game was to try to persuade the experimenter that you were introvert when you were really extrovert, and vice-versa. I never really believed Eysenck's models of introversion–extraversion because of such mean intractability in his human subjects.

The general attitude towards religion in the Institute of Psychiatry at that time can best be described as 'frosty'. Religious beliefs were generally equated with some kind of obsessional neurosis, possibly to be patronized, but certainly not to be taken seriously as claims to reality. Today there is a wealth of published data that supports a positive role for religious belief in mental health, but those data came later. Although the Institute generally had a hard-nosed reductionist attitude towards psychiatry and little time for the psychoanalytical schools that were popular in the US, Freud's antipathy towards religion still filtered down through the ranks. Having said that, there were also some Christian psychiatrists in the adjacent Maudsley Hospital and I met with them regularly for prayer and Bible study. Then and since I have always felt that it is important for Christians to get together for fellowship in their work context, not least to avoid the idea that faith and work are in any way divorced.

Two important extracurricular events took place around this time. First, whilst showing a coach-load of overseas students from London round Cambridge, I met my future wife; studying in London, but with a home in Cambridge, she happened to be helping out on the same trip. Our courtship involved many trips on the Honda, now nicknamed Bucephalus (the name of Alexander the Great's horse), with many cries from the back seat of 'Mind my legs!' as the driver weaved his way through the London traffic. Sadly, Bucephalus was eventually stolen one night, wheeled away from outside the Institute, as it had no lock. More happily, courtship led to marriage soon after my PhD was finished.

The second significant event was an approach by my elder brother, David, to write a book on science and faith. David had worked for eight years for IVP, a publisher specializing in Christian books, before branching out to start his own publishing house called 'Lion' with the aim of publishing Christian books for a broader, more secular readership. There were indeed very few sensible books on science and faith available at the time. Donald MacKay had not yet published much, Arthur Peacocke nothing, and there were just a few other authors in the field. In any event, I was told to write something 'popular' and, typical for an elder brother, David sent me a one-page summary outline of what should be in the book.

But first the thesis had to be finished, a task I completed at home on my father's old and cumbersome office typewriter. This involved making five carbon-copies using my one-finger typing; every time I made an error, this had to be corrected with 'Tippex', blowing on each page to dry it before being able to correct the one below. I like to tell this story to PhD students today, when they complain that the printer jammed once whilst printing from their laptop.

With the thesis out of the way, it was time to give attention to the book, eventually called *Beyond Science*: one of the very first books to be published by the fledgling Lion in 1972. I wrote it in the latter half of 1971 when I had just turned twenty-six. I now shudder at the arrogance of youth in thinking to write such a book, but at least it was fresh and spoke to my contemporaries, and it sold well. In fact I still come across people today who say how useful they found it in developing their own thinking: that science and faith were friends not foes, and that scientific advances were throwing up a host of questions that science itself was quite unable to address, but for which Christian faith had the answers. When it comes to writing, we're never too young to at least get started.

Science, faith and life in Turkey

During my student days, I had never lost the sense of God's call to work overseas. With *Beyond Science* nearly complete, I was verbally offered a teaching position at the Middle Eastern Technical University (METU) in Ankara, the capital city of Turkey. We waited eagerly for written confirmation in the last months of 1971, but nothing came. What did come was a telegram from our friends in Ankara saying, 'Flat rented, come now.' We went.

Loading a Ford Transit van with wedding presents and other paraphernalia we thought might be useful for a new home in Turkey, we set off for Ankara. I had visited Turkey once before, my new bride never. Unlike today, it was not then a well-established holiday destination and could best be described as 'developing'.

A week's drive brought us to Ankara, only to find that there was no job at METU; the hoped-for budget had never materialized. So I went to Haceteppe University (also in Ankara), where the Biochemistry Department had previously said that they had no openings, but where there was now a new Chairperson with new ideas. She was only too delighted to offer me a position as a *Yabancı Uzman* ('Foreign Expert' – in reality a glorified post-doc position). So began a pattern that continued throughout my life, of God opening some doors and closing others at the appropriate moment. I have always taken very seriously the promise of Jesus given in Matthew 6:33: 'But seek first his kingdom and his righteousness, and all these things will be given to you as well' – 'these things' referring to the daily necessities of life.

Eventually we spent fifteen years in the Middle East. People often ask what it was like to teach science and carry out research in the Muslim world. The answer I always give is, 'It depends which bit you mean', for in truth there is no such entity as 'the Muslim world' as if it represented some homogeneous geographical area. There are countries where Muslims are either a majority or a significant minority, but these in turn vary enormously.

Turkey was and is a Muslim country in the sense that 99 per cent of its inhabitants have 'Muslim' stamped in their identity cards as their religion. On the other hand, it is a more secular country than Britain, having a legal separation between religion and state. When Kemal Ataturk established the modern republic of Turkey back in the 1920s, he carried out a radical Westernizing programme of reform in which the political power of Muslim leadership was destroyed, the Arabic alphabet of Ottoman Turkish replaced by the Latin alphabet, and the population forced to adopt surnames to make them more like their European neighbours. In the 1970s, just as today, Turkey was continually pulled between East and West, with Ataturk's reforms under continued threat from those wishing to impose either fundamentalist Islam or ultra-nationalist agendas upon the Turkish state.

The most visible impact of Ataturk's reforms for me was that when I started work at Haceteppe, I was the only male in the Biochemistry Department. Turkey indeed has a good record of sexual equality in the scientific workplace, and today in the country's best universities, one third of the mathematicians and physicists, two thirds of the chemists and one fifth of the engineers are women. Proportionally there are higher percentages of women in different scientific disciplines in Turkey than in many non-Muslim countries.

After two years my contract at Haceteppe came to an end, but by that time a lecturing position had opened up down the road at METU, the very department to which I had originally intended to come. The university was and is operated totally in English, and my job involved setting up for the first time a neurochemistry lab and establishing a number of new courses, both undergraduate and graduate. One of the stimulating experiences of working in other countries is the way that you can be plunged into responsibilities at a much younger age than might otherwise be the case.

The equipment was not bad, but the shortage of consumables was chronic. I spent a lot of time scrounging consumables and radioisotopes from my old lab in London, who were very kind in sending out items. Somehow we managed. My very first Masters student now has her own lab in the USA; I discovered that another was now head of department when I went back to give a seminar in Ankara recently. But this also illustrates the challenge of much development work – to see trained people staying on in their own country to pass on the fruits of their experience to others.

At METU I found the Turkish version of secularism was based more on the French pattern of radical exclusion of religion from all state and official affairs (hence no headscarves on French campuses), as compared to the more British relaxed version (do what you want as long as no one is upset by it). The METU campus was entirely left-wing; the student body would not allow any right-wing students on campus, irrespective of whether they had a right to be there or not. Many faculty had been imprisoned and tortured by the military after the previous coup that took place shortly before we arrived in the country. There were frequent clashes between different leftist factions on campus, especially as the 1970s progressed and Turkish politics became increasingly fraught. The Maoists fought the Trotskyites, and the Trotskyites fought the Marxist-Leninists. Actually, half the time I don't think even the students really knew who was fighting whom. The Biological Sciences Department where I worked was right in the middle of the campus opposite the Rector's building, a favoured spot for confrontations, and on more than one occasion I was thankful for the large desk in my office, which I hid behind as shoot-outs took place outside. Nevertheless, despite endless chanting of 'Death to America!', the students were studiously polite and friendly when they came in for their biochemistry lectures afterwards: there was no personal antagonism involved.

A key element lacking in Turkey to a significant degree, is tolerance. Ataturk may have launched important reforms, but the idea intrinsic to the Western liberal tradition that you can hold individual beliefs quite different from those of others, yet still be valued as a citizen and even as a friend, seems quite alien to the Turkish psyche. What mattered is the *millet*, the nation, and what the nation wants. We in the West are so used to our individualistic freedoms that we forget the way in which communal thought and action are so much more valued in most parts of the world.

Certainly there was little tolerance shown towards the Christian faith during the years we were in Turkey. Leftist secularists were opposed to it because all religious beliefs for them were associated with backwardness. I have never heard such ready espousal of scientistic views as from my Turkish colleagues. This is the idea (quite fallacious, as it happens) that only science provides a reliable source of knowledge and that all other types of knowledge are unnecessary or based on 'mere opinion'. Right-wing nationalists, of whom there were many, opposed Christianity because they saw it as a 'new crusade', a

Western plot to subvert the nation. Islamists, of whom there are now more than in those days, viewed the Christian faith as a threat to Islamic hegemony. The idea that you could choose your own faith, yet at the same time remain a good Turk and loyal citizen, was not even countenanced.

All these factors eventually impinged on our own future. The late 1970s were years of increasing economic and political turmoil. The country ran out of money and could no longer pay for oil. Queues formed for everything, so that we started joining a queue as soon as we saw one, in the sure knowledge that some rare commodity (like margarine) was on offer. On one occasion I queued for twelve hours to buy sufficient petrol to take the family to the south coast for a weekend break. Inflation soared. Clashes between left and right increased in different parts of the country, until ten to thirty people were being killed each day. Civil war loomed.

There was no church building in Ankara where Protestant Turkish Christians could meet, so during this period we routinely welcomed into our home a nascent Turkish church consisting of a small handful of students and others coming together for regular worship and Bible teaching. In a secular state, where the legal right of religious assembly was protected by law, there was nothing illegal about such meetings. But the state thought otherwise, and in 1979 we received a deportation order. We duly tried to have this reversed and had some temporary success, but we were finally forced to leave the country in 1980 – just weeks, as it turned out, before the next army coup.

Life, science and faith in West Beirut

During a year back in the UK I was offered a position in the Medical Faculty of the American University of Beirut, to set up a laboratory of biochemical genetics as part of the National Unit of Human Genetics. Our three children were still young. If we were going to spend more time overseas, now was the time to do it. There was a major snag: I didn't know anything about the kind of genetic diseases that I was being asked to work on, nor about the specific techniques involved. 'Never mind,' came the reply, 'we have good links with the Paediatric Research Unit at Guy's Hospital in London, and we'll fund you there for two months whilst you learn your new field.' Human genetics, in a land where up to 42 per cent of some communities (the Druze) marry their first cousin, certainly seemed much more relevant than neurochemistry from a practical point of view. I accepted the offer.

When we arrived in West Beirut it was still ruled by the Palestinian Liberation Organisation (PLO), run like a slightly disorganized scout camp by Yassar Arafat. The city had never fully recovered from the civil war of 1975–6. But an uneasy equilibrium of a kind had been achieved, although the power of the state was rudimentary, most areas being controlled by different militias, of which the PLO was deemed the most powerful. The balcony of our apartment faced the Arab Bank where the PLO gold was stored, one benefit being that in the space in between, our car was well guarded.

The American University Hospital was modern, effective and well funded, the University being registered in the State of New York, with an American President (sadly assassinated during our time there). The University operated entirely in English. Our Genetics Unit represented just about every one of Lebanon's diverse communities: Armenian, Druze, Sunni Muslim, Shiite Muslim, Maronite Christian, Protestant and Orthodox. We all got on extremely well, with a communal meal once a week, each member bringing a meal typical of their community. Sometimes these communities were fighting each other bitterly outside, but at least peace reigned in the Hospital.

It was in the Genetics Unit that I encountered the first moral dilemmas arising out of my science. Working on ox brains had raised no pressing ethical concerns. Genetics was something quite different. It gradually dawned on me that I was being asked to set up prenatal diagnosis on as many lethal genetic diseases as I thought appropriate. In fact we established the first prenatal diagnostic clinic anywhere in the Arab world. There was no ethics committee to give advice: I *was* the ethics committee. The techniques of the time involved therapeutic abortions at 12–14 weeks in the case of an affected foetus. Families of 8–12 children or more were not uncommon. Sometimes we had parents coming for genetic counselling who had seen 3 or more of their young children die slowly and painfully around 6–10 years old. Typically such couples were both carriers of defective genes for enzymes used in lysosomes, the waste-disposal organelles of the cell. That meant that each child had a 1-in-4 chance of being homozygous for the defect. They would be normal at birth, but then the gradual accumulation of waste-products would lead to an untreatable cell pathology that would kill them in early childhood. At the same time there was still a strong (and horrendous) belief in less educated families that giving birth to a child that was or became abnormal was a judgment from God. There were stories of such children being left to die, hidden from the community in dark cupboards.

I took the pragmatic decision that if a gene defect had a 100 per cent chance of killing a child at a very early age, then we would develop the biochemical assay needed to do the prenatal diagnosis, but any disease that developed later would not go on the list. This was based on the firm belief that all therapeutic abortions are evil, and on the equally firm belief that allowing a child into the world that was destined to die slowly and painfully at a very early age, with all the agony that involved for not just the child, but also the parents and wider family, was an even greater evil. Quite often medical interventions involve choosing the lesser of two evils.

Today technical advances have changed the picture considerably. Chorionic villi sampling has enabled prenatal diagnosis to be carried out earlier in pregnancy. The advent of preimplantation diagnosis, involving the genetic screening of embryos prior to implantation, has rendered discussion of abortion redundant for an ever-wider range of diseases. Such technologies have raised new questions about how far to go. But as far as the really lethal diseases are concerned, I have never seen any reason to change my ethical position from that worked out 'on the hoof' in the maelstrom of early 1980s Beirut. Those holding to 'absolutist' views on such matters are often not those who have to face a mother who has seen several of her children slowly die from a devastating disease.

Re-entry

Turkey had gradually dissolved into political chaos during our time there, and Lebanon did the same. We were evacuated three times. Twice we returned once things had quietened down, but the third was our final exit. This took place because President Reagan had decided to bomb Libya in a crazy plan to kill Colonel Ghaddafi (they missed him, but killed one of his adopted children). The planes took off from a US base near Cambridge. Not surprisingly, the Arab world seethed in anger. Three Western hostages were killed in retaliation in Beirut, one of whom was the Director of the Language School where my wife was teaching. Our Lebanese friends said: 'We love you – please leave now!' We left within forty-eight hours with experiments sitting unfinished on the lab bench and children wailing as they said farewell to the family cats. As we drove across from west to east Beirut under armed escort, the British Ambassador greeted us in his bullet-proof car and took us all off to experience that great British response to all emergencies: a nice cup of tea.

Re-entry into British life proved more problematic than readjusting to British tea (with milk – ugh!) and the terrible weather. A life of research in the UK had never been on my agenda. Fortunately I had never left active scientific research and teaching, and had managed to get a few papers published in decent genetics journals whilst in Beirut. Fortunately, also, no one had told me that getting one's first job in academic science in Britain at the age of forty-one is impossible. Remarkably, a post as visiting researcher at what was then the Imperial Cancer Research Fund (ICRF, now Cancer Research UK) opened up. I was told very firmly that it could be for one year only, but in the end it continued for more than three years, giving a great opportunity to get a toehold back in the UK research community. The position necessitated shifting fields once again, this time to molecular immunology, but this returned me to my 'first love': protein phosphorylation (and dephosphorylation, just as important). Again through some rather extraordinary 'coincidences', the way then opened up for a position at the Babraham Institute in Cambridge, where later in the 1990s I became Chair of the Molecular Immunology Programme.

Return to the UK also stimulated a renewed interest in the science–religion debate, an interest that had never waned over the years, but had simply been squeezed out by the pressure of events. I became very involved with Christians in Science, and eventually took on the role of Editor of their journal *Science & Christian Belief*. Back in Beirut I had signed a contract with Lion Publishing to write a replacement book for *Beyond Science*, with the provisional title *Science and Faith at the End of the 20th Century*. Unfortunately the century wasn't long enough. The book finally emerged in 2001 with the title *Rebuilding the Matrix – Science and Faith in the 21st Century*.

Life in science for the Christian can indeed be an exciting adventure of faith. Sometimes it turned out for us a little more exciting than we had intended, but this can be useful in increasing one's dependency upon God. We have continually experienced the truth of Jesus' promise that if we seek first his kingdom, then the necessities of life will come along behind. Science and faith are not two different worlds, but different aspects of one world, God's world. All scientists have the privilege of uncovering just a little more of the wonders of God's creation, but scientists who are Christians have the added privilege of seeing this as part of their worship as they seek to use their science in the service of others.

CHAPTER 3

Spending a Life in Science and Faith

Derek Burke

Derek Burke was educated at Birmingham and Yale Universities; Professor of Biological Sciences, University of Warwick (1969–82); Scientific Director, Allelix Inc., Toronto, Canada (1982–87); Vice-Chancellor, University of East Anglia (1987–1995); Chairman, Advisory Committee on Novel Foods and Processes (advising UK Government, 1988–97); Member, Advisory Committee on Genetic Modification (1987–95); Member, Technology Foresight Steering Group, Office of Science and Technology (1993–95); Member, Council of the Cancer Research Campaign and its committees (1973–97); Member, Biotechnology and Biological Sciences Research Council and its committees (from 1994); Member, Engineering and Physical Sciences Research Council Societal Issues Panel (2005–2008); Member, Nuffield Council for Bioethics working parties on 'Genetically Modified Crops: the ethical and social issues' (1999) and on 'The use of Genetically Modified Crops in Developing Countries' (2004); Specialist Adviser, House of Commons Science and Technology Committee (1995–2003); Member, Science, Medicine and Technology committee of the Church of England (1995–2000); Past President of Society of General Microbiology and of Christians in Science; Past Chairman, Patterson Institute for Cancer Research (1992–97). Hon. LLD, University of Aberdeen (1982); Hon. LLD, UEA (1995); Hon. Fellow St Edmund's College Cambridge (1997). Member, EMBO.

I am not from an academic family; my grandparents were working-class people from north Birmingham and my parents moved into the middle class, my father becoming Managing Director of an engineering company in Birmingham, after leaving school at fourteen and signing his own apprenticeship papers (his father was an alcoholic). Neither of my parents were churchgoers at that time, but belief in God was widespread in the 1940s in Britain. We had all spent six years of the Second World War wondering what the future held for us, sleeping in shelters, queuing for food and, in my case, rescuing an incendiary bomb from the local park and carrying it on my bicycle to the local police station to do my bit. I came to faith in my early teens through the influence of the local Crusader class, and owe much to the faithful men who taught us weekly and at the summer camps.

I had always been interested in science, and in those days it was possible to own a chemistry set and use it in the kitchen at home. So I carried out all the experiments in the book and then tried some of my own, just mixing things up to see what happened. Although not proper science, I was driven by lots of curiosity about how the world worked. I loved natural history too. In those days it was perfectly all right to collect butterflies and bird's eggs as long as no more than one was taken from a nest. I remember, too, taking all my caterpillars on the back ledge of a car to a holiday in Devon in 1939. I was very fortunate in being well taught in the local grammar school by really bright men, people almost forced into teaching in the thirties by the industrial depression. In 1947, at just seventeen, I went to university, the first person in my family to do so. The war had only finished two years before; there was still rationing and men and women were still being demobilized from the armed services, so my first year at the University of Birmingham had 80 per cent ex-service people, mainly men. They included an ex-colonel in a bomb disposal squad, an ex-fighter pilot, both of whom were fortunate to have survived the war, and many others. They found academic work hard after all those years away, but were very fit and the standard of sports was high. I joined the Christian Union, and because of a leadership crisis, found myself President before the end of my first year. The President had to give an annual Presidential

Address and I chose to speak on John 14:6, 'I am the way, the truth and the life', taking the line that faith and science were both concerned with the truth about our world, and so must not conflict. It turned out to be a recurrent theme in my life.

Academic life

I graduated in Chemistry in 1950. My Professor called me in and just told me who I was going to work with and what I was going to work on for the next three years for my PhD. It was a project on steroids, trying to make cortisone from ergosterol. It never occurred to me to question my Professor's decision, but I grew more independent in those three years of research. On my own initiative I wrote to several North American universities seeking an opening, and was offered a position as a post-doctoral fellow at Yale University in September 1953 to work on some naturally occurring nucleosides from a Caribbean sponge, which turned out to have arabinose rather than ribose as the sugar component. Thus began an exciting time in both my academic and personal life.

In those days, no one flew to North America. I travelled on the *Georgic*, a one-class Cunarder, which was full of young people: Brits going to the United States and young Americans returning from a summer in Europe. We had a splendid time, and I met two people who personified the two main themes of my life. One was Malcolm Jeeves, well known now as a distinguished psychologist and a fine Christian, who was going to work at Harvard. The other was Jim Watson (already well known as an author with Francis Crick because of that famous paper in April 1953 on the structure of DNA), who was also going to Harvard. He moved later to Cold Spring Harbor and was to win a Nobel prize.

New York was amazing; I had been to France, Belgium and Norway since the end of the war, but no one I knew had been to North America. I was overwhelmed. The bustle of New York, the huge taxis, the skyscrapers; everything was bigger than I had expected. I sat on the train to New Haven, the home of Yale

University, wondering if I was going to be accosted by strangers since I had heard Americans were over-friendly. Luckily I was left alone, and arrived safely at the lodgings my Professor had found me with an elderly anglophile American landlady: a nice woman who had had an affair with a member of the House of Lords just before the war. I was the first Britisher she had met since then and I was treated well.

Before I had left England my vicar had teased me that I would marry an American since several Christian young men had gone the year before to North America and all had come back married. He pointed out that it would be cheaper to buy the ring here in England, but I protested vigorously that I was not going to marry an American. I was wrong. I met Mary in church on my second Sunday in the US. The young people of the church used to go to Howard Johnson's ice-cream parlour after the evening service – quite a shocking, even revolutionary idea to me after staid 1950s England – and among the group was Mary, who had come back to Yale to finish her PhD, working on the letters of James Boswell. Together we started a Bible study group in the Graduate School, and gradually fell in love. We got engaged in November 1954 and married the following May, returning to Britain later that year on the *Mauritania*.

We arrived in Southampton with a lorry-load of luggage and almost no money. Half our savings went on paying the duty on the camera I had bought just before we left the US. I had no job and was liable for military service, but we were young and trusted in God's benevolence for us.

There were a few jobs available which carried exemption from military service and I was offered one, working on rocket fuels on the west coast of Scotland for ICI. Although it was all there was, I turned it down and went after a job working on aircraft fuel development. While I was being interviewed for that, someone suggested I write to the National Institute for Medical Research in Mill Hill (NIMR), North London, where there were sometimes jobs. I did; there was a job, which had not been advertised. I was interviewed and offered the job on the spot – working on the biochemistry of influenza virus. Thus was set the course of my research life.

We had nowhere to live. We were so young and naive, that we thought we could just go to London for a day to find a flat. But God's gracious care prevailed. We stumbled on a flat in Hendon, lived there for the next four and a half years and had two children there, despite the landlord having said at the beginning that he was not prepared to let the flat to Americans or to couples with children.

My first project at NIMR was in the Chemistry Division working with Alick Isaacs, a brilliant young virologist. The task was to determine the nucleic acid content of the influenza virus, known to be an RNA virus, but how much RNA? Near its successful conclusion, Alick suggested that I should help him 'with something interesting that we are doing on interference'. 'We' was Jean Lindenmann and himself. It was March 1957, and their discovery, which they named interferon, was only a few weeks old. The name was new – Alick once explained that it was 'time that biologists had a fundamental particle, for the physicists have so many: electron, neutron, proton etc.' That did not stop Lord Hailsham, then Chairman of the Medical Research Council, objecting to such a nasty hybrid word with both Latin and Greek roots! But by then the name had stuck. Little did I know that I was to work on interferon for the next twenty-five years.

Interferon had been discovered as a result of testing an incorrect hypothesis. It was the steam age of virology (as a very senior virologist said, referring rather disparagingly to the dream age that would follow – molecular biology and all that), and no one really knew how animal viruses worked – indeed it was suggested that the viral coat was left outside the cell, like bacteriophage. Alick and Jean tested this by seeing whether any viral property – and they chose interference – was still associated with the outer membrane of the cell, and could be washed off. What they found was not the viral coat outside the cell, but the interferon newly made inside the cell.

The system was crude. The experiments took hours to titrate, involving little more than purely mechanical operations, and this left time to talk. Alick led in conversation, and ideas for new experiments, political discussion, or identification of snatches of opera that he would sing made the time pass quickly. It was a lively time. Two scientific papers had already been published, but there was much to do. We worked quickly, and published the results in a series of five papers. Though I say so myself, this was quite an achievement for a young post-doctoral scientist on a meagre income, with a wife and two small children to support! I still have my laboratory notebooks, and my first experiment, dated 'March 4th, 1957', was headed 'Dialysis of interferon' – we did not even know whether interferon would pass through a dialysis membrane. The second experiment, started the same day, was to test whether interferon activity was destroyed by shaking with ether. It was; another clue that interferon was a macromolecule. A series of experiments strongly suggested that interferon was a protein, and if so, then presumably it could be purified, perhaps quite easily. The conclusions were correct, but purification took a long time and was much more difficult than any of us had expected.

Interest in interferon was growing. Alick and I wrote an article titled 'Interferon: A possible check to Virus Infections' in the *New Scientist* in June 1958. Interferon even made it into a Flash Gordon cartoon! We were invited to present our results at a Conversazione for the Fellows of the Royal Society in May 1958. We had to wear dinner-jackets. Then we were asked to present our demonstration a second time at an event to which only the 'great and good' were invited. For that we had to wear white tie and tails, which I had to hire. I vividly remember dressing up in our very modest little North London flat, and sitting down with my wife at the kitchen table to eat before the great event: me in my splendour, while she put on an evening dress as a compliment and complement. It was a heady time; I was only twenty-eight.

Meantime, my time at Mill Hill was running out. My three-year appointment had been extended for another two but it was only in the middle of the fifth year that I found another suitable post. I had decided that I wanted to stay working on the biochemistry of viruses and needed a collaborator who could help me with the virology, and there were very few universities with any virology at that time. However, I was offered a lectureship in biological sciences in Aberdeen University starting in April 1960. That meant my work on interferon purification had to be rounded off very quickly. We also had to say goodbye to the good friends we had made, especially in the Baptist church just along the road which had become an intrinsic part of our London experience. It was in London too that I first learned to appreciate the Research Scientists' Christian Fellowship – later Christians in Science – with its excellent annual conferences, where we rather floundered around in the philosophy, until Donald MacKay would crisply and precisely sort us out. I confess that I did not always understand what he said, but it was good to have our minds stretched in this way. I worked in the laboratory until absolutely the last minute; it was only after the van had departed for Aberdeen with most of our furniture that I finished the last experiment. My wife was very tolerant.

Aberdeen was a new and challenging experience. The department was tiny; there were only three other lecturers and a Professor, who had been blinded in a laboratory accident thirty years before, teaching the whole of a biochemistry degree plus two years of biochemistry to medical students. I was given an absolutely empty laboratory without a single piece of glassware. There was a little money from the department and at the second attempt I secured a modest grant from the Medical Research Council. So we continued work on the purification of interferon and started work on the mechanism of its production. But it was a slow start and but for the students and some outstanding post-doctoral workers who joined me, I, like many other young academics in the sixties, would probably have died without trace, quietly giving up research. I resolved to change the system when I got the chance, and I did later at Warwick, when we built up research groups from the beginning.

In Aberdeen, we were Presbyterians for a time, until the long sermons and the continued promise of judgment from God on the Scottish people who had so sadly neglected their covenant with God, so depressed us that we moved into a small, friendly Baptist church. The church was helpful, but what really kept us going was the Graduates Fellowship, which met monthly in a home and provided us with Christian friends from across the city, many of them working in the University or local Research Institutes. We bought a house, and two more children were born. But we were isolated scientifically – it was a three-hour drive to Glasgow for seminars – and I tried several times to move. At last, in the spring of 1969, I was appointed as the first Professor of Biological Sciences at the University of Warwick, close to where my ageing parents lived. There again, looking back, God's care was shown; I had applied for other jobs but not got them and was rather discouraged. Then at a small meeting on interferon, Sydney Brenner, already a powerful person in molecular biology, told me that there was a job at Warwick which I should apply for. I did as I was told, reasoning that if I didn't he would never make any other suggestions. But I had no high hopes – especially as I later found out that he was backing another candidate.

But I got the job and we moved to Warwick to start a new department in a thriving and very lively institution. It was a difficult era; Paris had been in uproar in 1968, and some of the turmoil had spread to the UK. There was a major sit-in at Warwick in the spring of 1970. Change was needed, and as a young Professor, I was appointed to a small working party 'to consider the governance of the University of Warwick'. It was, looking back, my first experience of management in a university, and I found it very stimulating. The second came a little later. I was a Pro-Vice-Chancellor, and while the Vice-Chancellor was abroad, a student demonstration in London went wrong, and one of our students was killed accidentally. A major storm broke over the university. I found that I very much enjoyed working with colleagues from different departments, trying to find solutions we could all live with. Without knowing it at the time, this later led to a major change in career direction.

Research went well: I set up the research groups that I had been dreaming of, and we recruited fifteen new staff members to work in four research groups. I led a virology group, working on the molecular biology of RNA viruses and on interferon. The molecular biology of influenza virus turned out to be an unexpected gold mine, while interferon continued to attract international attention. I travelled widely to conferences, but always with the pressure of producing new and interesting results. We succeeded in cloning two interferon genes, but we were third in the race. On the other hand, we were the first to make a monoclonal antibody to interferon alpha. Things were going well but I was running a group of about fifteen people and working sixty hours a week. I began to ask myself whether I wanted to do this for the rest of my life, even though we were happy at Warwick and in our local Anglican church.

Academia to industrial life

In 1981 I had been at Warwick for nearly thirteen years, had fifteen years to go to retirement, and wanted something new to do. Out of the blue, I was phoned by a head-hunter asking if I was interested in a job in a new Canadian biotechnology company. Rather reluctantly, I went for interview – it was a busy time and I wasn't very interested. As soon as the interview started, I decided that this was not my job, for they were looking for people with different scientific backgrounds to mine. So I relaxed and chattered away, declined to stay for lunch and went home. To my astonishment, I was phoned the next working day and asked to go to Canada for a second interview, and suddenly we had to decide whether we really wanted to pursue this or not. We were ready for a move, our youngest was soon going off to university, and Mary and I did not want to stay at home feeling sad about the empty nest. So when I was offered the job, I accepted and we emigrated to Canada to help start the new company in January 1983.

The job turned out to be very tough. I was the fourth employee; we had an empty laboratory, no strategy, no equipment and no scientists. It was my job to remedy all this. It became clear very quickly that once this had been done, I would be surplus to requirements, and within a few months, we had decided the job would not last until retirement. But we loved Toronto, found many new things to do and were very happy in the local

Baptist church where there was a real feeling of support and comradeship, with lots of people struggling with difficult jobs. We made very good friends, but the job was not going to last. After three years, I started looking around. Again God's benevolence showed itself; I was back in the University of Warwick for a learned society meeting and someone from Norwich asked me whether I knew that they were looking for a new Vice-Chancellor at the University of East Anglia. I said nothing but made a few inquiries, and a little later received a very gracious letter from the Registrar asking if I wished my name to be considered, and if so would I send them a CV.

Back to academia – and national involvements

So started the last chapter of my working life. When I came over on my own for the first interview, I did not think it had gone well, and phoned home to tell my wife. But within a couple of days I had a phone call asking when could I come for a second interview and would I bring my wife? We went first to our youngest's graduation from Sheffield University, then to UEA, where I was offered the job, and then on holiday in west Wales. A few months later, we moved back across the Atlantic with all our furniture and our two dogs, which had to spend six months in quarantine. Thus I commenced a very happy nine years working as Vice-Chancellor in Norwich. There was a huge amount to do and it wasn't easy, but in a way that I could never have anticipated or planned, it drew all my previous experience together. I could read a balance-sheet, talk to business people, write a strategic plan, but most important of all, I had learned that the motivation of highly qualified staff is the key to managing change. Academics work for themselves, and unless they are valued by their institution and want to embrace the future, they can be very hard to move! It also gave Mary and I a chance to work together in entertaining and being entertained in houses large and small all over Norfolk and Suffolk, meeting a huge variety of people in a job I loved.

I approached retirement in 1995 with real trepidation, because I knew I would miss the stimulus of the job and working with such splendid senior colleagues, so I decided to keep working as long as I usefully could and started picking up new jobs in my last year at UEA, some with the churches and some in science policy. We moved from Norwich to Cambridge because I didn't want to be on top of my successor, like a vicar remaining in his parish after retiring. Friends in Cambridge helped me to break into the system there – not an altogether easy thing to do – but with a couple of college links, I gradually learnt how that extraordinary university worked. Most of my jobs were in London and an excellent train service made that very easy.

What opened up, quite unexpectedly, was the consideration of the concerns that the public had over the social and ethical issues arising from new advances in the biological sciences. This arose naturally from a job I had been doing for the Government on the regulatory approval of novel foods, which included all foods using genetically modified material. Initially this was straightforward. A tomato paste made from genetically modified tomatoes had appeared on supermarket shelves without any upset, and had sold well; the product tasted better, it was cheaper and since it was labelled, there was choice. But when the flour from genetically modified soya plants appeared in the early-to-mid nineties, it rapidly became the centre of a very professional anti-GM campaign – based not only on possible risks to health (based either on flawed evidence or on conjecture – 'unknown-unknowns'), but also on resistance to accepting products from a large American multinational, concerns over the patenting of life forms, and 'playing God' with the natural world.

Since that time, I have spoken and written a lot about such issues. But the public were not persuaded: there was no advantage to them in choosing GM foods, and there might just conceivably be a problem. So they avoided them, literally like the plague. I believe that this has been not only a real rebuff to British science, but also a setback to faith, for in my understanding of Christian faith, reason and evidence are more important than inchoate feelings. It became increasingly obvious that the influence of postmodernism, which says that there are no grand narratives and no 'truth' out there, is having a corrosive effect on both science and faith. However, everything is not lost; evidence of the safety of GM foods continues to accumulate and food sustainability has become an important issue. I have no doubt that ultimately the British public will get used to eating foods made from genetically modified plants, as they have done in North and South America and increasingly in Southeast Asia.

Other new jobs opened up too, several working for the Research Councils and a very interesting five years as a Specialist Adviser to the House of Commons Science and Technology Committee where I had the opportunity to influence what questions MPs ask (all prepared beforehand) and also to draft the reports for the Committee. One report in particular stands out, which was concerned with the more effective channelling of basic cancer research into clinical practice. We wrote a report which became the core of a Government White Paper, and that led in turn to substantial changes in policy. This struck a deep personal note, for about this time our middle daughter contracted breast cancer and died in April 2004, leaving three children under six.

In 2006 we moved back to Norwich to pick up old friendships, to be closer to our cottage on the Suffolk coast and to pick up connections to the University, for three Vice-Chancellors had come and gone since I had retired, and I was no longer treading on anyone's toes.

But concerns in the public's minds about developments in science continue and seem to intensify. I still work on two committees on these issues, one for the EPSRC and one for the BBSRC, and 'Synthetic Biology' is a new issue that has arisen just within the last few months. People are troubled about the synthesis of life forms, and again the spectre of 'playing God'.

Christian faith has a profound insight in describing life as a pilgrimage, with us as pilgrims, each with a life to spend, and to spend it just once. Looking back, I could never have planned a career which started in organic chemistry and finished in such a mixture of political, societal and ethical issues. But there has been a path throughout. I can see the connections between the different jobs and the way in which they have fitted together, so I will work on for as long as I can, in the meantime thanking God for all the opportunities I have had.

CHAPTER 4

Borderlands
Gareth Jones

Professor D. Gareth Jones CNZM, BSc, MBBS, DSc, MD, FI Biol. Born 1940. Deputy Vice-Chancellor (Academic and International) at the University of Otago, Dunedin, New Zealand, where he has been Professor of Anatomy and Structural Biology since 1983. Prior to this he held positions in the University of Western Australia, and University College London. He is a Visiting Fellow at St Edmunds College, Cambridge, and a Visiting Professor at Liverpool Hope University. In 2004 he was made a Companion of the New Zealand Order of Merit (CNZM) for his contributions to science and education. He holds the degrees of DSc and MD, for his publications in neuroscience and bioethics respectively. He is a member of the New Zealand Government's Advisory Committee on Assisted Reproductive Technology. Recent books include *Valuing People: Human Value in a World of Medical Technology* (1999), *Speaking for the Dead: Cadavers in Biology and Medicine* (2000; 2nd edition, 2009), *Clones: The Clowns of Technology?* (2001), *Designers of the Future* (2005), *Bioethics* (2007). He is co-author with Alastair Campbell and Grant Gillett of *Medical Ethics* (4th edition, 2005). He is editor with Mary Byrne of *Stem Cell Research and Cloning* (2004), and with John Elford of *A Tangled Web: Medicine and Theology in Dialogue* (2009).

Getting into science

When I set out on my university studies, my goal was to be a medical doctor; nothing could have been further from my mind than science. However, I soon realized that what set me on fire were ideas rather than patients – in the sense that while I could empathize with patients, I was driven by ideas. What changed my direction overnight was a research seminar given by a leading cell biologist during my second year in medical school. As I listened to him describe the then newly discovered unit membrane of the cell, I was entranced. It was like a conversion experience into scientific research; it was to prove my way into academic life, a life from which I have been unable to escape over the succeeding forty or so years.

But all was not straightforward. At that time I was a relatively young Christian, and my research put me into a climate of scientific positivism and aggressive scientific humanism. It was a world antipathetic to Christianity. Science was, supposedly, on course to solve all the problems of humanity, and alongside this triumphalism, Christianity seemed insignificant and academically very puny. It was hardly surprising that most of the Christians with whom I had contact were exceedingly suspicious of science. There were no problems in being a doctor, since this was still seen as a caring profession (the taxing ethical issues that would one day swamp medicine lay many years in the future). But being a scientist was quite different.

More often than not, as I consulted people whom I respected for advice, I was warned against going in this direction because I would probably not survive as a Christian in such a hostile and unsympathetic climate. However, in the years before becoming a Christian, I had read widely in the literature espousing evolutionary humanism, a philosophy that attracted me considerably. I had looked very hard at what it offered intellectually, and my conversion to Christianity entailed a deliberate rejection of this worldview. Consequently, for me, a career in science would be undertaken within a theological framework that enabled me to appreciate the power of the methodology of science as well as the limitations and distractions of scientism as a philosophy. Hence, I came to recognize that a life in science (and in academia) was a 'calling' whereby I was to stand as a Christian in whatever environment I found myself.

What I did not realize at the time was that my career was to involve far more facets than I could ever have imagined. My scientific endeavours in neuroscience were to be supplemented by increasing involvement in bioethical issues, and by major administrative responsibilities at departmental and central levels in universities. But all these have revolved to varying degrees around science, and I have aimed to bring to all of them my Christian perspectives. What has surprised and often disconcerted me, has been the contentious nature of so many of the scientific issues with which I have had to deal, often more controversial within Christian communities than among the general populace.

Early influences

It is interesting as one looks back to assess those influences that made a major impact on one's life – in this case my life as a scientist and Christian. Within biology, a major influence was J. Z. Young, the Professor of Anatomy at University College London. J. Z. was at the height of his powers in the 1960s during my time there as a student and junior academic staff member. His interests ranged from the nervous systems of octopuses and memory systems in the brain, to how nerves function, to doubt and certainty in science (the title of one of his books), to evolutionary questions, and to the underlying principles behind mammalian and vertebrate systems. His lectures were *tours de force* and individual tutorials with him veered from terrifying to immensely stimulating (as long as you were capable of thinking creatively).

This was but a start. J. Z. was also intensely interested in religious questions. Indeed as the years passed, his writings on science took on more overt religious overtones, although he remained staunchly agnostic. He was a scientific humanist of immense proportions and this forced me to analyze all my thinking as a Christian by very rigorous standards. There is no better school in which to develop one's own worldview than alongside someone who does not share one's preconceptions. You cannot get away with sloppy thinking, and you learn that sloppy thinking should have no place in one's own repertoire.

Science is about testing and retesting conventional notions: always striving to come up with better solutions. It is exposing yourself to the gaze of those who want to overthrow your own ideas. But if this applies to science, it should also apply to one's Christian faith, especially where one's faith impacts on science, and *vice versa*. My training provided fertile ground for both the development of my scientific thinking and the development of my science and faith. I could never be satisfied with a sophisticated science linked to a kindergarten faith. It was essential that my faith grew intellectually alongside the growth of my science.

The second person to have an immense influence on me was poles apart from J. Z. Young. This was Martyn Lloyd-Jones, the minister of Westminster Chapel, London, the church I attended for the first four years of my time as a student. This famous preacher had started out as a medical doctor, and it was he above all others who taught me to think. His sermons were lessons in diagnosis, analysis, application, careful exegesis, and a determination to demonstrate how Christianity is relevant for every aspect of existence. My eyes were opened and my horizons expanded. I learned how to think theologically; it illustrated how Christianity applies to everything in life, including science. Every part of our thinking and attitudes is to be infused with Christian precepts, including, of course, science. Never again could I doubt the place of the mind within the Christian life, and never again could I view science in isolation to Christianity. I learnt that it was possible to develop a vigorous faith that could stand tall in any culture, no matter how antagonistic to Christian aspirations. This was to have considerable repercussions for much of my later neuroscientific thinking, when I came to recognize the centrality of our brains for who we are as people.

The third person to influence me was a senior academic in my university department; he was Jack Aitken, whose strong, quiet faith influenced many generations of young medical students and doctors. He demonstrated the importance of a winsome Christian faith and was always there when needed; he was the great encourager; he had the word of advice, and an ever-ready smile.

What I learned from him was that scientists can be human, and that human values can and should shine through. No matter what the questions that were being asked, or the experiments that were being conducted, there was a human face to science. Through the influence of this one man, I learned that science had to be applied in ways that would benefit humankind.

A further influence was Donald MacKay, who came into my life a few years after I had commenced an academic career. Not only was MacKay a mixture of a physical scientist and a biologist, he was one of the most incisive thinkers I had ever come across. His incisiveness stemmed from his love of God and his love of science. It illustrated his commitment both to the book of Scripture and the book of nature. His science and his faith complemented each other perfectly. He totally rejected sloppy thinking, which by definition for him could not bring glory to God. Furthermore, he rejected loose thinking to bolster viewpoints put forward as Christian ones.

From time to time this got him into trouble with those who felt he was rejecting enshrined Christian truths. For MacKay this could never be the case, since his love of the truth shone through in everything he said and wrote. But he was not prepared to accept positions simply because they were put forward as being Christian. For him, if anything truly was Christian it could be argued for and supported from Scripture. He also cautioned against arguing too strongly from the silence of Scripture. But this was part of his incisiveness, and of his longing to be true to what Scripture has to say, rather than to what we think it should be saying. Little did I know at the time just how relevant this model would prove for me when, in later years, I repeatedly found myself in very contentious territory.

Neuroscience and reproductive technologies

Throughout my academic life I have found it impossible to separate my science from my faith and my faith from my science. In the early days, I concentrated on creation – evolution issues – and came to what I regarded as a satisfactory synthesis. However, as this was somewhat peripheral to the science that I was actually undertaking, I began to think about issues closer to my professional concerns; initially neuroscientific ones. These were soon added to by reproductive issues, where the debate at that time was far more vociferous, revolving around abortion. I soon realized (this was in the 1970s) that the debate would come to focus on the nature and status of the early embryo; at the time *in vitro* fertilization (IVF) was emerging as a viable clinical procedure.

My neuroscientific interests centred on the cerebral cortex (grey matter) of the brain, and in particular on its synaptic connections – the junctions between nerve cells. My studies have been dominated by the notion of synaptic plasticity – that is, the flexibility and malleability of synapses in response to functional demands placed upon them. This is the basis of memory and adaptability. Of course, it constitutes only one part of these complex stories, but it is an essential part. This plasticity may change with time, and older people tend to have brains that are less plastic than those of younger people. While we cannot be too dogmatic, there seems little question that it is advantageous to stimulate our neural capacities throughout life. Not only this, a greater understanding of plasticity is also of importance for those who have suffered brain damage and are recuperating. How much recovery of function can we expect, and are there ways in which it might be maximized?

Although my work has been in fundamental research, I have constantly been aware of the world of applied science and over the years I have attempted to relate my work to different medical issues. These have included the effects of malnutrition on the development of synapses in the brain, the effects of alcohol and various other drugs on synaptic development, and the changes incurred by synapses in the ageing brain and particularly in dementia.

This has meant that as I have carried out experimental studies, I have attempted to relate the narrow scientific focus of my research to broader social issues. After all, as a scientist I have always recognized that I am a moral agent, and that I cannot and should not act as a mere technician. It has been my responsibility to determine as far as I can that my work fits into priority areas that will benefit humans and human society. I have seen this as an outworking of what I am as a Christian.

More recently I have become involved in neuroethics (and perhaps even 'neurotheology'), which has emerged as people struggle with the ever-increasing intrusiveness of non-invasive means of analyzing human brain function, via neuroimaging (functional magnetic resonance imaging or fMRI) with its ability to examine neural activity and relate it to behaviour. This facility forces one to ask whether there are neural correlates for moral choices and spiritual activities. Also, since almost every behavioural disorder has become amenable to drug-based treatment, one has to question whether traditional spiritual means of helping people should be complemented by neuroscience. Have traditional approaches using prayer been replaced (or at least augmented), and where do drugs such as Prozac fit in?

Damage to certain brain regions may have grotesque ramifications. This is because memories, emotions and higher thought processes as well as motor functions and sensory awareness have physical correlates in the brain. Crucial as are these observations, they have hardly featured in Christian thinking, which still concentrates on 'the heart' as the organ *par excellence* underlying human responsiveness to God. A theology of the brain is urgently needed. My own approach is to advocate concepts based on a personal model of the brain, using what is known of the plasticity of the brain and its responsiveness to environmental stimuli, rather than a machine analogy. Indeed the brain cannot be isolated from what an individual is and stands for, nor can it be replaced by another brain without destroying the integrity of that person as an individual. I have no doubt that our biological uniqueness as individuals mirrors our theological uniqueness as persons created by God. Throughout, my contribution is to bring a neuroscientific understanding to theological and social debate, in an attempt to forge new paths that take account of both neural explanations and spiritual dimensions.

Alongside these neuroscientific interests, there have been reproductive ones. In the early 1970s I became attracted to the nascent debate concerning artificial reproductive technologies (ARTs). At the time, the arguments had not become highly polarized, unlike in the abortion debate. Few Christians showed any interest in the ARTs, but it was clear to me that the status of the human embryo was one of the most challenging of all areas for Christians. It was exciting territory and I wanted to be part of it. Not only this, I could see that this was an area within anatomy where I could apply my Christian thinking and bring the two sides of my life together; my theology and science could interact and inform one another.

In this way, bioethics became a hobby of mine. In the early 1980s I had no idea how much it was to feature in my life and that a hobby would become transformed into a serious academic pursuit. The turning-point was the publication in 1984 of my book *Brave New People*, one of the early attempts to reflect theologically and scientifically on the burgeoning ARTs. For me this book was to be a one-off, my one and only foray into the ARTs, but this dramatically changed with the intense debate aroused by this book within American Christian circles. Totally unexpectedly, I found myself the centre of controversy. I had hit a spiritual nerve by refusing to accept that human embryos are always and under all (or almost all) circumstances inviolable. The integrity of the relationship between my Christian faith and my science was called into question, to such an extent that I could have despaired. Rather, I set out on two new directions.

On the one hand, I was forced to look far more closely at the theological and ethical issues at the beginning of human life. This led to the publication of *Manufacturing Humans* in 1987, and to a string of subsequent books aimed at a Christian readership. The other new direction was to begin to publish in academic ethics journals, rather than confine myself to Christian publications. Implicit in this latter decision was the realization that there is far more scope to develop ideas in the secular arena than there is in the far narrower confines of Christian publishing. This has enabled me to explore territory and ideas crucial to the flowering of ethical ideas, but always with the goal of unpacking values that are in my view consonant with Christian imperatives. The result was that bioethics became a serious academic pursuit for me, the origins of which lay squarely within my Christian commitment.

In this regard it is important to make the point that my approach to bioethics is thoroughly informed by my scientific background as well as by my Christian framework. I am wary of writers in bioethics who know little about the science underlying the issues at stake. Whenever this happens debate becomes mired in vast generalizations, all too often driven by extremist scenarios and possibilities or by idealistic expectations. This is counter-productive; a scientific input is essential if the debate is to be grounded in reality – what is feasible now or may be feasible within the foreseeable future.

Anatomy and ethics

When I arrived in New Zealand in 1983 to take up the Chair of Anatomy in the University of Otago, some people were extremely surprised to learn that an anatomist would have any interest in ethics. The underlying assumption appeared to be that there was nothing of ethical interest in anatomy. After all, anatomists only deal with dead human bodies, and these are ethically neutral, or so it was thought. Apart from the human cadavers, the department housed histology slides of human material, human embryonic and foetal material, human skeletons, Maori and Polynesian skeletal material, a museum with an extensive range of archival and recent human organs and body parts, together with a constant supply of experimental animals. All these seemed to be accepted as of no ethical consequence. We were legally allowed to have them and study them, and that was it. We were certainly not expected to talk about them too openly in public or use them as matters for debate.

One can now look back on those days of twenty-five years ago, and wonder at the naïvety of serious and reasonable anatomists who thought like that. They had somehow managed to isolate the professional practices in which they indulged from the remainder of their existences, permeated as they must have been by moral values and swirling ethical debates of strident intensity. And yet what was true of anatomy was undoubtedly true of many other disciplines and professions. This is not to say that there was no awareness of ethical matters; there was. But it tended to be highly focused and selective, and generally lacked intellectual rigour.

For me, it was impossible to act in this manner, since I felt compelled to relate as best I could my Christian faith and my professional responsibilities. This necessitated a serious ethical analysis of all these practices in which anatomists were engaged. In the preface to the first edition of my book, *Speaking for the Dead*, I explained why I thought such an analysis is required:

> The manner in which we respond to the dead, the use we make of their skeletal remains and their tissues, the ways in which we learn about ourselves by studying them, all raise queries that go to the heart of what it means to be human. Hence, the apparently unfathomable gulf between the dead and us is far less unfathomable than we often imagine, and presses upon us the importance of exploration and understanding of the many links between the living and the dead.

While this book and its subsequently updated second edition was written for an academic readership, it was intended to reflect Christian underpinnings in bridging the worlds of science and ethical practice. It is fascinating to ponder on ways that the treatment of the dead human body has ramifications for a wide array of ethical conundrums implicating human tissue and human material: from embryo research (including the derivation of embryonic stem cells) to definitions of brain death, from the use (or abuse) of body parts to contemporary ways of preserving and exhibiting human cadavers, and from the utilization of dead human foetuses in neural grafting to attempts at enhancing human bodies and 'curing' death.

In approaching ethical issues in this manner I have attempted to view them within the context of the human body rather than tackle them as isolated ethical problems. While I cannot claim Christian credentials for acting thus, I contend that it brings out the ethical significance of myriad aspects of human relationships – with one another, with the marginalized, with those who have died, and with those as yet unborn. Anatomy, traditionally the province of the dead human, is brought into the same conceptual world as that of clinical and research ethics, so it is becoming obvious that anatomical study is far from ethically neutral. Indeed it is pervaded by ethical queries of the utmost gravity for the human condition. Christians should be keen to search for ways in which their insights into human dignity and human value – based as they are upon our creation in the image of God – can be applied consistently to human existence before and after birth, debilitated as well as in health, in death as well as in life. Moreover, our concern for humankind should extend to those of all cultures, an issue of considerable relevance when determining how to treat skeletal remains of indigenous groups and the manner in which organs and cadavers available for therapy and research have been obtained, not least in societies with diametrically different worldviews from one's own.

Are Christians in science in a perilous position?

This is a question that has to be asked, by scientists as much as by others. Many years ago I determined to go into a scientific career in spite of the concern shown by some senior Christian leaders. I now need to ask whether that was a mistake. Of course, it would be even more valuable to ask those who advised me against science all those years ago what they now think. That is impossible, but it is a salutary consideration.

Some Christians may think I have abandoned the true faith, or at least have a second-class faith. I profess to be a Christian; those working with me know me as a Christian; I write a great deal as a Christian in controversial areas. The problem is that I constantly ask difficult questions. I refuse to accept superficial answers, and I refuse to be labelled in any of the neat ways beloved of many Christians. I spend my time in intellectual territory where Christians are often uneasy – issues such as the beginning and end of life, abortion, euthanasia, brain death, neural transplantation, dementia, genetics, artificial reproductive technologies, homosexuality, and so on. Each one of these is highly controversial for some groups of Christians (as well as others). Why, then, don't I stick to straightforward non-contentious topics, where most Christians would feel more at home?

The answer is simple. I believe I have been called into these realms of uncertainty and cultural disquiet. This is where I am to integrate my faith and learning. If I am a human anatomist, with a particular interest in the brain and in human development and ageing, these are the areas where I am to spend most of my efforts at integration. I am to be prepared to give an answer to anyone who asks me how I live as a biomedical scientist and a Christian.

I do not want to keep my science and faith in separate watertight compartments. I am unwilling to live with a vast chasm between the two. I am determined to relate my faith to the science in which I am engaged, and not to some other branch of science that is not my own professional area. I think this would be unhelpful, in that my scientific expertise would not be informing the faith/learning dialogue. This would also allow me to function in my own scientific area in unexamined ways.

A Christian faith must surely seek to influence science and likewise science must influence our faith, as long as our faith is firmly controlled by a biblically based ethos. Some may be alarmed at a statement like this, seeing it as smacking of a relativistic faith. However, I would make a similar statement about accountants, shop assistants, school teachers, or counsellors. Integration of our faith with any aspect of human existence and experience has its dangers. On the other hand, lack of integration leaves our Christianity isolated from ordinary life; its purity may go unchallenged, but its ability to inform and transform daily existence is limited. Jesus was striving for integration when he recounted his parables of the light and salt, the wheat and tares, the talents, and the unscrupulous servant, and when he urged his followers to be in the world but not of it. He mingled unashamedly with prostitutes and tax-gatherers, the outcasts of respectable society. This is how he himself lived; and he calls us to follow in his footsteps.

Being a scientist and a Christian

I have little doubt that being a scientist affects what I am as a Christian. However, I am convinced that scientists bring invaluable challenges to Christianity because of some of the characteristics they have gained from their science. For myself I think the following apply.

The first is constant inquiring and searching. I am prepared to ask awkward questions, and sometimes even to think the unthinkable. Nothing is above analysis and assessment, just as nothing is above questioning in any true, scientific realm. It is basic to who I am as a Christian. Faith grows as it is exposed to challenges, whether these are in the form of suffering or hardships, or by being challenged intellectually.

Allied to this is the search for truth, and the importance of honesty and openness in this search: these are inseparable characteristics of science (even if on occasion they are tragically missing when fraud and deception raise their ugly heads). Any proper scientist will demonstrate a free spirit of enquiry. Likewise, Christians should love the truth and should do everything to base their beliefs and lifestyles on it. We should be ready to admit when we are wrong and we should be ready to correct error (especially in ourselves – Matthew 6:4–5). All ideas and views are open to being tested and revised. Scientists who are true to their craft have an aversion to dogmatism, and this is an important feature of the Christian character as well.

From this it follows that, as Christians, we should refrain from setting ourselves up as authorities. There is only one authority and that is Christ, to whom we are always to be subject and from whom we are always to learn. Our interpretation of Scripture may be wrong and our dependence on the Holy Spirit may be inadequate. In all this, many of the characteristics of the good scientist functioning as a scientist are those of the Spirit-filled Christian.

CHAPTER 5

And Information Became Physical

Andrew Briggs

Andrew Briggs is Professor of Nanomaterials at the University of Oxford, and Director of the Quantum Information Processing Interdisciplinary Research Collaboration. He is Professorial Fellow of St Anne's College, Emeritus Fellow of Wolfson College, Honorary Fellow of the Royal Microscopical Society, Fellow of the Institute of Physics, and Liveryman of the Clothworkers' Company. He has a degree in theology and a private pilot licence. He has over 500 publications, the majority in international scholarly journals. His research focuses on carbon nanomaterials and their properties for quantum technologies.

In 1972 the Cavendish Laboratory of the University of Cambridge moved to a new set of buildings. It had previously been located in the centre of the city, with its main entrance in Free School Lane. In the course of its history it had been presided over by some of the most distinguished physicists alive. On the doors of the original laboratory had been carved, almost certainly at the instigation of the first Cavendish Professor, James Clerk Maxwell, a verse from Psalm 111, '*Magna opera Domini exquisita in omnes voluntates ejus.*' Professor Sir Brian Pippard has related how, 'Shortly after the move to the new buildings in 1973 a devout research student suggested to me that the same text should be displayed, in English, at the entrance. I undertook to put the proposal to the Policy Committee, confident that they would veto it; to my surprise, however, they heartily agreed both to the idea and to the choice of Coverdale's translation' (Pippard, 1987). It was carved on mahogany by Will Carter, and placed over the new entrance. It reads:

The works of the Lord are great,
sought out of all them that have pleasure therein.

I was that research student. I love this text, because it says that what we scientists are doing is studying how God makes the world work.[1] I find that many of the challenges in relating science and faith spring from an inadequate appreciation of what this means. Conversely, just as there is an added dimension of pleasure in enjoying the creative work of someone you know, so there is an added pleasure in studying the world if you know the creator.

I grew up in Cambridge, where the reputation of the Cavendish Laboratory is part of local folklore. I remember my mother telling me that this was where Rutherford had split the atom. As an undergraduate I studied physics at Oxford, returning to Cambridge for my graduate studies. After my PhD I planned to be ordained in the Church of England, and I took the Cambridge Theology Tripos. But the call of science was too strong for me, and after a short period of post-doctoral research in the Cambridge University Engineering Department, I joined Sir Peter Hirsch at what was then the Department of Metallurgy and Science of Materials at Oxford. I became obsessed with microscopy, and the ability to study materials on an ever smaller scale. This was the beginning for me of what is now known as nanotechnology. In due course the University of Oxford created a Chair in Nanomaterials, and I was appointed as the first Professor of Nanomaterials.

Nanotechnology and quantum computing

As you make things smaller and smaller, you can ask the question, 'How is small different from big?' The answer may take many forms. It may be that the surface begins to dominate in importance over the bulk, so that adhesion becomes more important than inertia, with consequences for nano-electro-mechanical systems. A higher proportion of the atoms are at the surface, with consequences for chemical reactivity and catalysis. As you make things very small, so discrete quantum states emerge, and these can be studied and manipulated. This has led to the emerging discipline of quantum nanotechnology.

In 1997 I spent a sabbatical year at the Hewlett-Packard Laboratories in California. I had become interested in the growth and properties of quantum dots which could form during the growth of semiconductor wafers. Germanium atoms are slightly larger than silicon atoms, so if you try to grow germanium on a silicon wafer, the germanium atoms are under compression. The germanium can grow like this for a few layers, but then the strain becomes too great, and tiny islands of germanium spontaneously form. These grow into quantum dots. At Hewlett-Packard I participated in some experiments to study such materials systems with atomic resolution, and to try to account for the distributions of shapes and sizes of the resulting dots. While I was there I learned about quantum computing. At the time I could not think of any experiments that I could do that would contribute to building a quantum computer, but I found the subject deeply fascinating and I determined to learn more.

The discipline of quantum information processing owes much to the insight that information can be described physically. In the 1940s Claude Shannon had perceived how information could be described mathematically. He found that equations describing information – for example, how it could propagate in an imperfect channel – had the same form as equations which had been developed in the nineteenth century to describe the thermodynamics of particles. This is why terms such as entropy are often used to describe information. At about the same time that Shannon was developing his insights about the mathematical nature of information, Alan Turing was developing ideas about a universal machine for computing (Turing, 1936). Half a century later, David Deutsch at Oxford published a paper which in many ways has served as a manifesto for quantum computation (Deutsch, 1985). He built on Turing's insight:

> Every 'function which would naturally be regarded as computable' can be computed by the universal Turing machine.

David Deutsch picked up on the point that although Turing was writing about a machine for computation, he did so in an abstract way:

> The conventional, non-physical view interprets it as the quasi-mathematical conjecture that all possible formalizations of the intuitive mathematical notion of 'algorithm' or 'computation' are equivalent to each other.

He criticized formulations such as Turing's as being vague, for example in speaking of 'what would naturally be regarded'. He re-expressed Turing's formulation as a physical statement:

> Every finitely realizable physical system can be perfectly simulated by a universal model computing machine operating by finite means.

Deutsch preferred this as both better defined and more physical, because it referred exclusively to objective concepts such as 'measurement', 'preparation' and 'physical system', which are already known in measurement theory.

This may sound like mere philosophical nitpicking, but it turns out to have immensely practical consequences. If information is to be subject to computation in a physical system, then it had better be regarded as quantum, because at the relevant level physical systems are quantum. And if it is quantum, then whatever you can do with a quantum object you can do with information. The discipline of quantum information processing rests on this fundamental understanding. It was further articulated by Rolf Landauer of IBM in a paper on *The physical nature of information* (Landauer, 1996). The opening paragraph is headed 'Information is physical':

> Information is not a disembodied abstract entity; it is always tied to a physical representation. It is represented by engraving on a stone tablet, a spin, a charge, a hole in a punched card, a mark on paper, or some other equivalent.

This ties the handling of information to all the possibilities and restrictions of our real physical world, its laws of physics and its storehouses of available parts.

Landauer was initially sceptical about the feasibility of quantum computing, because quantum superposition states are so delicate that it seemed that it would be impossible to preserve them for long enough to do sustained calculations. He changed his mind when he learned about methods for fault-tolerant error correction in quantum computing, one of them invented by my colleague Andrew Steane at Oxford.[2]

During the year following my return from California, I began to think more and more about how you might use quantum properties of materials to build a quantum computer. At the time I was a visiting professor at the Ecole Polytechnique Fédérale de Lausanne, and we were engaged in some experiments to measure the mechanical properties of carbon nanotubes (Salvetat *et al.*, 1999). These consist of sheets of carbon atoms rolled up to make tubes that are so tiny that if you put 50,000 of them side by side, that would be about the width of a human hair. I thought about how you might put spins inside a carbon nanotube to create an array for a quantum processor. The ideas grew, and there is now a sizable community of us at Oxford and beyond studying the properties of carbon nanomaterials for quantum technologies (Benjamin *et al.*, 2006). One of the most remarkable molecules for this purpose is a cage of sixty carbon atoms, arranged like the vertices on a soccer ball, inside which we can place a single nitrogen atom. This atom behaves as though it were almost perfectly isolated, so that we can manipulate the quantum states of its electrons and its nucleus with exquisite precision. The accuracy with which we can do this, and the time over which the quantum information can be retained, are sufficient for this to be used as a component for a solid-state quantum computer.

God, creation and history

Quantum computing is not the only field of science where what might previously have been described by an abstract noun is now seen to have a physical embodiment. There is a growing amount of experimental data showing how behavioural attributes, such as personality and character, correspond to physical states and processes in the brain (Jeeves, 2004). Such advances in neuroscience prompt afresh questions of human freedom and responsibility in the light of the mechanisms of the brain. Can the new understanding of the physical nature of information similarly stimulate fresh insights about the nature of God's involvement in the world?

I find that it is essential to appreciate the continuity between God's activity in creation and his subsequent activity in history. The connection is so close that although these two can be distinguished they cannot usefully be separated. At least four different belief paradigms can be identified, using Oxford English Dictionary definitions:

- **Atheism:** Disbelief in, or denial of, the existence of a God. 'A little superficial knowledge of philosophy may incline the mind of man to atheism' (Francis Bacon, 1561–1626).

- **Deism:** Belief in the existence of a God, with rejection of revelation: 'natural religion'. 'Deism being the very same with old Philosophical Paganism' (Richard Bentley, 1662–1742).

- **Agnostic:** One who holds that the existence of anything beyond material phenomena cannot be known (coined by Thomas Henry Huxley, 1825–95).

- **Theism:** Belief in a deity or deities, as opposed to *atheism*. Belief in one God as creator and supreme ruler of the universe, without denial of revelation; in this use distinct from *deism*.

Since atheism denies the existence of God, an atheist believes neither that God created the world nor that he subsequently sustains it; there is little more to be said. Deism asserts that God created the world, but that he subsequently left it to itself and has no further interaction with it. A consequence is that there is no revelation from God to man. Knowledge of God comes instead through so-called natural theology, whereby man is able to deduce through the exercise of his reason what God is like. The sciences play a special role in this, since they provide the empirical evidence to which reason is applied. Robert Boyle may have unintentionally contributed to the rise of Deism, through likening the universe to a famous clock at Strasbourg whose mechanism can be studied; the clock does not need the subsequent intervention of the clockmaker for each tick (if regular winding and occasional repairs are disregarded).

Joseph Addison was born on 1 May 1672 in Wiltshire. He studied at Queen's College, Oxford. His Latin verses gained him admission to Magdalen College as a demy; he was elected a Fellow of the College in 1698. Having written several works of poetry and prose, he turned to essay-writing for the *Tatler*. In 1711 he published the first issue of the *Spectator*. He died of asthma complicated by dropsy in Warwickshire in 1719. Joseph Addison's famous 'Ode' to the glory of God (after Psalm 19:1–6) first appeared in *The Spectator*, no. 465, 1712. It was set to music by Benjamin Britten in his *Noye's Fludde*:

> The spacious firmament on high,
> With all the blue ethereal sky,
> And spangled heav'ns, a shining frame,
> Their great original proclaim:
> Th' unwearied Sun, from day to day,
> Does his Creator's power display,
> And publishes to every land
> The work of an Almighty Hand.
>
> Soon as the evening shades prevail,
> The Moon takes up the wondrous tale,

And nightly to the list'ning Earth
Repeats the story of her birth:
Whilst all the stars that round her burn,
And all the planets, in their turn,
Confirm the tidings as they roll,
And spread the truth from pole to pole.

What though, in solemn silence, all
Move round the dark terrestrial ball?
What though nor real voice nor sound
Amid their radiant orbs be found?
In Reason's ear they all rejoice,
And utter forth a glorious voice,
For ever singing, as they shine,
'The Hand that made us is Divine.'

Addison assumed that the Earth's rotations take place in silence because God does not speak; it is only the observations of astronomy that enable human reason to deduce the power of God. This is wrong not so much for what it affirms but for what it denies. I prefer what my grandfather, George Wallace Briggs (1875–1959), a Canon of Worcester Cathedral, wrote in 1953 about how God communicates. I find that this reflects more accurately both what I find in the Bible and my experience of the Christian faith:

God has spoken by His prophets,
Spoken His unchanging Word,
Each from age to age proclaiming
God, the one, the righteous Lord.
Mid the world's despair and turmoil,
One firm anchor holding fast;
God is King, His throne eternal,
God the first, and God the last.

God has spoken by Christ Jesus,
Christ, the everlasting Son,

Brightness of the Father's glory,
With the Father ever one;
Spoken by the Word incarnate,
God of God, ere time began,
Light of light, to earth descending,
Man, revealing God to man.

God yet speaks by His own Spirit
Speaking to the hearts of men,
In the age-long Word expounding
God's own message, now as then;
Through the rise and fall of nations
One sure faith yet standing fast,
God is King, His Word unchanging,
God the first, and God the last.

A HYMN SUNG TO THE TUNE OF BEETHOVEN'S 'ODE TO JOY'

Deism did not survive. Ian Barbour (1966: 61–62) explained why:

> The waning of Deism can be attributed primarily to its own inherent weaknesses. The Cosmic Designer, who started the world-machine and left it to run on its own, seemed impersonal and remote – not a God who cares for individuals and is actively related to man, or a Being to whom prayer would be appropriate. It is not surprising that such a do-nothing God, irrelevant to daily life, became a hypothesis for the origin of the world or a verbal formula which before long could be dispensed with completely.

Thomas Huxley coined the word 'agnostic' in 1869 at a party held to mark the formation of the short-lived Metaphysical Society, allegedly taking it from Paul's mention of the altar to 'the Unknown God' in Acts 17:23.[3] Uniquely of the four belief paradigms, the term for this one was created by its advocate; the others were each initially derogatory. Huxley quickly lost control of the meaning. There is a story that Benjamin Jowett, the Master of Balliol College, Oxford, replied to an undergraduate who proclaimed himself an agnostic, 'Young man, in this university we speak Latin not Greek, so when speaking of yourself in that way, use the word ignoramus.' It was quickly recognized that agnosticism could be a veneer: 'In nine cases out of ten, Agnosticism is but old atheism "writ large".'[4]

If old-fashioned deism is less prevalent now, it may be regarded as being to some extent superseded by its apparent opposite, first in the form of creationism, and more recently in the form of so-called intelligent design. Creationism, in its most extreme form, denies much of the scientific consensus about the processes of evolution in the origin and development of species. It is often associated with a belief that the universe is much younger than the generally accepted value of 13.7 billion years or so. The intelligent design movement has complex origins. Politically it arose from the requirement in America to eliminate instruction about God from state education, and hence to abandon any insistence that creationism should be taught as an alternative model to evolution. Intellectually it arose from the writings of people such as Phillip Johnson, a law professor at the University of California at Berkeley who sought to argue that scientists, with an astonishing degree of apparent collusion, were pursuing a materialist (= atheistic) agenda.

Intelligent design identifies phenomena in biology whose evolutionary origin demands further explanation, and claim that such phenomena provide evidence for 'Intelligent Design'. To avoid mixing education and religion, the advocates may not be allowed to identify the designer as God, but this is the clear implication. Some writers in the ID movement, such as Michael Behe, go further, and claim that the complexity of the biological world could not have arisen without some independent steer from the intelligent designer (Behe, 1996). I do not know of any colleagues at my own university who find such arguments either convincing or useful. Even for organs such as eyes there is a growing amount of evidence that evolutionary development has occurred through several independent pathways.[5] But no less important is the theological argument.

Suppose the set of all observed phenomena is drawn as a circle in a diagram. Now imagine a boundary separating those phenomena which we understand at some level from those which we do not understand. If we ascribe those which we understand to science, and those which we do not understand to God (or at least to an intelligent designer), then as science progresses, more and more can be explained by science, leaving less and less to God. This may be how some people view the demise of faith in the face of the inexorable advance of science. But such a picture is wrong in almost every respect. First of all, the size of the circle is growing rapidly, and it may well be growing faster than the area of the territory containing what we understand. Indeed, to say that we understand something is an imprecise statement; the best that we can usually do is to understand an observation to a given level of explanation. Both of these objections are trivial compared with the fundamental mistake of ascribing phenomena either to science or to God, as though these were alternatives. As the inscription over the entrance to the Cavendish laboratory says, in our scientific studies we are discovering how God makes the world work.

A Jewish colleague recently told me how much he had enjoyed reading *The Language of God* (Collins, 2006, see pp. 246–60, below). He is a believer, and writes with considerable authority about the composition and function of genes. My colleague commented that he detected the greatest sense of worship in the book when Collins was writing about science that is now very well understood, and he contrasted this with those who claim to feel most secure in their faith when they find topics in science that have not yet been elucidated. As the founding Professor of Theoretical Chemistry at Oxford wrote, 'When we come to the scientifically unknown, our correct policy is not to rejoice because we have found God; it is to become better scientists' (Coulson, 1958: 16).

The God who reveals himself

For me the only tenable position is the one designated 'theist'. God's activity in creation and his activity in history are of a single piece. While there are successive stages in the narrative in Genesis, there is no satisfactory point which would function as a divide between creation and subsequent history. On the contrary, the opening chapter seems to be put there to say, in effect, the God whom you are going to read about in the following pages, and whom you may know through your community and through your own experience, is exactly and precisely the one who is responsible for the whole physical existence of the universe and your place in it. This is why the believer can enjoy complete integrity between worship in church and research in the laboratory.

The fusion of the world of information and the physical world should not come as a surprise to the Christian believer. This was foreseen in the Old Testament, where the word of God often has the properties of something that is effective in the world. In the opening chapter of his gospel, John describes how the Word became physical. The term $\Lambda \acute{o} \gamma o \varsigma$ (*Logos* or 'Word') conveys a *double entendre*, no doubt intended. In Jewish thought it could describe God's revelation in which his thought was communicated through his speech. In Greek thought it was the rational principle of the universe of Stoic and Platonic philosophy. John takes both of these meanings and explicitly identifies them with God himself, and then states that in Jesus the $\Lambda \acute{o} \gamma o \varsigma$ was physically embodied. The early Christians were quick to see the implication of this for every aspect of their lives. What is probably one of their earliest hymns bases the attitude which they should have to each other on what they find in Jesus:

> He was in the form of God; yet he laid no claim to equality with God, but made himself nothing, assuming the form of a slave. Bearing the human likeness, sharing the human lot, he humbled himself, and was obedient, even to the point of death, death on a cross!
>
> PHILIPPIANS 2:6–8

The resurrection is the best-documented miracle of the Christian faith, but the incarnation is at least as significant. 'The central miracle asserted by Christians is the Incarnation. They say that God became Man. Every other miracle prepares for this, or exhibits this, or results from this' (Lewis, 1947: 131). We have yet to see what the eventual impact of quantum information processing will be. The significance of the Word becoming flesh is already well established.

NOTES

1. Berry, R.J. (2008). 'The research scientist's psalm'. *Science & Christian Belief*, 20: 147-161.
2. Steane, A. M. (1996). 'Errot connecting codes in quantum theory'. *Physical Review Letters*, 77: 793–97.
3. R. H. Hutton, owner of the Spectator, in a letter dated 13 March 1881.
4. *Saturday Review*, 819 (2), 26 June 1880.
5. See Chapter 15 by Simon Conway Morris.

CHAPTER 6

A Belief in Climate
Mike Hulme

Mike Hulme is Professor of Climate Change at the University of East Anglia (UEA) and the founding Director (2000–2007) of the Tyndall Centre for Climate Change Research. After geography degrees at the Universities of Durham and Swansea, he lectured in geography at the University of Salford, before joining the Climatic Research Unit in the School of Environmental Sciences at the UEA in 1988. He has advised numerous organizations, companies and governments about climate change, and as a member of the United Nations Intergovernmental Panel on Climate Change from 1996 to 2002, he was a joint recipient of the 2007 Nobel Peace Prize. He worships at an Anglican church in Norwich.

Early influences

I have lived with the weather for all of my adult life. Or more precisely, I have lived and breathed the numbers we use to describe the weather. I first started following the daily TV and newspaper weather forecasts when I was a teenager, anxious to know whether or not my school cricket match or England's Test Match was going to be cancelled owing to poor weather. I first tested the accuracy of weather forecasts using a max–min thermometer in our mini-conservatory at home, each day checking to see whether the temperatures matched those that had been forecast the previous day. This interest developed as part of a much broader fascination. My curiosity about the nature of the world around me – both its human and physical dimensions – made for an easy choice of subject to study at university. Three years of an undergraduate geography degree at the University of Durham did not sate my thirst for the subject and I went on to work at the University College of Swansea for a PhD in rainfall variations in Sudan. I had embarked on a career that was to lead me to the study of global climate change: how we construct knowledge about future climate and what we do with that knowledge once it is formed.

My three years at Durham did more than provide an academic springboard for my later career. While there I had confirmed for myself the Christian faith in which I had been brought up. My parents were Christian converts from the 1940s and their strong evangelical convictions provided a framework for living into which I was inducted. Looking back on my parents' faith – their 'way of living' which, through osmosis, I had absorbed as being the norm – I recognize its three main dimensions: moral, spiritual and intellectual. There was no escaping the strong Christian morality at home. Boundaries of personal behaviour were made clear and the desirability of various forms of public morality in the social realm was often discussed at meal-times. The spirituality of my parents was evident in their devotional prayer life and in the strength upon which they drew to offer hospitality and support both to neighbours and strangers. The latter were often students from the university where my father worked, many of them international students, especially from Africa.

It was the intellectual dimension of my parents' Christian faith that was perhaps the most striking, especially that of my father. The Baptist church that we attended had only a very small youth group and all of the members were girls. My parents took pity on me and I wasn't made to attend. Instead, after a year of joining in a rather distant Crusader class on Sunday afternoons which didn't go very well for me, my father enrolled me in his own idiosyncratic course of Christian education. Each Sunday evening we would spend an hour or so together, during which he would set me some reading or a mini-research project for the following week. This home-spun syllabus covered not only what one might have expected – biblical study and some church history – but it also introduced me to a much wider set of Christian biographies and ideas, critiques and commentaries than most fifteen-year-olds would have encountered. I thus read some of the great Christian apologists of my father's generation, who had written on subjects such as the history of science (Reijer Hookyaas), English literature (Ruth Etchells), the philosophy of science (Donald MacKay), philosophy and apologetics (C. S. Lewis), poverty and ethics (Ronald Sider) and modern culture (Francis Schaeffer).

This rather curious introduction to an eclectic intellectual Christianity did two things for me which in retrospect were significant. The first was the licence my father gave me to read, think and question, rather than to blindly accept the rather superficial and platitudinous theology one sometimes heard in church. The authors to whom I was introduced were all prepared to tackle some of the most perplexing and controversial aspects of how the Christian faith related to secular knowledge. Being exposed to such writings at an impressionable age taught me that there are no questions that are too difficult for a Christian to engage with. The second thing I learnt was that there were people and thinkers far greater than I who had wrestled with the same sort of questions that troubled me; Christians who were no one's intellectual debtors. I ended my home schooling in the Christian faith with no doubts that whether one was an artist or a philosopher, a scientist or a novelist, it was possible also to be a man or woman of convinced Christian faith.

Yet whilst these discoveries impressed themselves on me, I was still a nervous and timid eighteen-year-old when I left home for university. I was not entirely sure whether I had the inclination or determination to become a person who lived by faith or simply a person who knew a lot about what the Christian faith meant to others. If pushed, I might well have said I was a Christian, yet I remained sheltered from the challenges and demands of adult life. These challenges probe deeply into our spiritual and ethical resources. If we are to survive them we have to discover and nurture a depth of character capable of withstanding considerable pressures and distractions.

Nineteen seventy-eight was a critical year for me. It involved a number of encounters, two of which stand out as particularly significant. In the summer before I started at Durham, my parents encouraged me – I still can't quite work out how they managed to persuade such an unsociable teenager – to attend a three-week work-camp in the south of France under the auspices of the International Fellowship of Evangelical Students. Here I laboured and relaxed under an endless sun with a couple of dozen other young British Christians. I vividly remember one lazy afternoon sitting by a stream with one of the adult leaders who asked us what we wanted to be in our later lives. My answer was entirely instinctive and I said I would like to work for the United Nations in some capacity, perhaps using my interest in geography. This surprised me as much as it surprised anyone else.

The other incident occurred during my second term at Durham. I had tentatively identified myself with the Christian Union in my College and was beginning to find it possible to stand on my own two feet away from home. Late one evening over coffee with a group of sporting friends who weren't Christians, we entered into a lengthy discussion about the evidence for the Christian faith. This topic had certainly not been sought by me and yet it ran and ran until about five o'clock in the morning. From what I remember, it was a good-natured discussion and although outnumbered, I was somehow able to respond to most of the issues that ran through the night: the evidence for God, the nature of science, the reliability of the Bible, the evidence of the resurrection of Christ, the diversity of religions, and so on. One incident remains with me: my friend Lincoln claimed at one point that if there was a Supreme Being, he surely would not choose to reveal himself in a book (meaning the Koran, the Bible or the Bhagavad Gita). And my point was exactly this: the unique claim of the Christian faith is that God's ultimate revelation has been in the form of a person, not a book – a living human being to whom we can relate and with whom we can identify. If Jesus Christ is not 'God made flesh', then Christianity loses its foundation; no amount of wisdom contained in all the holy books of the world could compensate.

This line of reasoning pre-dated my later discovery in the writings of C. S. Lewis – for me, the greatest of Christian apologists and communicators – of a similar logical apologetic for the nature of divine revelation. Drawing upon the analogy of a biologist, Lewis argues that lower forms of being can only know the essence of higher forms of being if those higher forms choose to reveal themselves, yet the higher forms can know the lower forms by imposing their superior power. Thus the microbiologist can study phytoplankton under a microscope without the co-operation of the phytoplankton. And a botanist can study the functioning of the vine without the co-operation of the vine. When it comes to the higher forms of animals, the zoologist may have a harder time studying the robin or the field-mouse, but it can generally be accomplished, although the study of the gorilla will generally require a degree of co-operation from the subject. With human relations we can only truly get to know someone if they are willing to disclose themselves. If they do not, our knowledge of them will remain superficial. In the case of a Supreme Being we, as the lower form of life, have no chance of knowing anything meaningful about such an entity unless he[1] should choose to reveal himself to us. We cannot know such a Being from a distance and we cannot subject him to our experiment or control.

It is in this sense that God's revelation of himself in the person of Jesus Christ is the only true and satisfying way that we, his creatures, can ever enter into relationship with him. As my later field research was to show me, there are places on Earth where transcendent experiences can be found – for me, sleeping under the stars of the Sahara Desert was the most powerful of these – but such experiences are no more than pointers to a Supreme Being. The encounter only becomes personal and satisfying through the person of Jesus Christ, God's chosen means of self-disclosure to humankind.

The science of limits

Twelve years almost to the day after surprising myself with my expressed desire to work for the United Nations, in early August 1990 I found myself in the headquarters of the UN Environment Programme (UNEP) at Gigiri, Nairobi. I was by now working as a contracted researcher in the Climatic Research Unit at the University of East Anglia, one of the first research groups in the world to take seriously the study of climate change on human time-scales and the role of humanity in influencing the world's climates. Just turned thirty, I was in Kenya on a week's consultancy mission to help UNEP with their global assessment of desertification. I was to provide for them climatic data which would underpin their analysis of the extent and distribution of the world's drylands, within which the processes of land degradation were at work.

In 1988 the idea of the 'enhanced greenhouse effect' – or 'global warming' as it is now more popularly termed – exploded from being a subject of academic study onto the national and international policy stage. This was the summer when I moved from an academic job at Salford to Norwich to take up a research post. I found myself working on and developing global climate datasets and using them to evaluate the performance of climate models. Dealing with millions of individual meteorological measurements from around the world, I now had my fill of numbers, statistics and weather.

The idea that humans are altering global climate, potentially in quite significant ways, struck me early on as carrying with it a range of ethical and spiritual considerations. I wrote an article about climate change for a Christian magazine in 1990 and starting giving talks about its significance in my church and to Christian groups elsewhere. For me, this was not just an abstract or intellectual question: my own lifestyle decisions were now influenced by my desire to 'live more lightly' on the Earth and in particular to minimize my energy consumption. Our decisions as a family in the early 1990s to retrofit our home with low-energy bulbs and insulating materials, to live within walking distance of as many as possible of our key local venues – work, church, schools, shops – and, a few years later, to buy one of the early Toyota Prius hybrid cars, were all motivated by this desire to align my lifestyle choices with my academic research and Christian faith.

However, I have found that the sorts of questions it raises in my mind have changed as the issue of climate change has increasingly impacted on the public conscience and risen higher up the policy agenda. I do not believe that we need to preserve for all time a pre-industrial nineteenth-century climate, or even to regard today's semi-altered climate as the norm. Neither do I believe that humanity is capable of eventually mastering the world's climate and maintaining its stability, whether through social, political or technological interventions. There is a danger of hubris in setting out on such an over-reaching mission, a danger to which humans have been attracted ever since they attempted to build the tower at Babel.

Indeed, I don't think that climate change is the fundamental problem. For me, the idea of climate change – that the reach of humanity is now so great that the functioning of the entire planetary system (not just its climate) is being altered by our collective actions – is merely a magnifier for many of the other ills in our world, ills that we humans are deeply implicated in.

- Climate change may make hunger worse amongst the 'bottom billion', but hunger in our world is already a scandal.

- Climate change may accelerate the extinction of some species, but through our demanding use of the land we're doing a pretty good job of applying the squeeze already.

- Climate change may bring us somewhat more speedily to the limits of fresh-water use in some parts of the world, but our growing and increasingly demanding populations will get us there anyway.

- Climate change (through rising sea-level) will put more people at risk of inundation from tidal surges, but the

burgeoning mega-cities of the Asian coastal zones and
their hoovering-up of the rural poor are doing that
already.

We live in a distorted and unjust world, with problems that are
always easier to solve through rhetoric than to eliminate in reality.
Our clumsy and distorting fingerprints can be found everywhere
and they are now found tampering with the very climate of the
planet itself. Symbolically I believe this is significant; it rings
warning bells that, collectively, we have gained an unsought
power rivalling that of the sun. But in a substantive or material
sense I don't think climate change is the ultimate evil. We are not
depleting the climate in the way we are depleting other resources.
There will be just as much 'weather' each day as before, although
it will be redistributed according to different rules. The point isn't
whether we are making the climate better or worse: such moral
categories do not apply to climate (is a drought an absolute evil,
or is a calm tropical day an absolute blessing?). The real question
is whether we are willing and able to live with the climates we
are newly making and whether we are paying enough attention
to those less able to survive and thrive under these new regimes.
This has been our challenge from the days when we first started
living in societies with technological and organizational cultures.
Climate change may make that challenge more demanding, but
it has not created it.

The limits of science

If my professional work on climate change has introduced me
to new ways of thinking about the science and ethics of climatic
limits, the interweaving of my Christian faith with my scientific
and social scientific practices has opened up for me different
ways of thinking about the limits of science.

With my father's multidisciplinary syllabus of humanities,
ethics and science behind me, it is not surprising that I have long
been suspicious of some of the brasher claims of science to offer

the only route to legitimate knowledge. While still a geography student at Durham, I sketched an outline for a book to challenge such claims of science and criticize the emergence of a new scientific priesthood. Needless to say, the book never got written, but whilst for most of my professional life I have worked as a scientist amongst scientists, I have always maintained a degree of scepticism about science's more over-reaching claims. Bishop Tom Wright puts it well: 'Somehow, as most admit and I suspect all know in their bones, science in the strict sense can never be enough, enough that is for a full and flourishing human life in all its dimensions' (Wright, 2007).

A few months after my daughter was born – with significant life-threatening complications which required immediate surgery – I was asked by the minister of my church to speak about how I made sense of that experience and, more generally, how I made my faith and science work together for me. I used the opportunity to consider the question of truth and what types of evidence we believe are legitimate to lead us to make true statements. It is true, I said, that greenhouse gases such as carbon dioxide act to trap infra-red radiation and thus contribute to a warming of the planet. It is also true, I said, that I love my six-month-old daughter. True statements both, yet based on categorically different types of evidence: one universal and scientific, the other personal and experiential. The wider point here is that there are limits to the role and efficacy of science in truth-seeking. Not all scientific statements are true and not all true statements are scientific.

Science also reaches its limits when it comes into contact with the need for judgments which can only be made on the basis of ethical and moral arguments. Science is a very powerful method for revealing how the physical world works, but it is only the mad or the evil who will use science to tell people how they should live. This limitation of science is frequently encountered in debates about climate change. What level of climate change is deemed to be dangerous – a key question at the heart of climate policy – cannot be discovered by science. Scientific research can reveal and suggest what types of biogeophysical changes may occur on the planet with different magnitudes of warming, but which of these scenarios is deemed to be dangerous requires value judgments to be made, judgments that lie beyond the competence of science. Dangerous for whom and against what criteria? Dangerous for the rich or for the poor? Dangerous for this generation or for future generations? For many people living today the risks associated with the existing climate are already dangerous, without having to wait for those risks to grow because the climate changes.

It is because climate change opens up so many questions of judgment and policy which demand strong ethical positions that we are finding an increasing number of religious organizations entering into debates about climate change. For example, a recent report from the Climate Institute of Australia presented short statements about climate change from all the major faith communities, including Christians, Hindus, Buddhists and Muslims. A statement introducing the report declares, 'The Climate Institute encourages this new and vital focus on morality and spirituality in the environmental conversation. We hope the moral dialogue may bring greater light into the debate' (Climate Institute, 2006). In the United States many evangelical Christian churches have joined in 'The Evangelical Climate Initiative', calling upon America's Christians to pay heed to the practical and ethical demands of climate change. Science remains therefore a necessary, but insufficient, basis for guiding any systematic response to the questions raised by climate change.

Humility: a shared virtue

I believe that there are many parallels to be drawn between the practice of science and the practice of faith. In neither enterprise can one afford to be dogmatic, to close one's mind to new discovery, or to believe that one has a surer grasp of the truth than is warranted. This may seem a surprising conclusion for a Christian believer. Atheists and agnostics often characterize religious adherence as being a dogmatic 'blind faith', implying an attitude closed to evidence and resistant to any challenge.

This is far from the case. I believe my faith is rooted in 'reasonable' evidence, evidence that can be debated and found either wanting or convincing. This evidence includes the nature of reality, the historicity of Jesus Christ and his resurrection and the lived personal experience of my spirituality. These types of evidence are each very different, but they can be subject to rational debate and they can be scrutinized. Having examined other religious beliefs, and also considered the beliefs of atheists, I remain convinced that Christianity is the most plausible explanation for my experience of life in this world – of the order and stability of the physical world; of the existence of the moral categories we call 'good' and 'evil'; of my own encounter with the transcendent or the spiritual; of the very fact of being.

If someone would convince me that Jesus Christ never lived or, more importantly, never rose from the dead, then I would cease being a Christian and search for alternative ways to make sense of the world we live in. As it is, the evidence for the resurrection of Christ has long convinced me of its historicity. As a student I read the book *Who Moved The Stone?* written by a sceptical journalist who set out to demonstrate that the evidence for the resurrection was fabricated. Instead, after weighing the evidence and subjecting it to an imaginary legal cross-examination, Morison ended up convinced that the evidence pointed powerfully towards a bodily resurrection (Morison, 1930). The Anglican Bishop Tom Wright offers a more recent examination of the same sceptical arguments in his 2007 Faraday Lecture. Wright treats this question as an historical one: 'God has given us minds to think; the question has been appropriately raised; Christianity appeals to history, and to history it must go. And the question of Jesus' resurrection, though it may in some senses burst the boundaries of history, also remains within them; that is precisely why it is so important, so disturbing, so life-and-death.' I would urge anyone, scientist or otherwise, who dismisses the possibility of Christ's resurrection to investigate for themselves this staggering historical claim made by Christians; *Who Moved the Stone?* is still well worth reading.

If historical evidence has to be scrutinized by the person of faith, so one's scientific beliefs need to be open to scrutiny and subject to new empirical and theoretical evidence. Climate change illustrates this nicely. The various assessments of the UN Intergovernmental Panel on Climate Change have increasingly converged on the judgment that the best theoretical, observational and modelling evidence indicates that most of the recent warming of the Earth is related to increasing human emissions of greenhouse gases. This judgment has been disputed by a diminishing number of scientists and some continue to argue that natural factors – variations in cosmic rays, for example – provide an alternative explanation. This is a plausible hypothesis, but it lacks any empirical evidence at the present time.

Such doubting scientists are often pejoratively called 'sceptics', but all scientists should be sceptics in the sense that we should always be critical of the theories we believe and the measurements that we make. All scientific knowledge in the end is provisional, some more so than others. And all truly religious people – Christians or those of other faiths – understand that they are grasping knowledge of God only tentatively. As a Christian, my religious faith battles constantly with doubt, mystery and uncertainty (even as I also rejoice in the forgiveness, hope and love that this same faith brings). Any other description is a caricature of what it means to live as a Christian. Likewise, my beliefs as a scientist about climate change have constantly to grapple with ignorance, incomplete knowledge and uncertainty. This state of contained ambiguity is not paralyzing for me, neither as a believer nor as a scientist. It is in fact truly humanizing and liberating. As argued by science-and-policy scholar Professor Sheila Jasanoff, this condition of humility is one that must be more widely recognized if we are to make good decisions under conditions of irredeemable uncertainty (Jasanoff, 2007).

This is why, as well as seeing a deep parallel between the practice of a scientist and the practice of a Christian, I also see an unfortunate parallel between Christians and scientists who forget this virtue of humility. By proclaiming they have an inside track to the very mind of God in every situation and on every controversy, fundamentalist Christians risk the perversion of their faith. And strident atheistic scientists who claim that there is no knowledge beyond the reach of science make a similar mistake and share the same fundamentalist attributes as those religious believers they lampoon. I think the psychology of extreme fundamentalism – whether of the scientistic or Christian variety – is the same: the inability of someone to live in humility with doubt and mystery.

Robert Pollack, the Director of the Earth Institute's Center for the Study of Science and Religion at Columbia, says: 'I don't think the categories, the "magisteria", are science and religion. The magisteria are of those who believe everything is understandable and of those who believe that some things are intrinsically not understandable. You will find scientists and religious people in both categories… the world in which people say, "What is known now or will be known by human beings is all there is" is a world of rigid fundamentalism, both in religion and in science' (Clayton & Schaal, 2007: 234–35). I illustrate these distinctions schematically in Figure 1 overleaf.

This humility – whether of the religious or scientific variety – in the face of the mysterious and the unknown is not the same as religious agnosticism. Humility is not to be equated with lack of belief, but with an appreciation that though we do believe, we wrestle with our belief and find that faith grows through being exercised. In the Gospel of Mark, the father of a mute boy brought to Jesus for healing captures this well when he cries, 'Lord, I do believe; help thou my unbelief' (Mark 9:24).

Scientific knowledge can only be acquired given a certain commitment of the scientist to the efficacy of the scientific method and a belief in the rationality of the universe. If one remained agnostic about science, then little scientific knowledge would be found to be secure. So too for Christianity. Agnosticism about the existence of God and the claims of Jesus Christ is of course a possible position, but such a lack of commitment – a lack of faith – excludes this person from certain ways of knowing. 'Believing is seeing' has greater power for both the scientist and the religious person than its sometime companion, 'seeing is believing'.

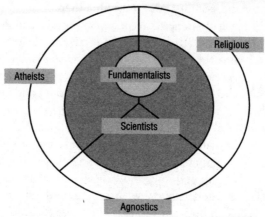

Figure 1. If people are grouped into atheists, agnostics and religious, then scientists (the shaded circle) can be found in each grouping. Those scientists who believe that in principle everything is understandable and knowable (the innermost circle), one of Pollack's two 'magisteria', could be classed as fundamentalists, whether they be atheist or religious.

Our understanding of climate change and its consequences is incomplete and will remain so to a greater or lesser extent for my lifetime and beyond. Likewise our grasp of God's purposes in this universe. The practice of science and the exercise of Christian faith – modes of living and thinking both of which, to be effective, require an *a priori* commitment from me – will help me navigate through this future. Yet I remain just one small creature in a vast, fruitful yet frustrating world. In the face of an awe-inspiring universe and bewildered by the amazing potential for both good and evil we see in ourselves and our fellow human beings, I keep returning to the prophet Micah who expresses it better than anyone: 'And what does the Lord require of you? To act justly and to love mercy and to walk humbly with your God' (Micah 6:8).

NOTES

1. A Supreme Being or indeed the Christian God has no gender in the human sense; the male pronoun is used here for the sake of convention only.

CHAPTER 7

Strive First for the Kingdom of God and His Righteousness

Ian Arbon

Ian Arbon is a Chartered Engineer, Registered European Engineer and Chartered Environmentalist whose career has involved working for, and eventually running, turbine and compressor manufacturing companies in the Netherlands, Germany, the United States, England and Scotland. He now runs his own consultancy partnership specializing in sustainable energy demand and supply. He is a Fellow of the Institution of Mechanical Engineers, the American Society of Mechanical Engineers, the Energy Institute, the Institute of Refrigeration and a Member of the Institute of Directors. In addition, he has an MBA and an MSc in Renewable Energy and the Environment. As well as his consultancy work, Ian is a Visiting Professor in Alternative Energy Systems at Newcastle University and is currently developing his farmhouse in southwest Scotland as a sustainable energy demonstration centre.

My title comes from Matthew 6:33. I can think of no other verse which so succinctly sums up my life's aspiration, particularly in the NRSV translation, where we are told to '*strive* for the kingdom of God', which seems much stronger than the more familiar urging to 'seek'. It speaks of striving to see God's kingdom established on earth *now*, not simply at some future point, and living a life that is characterized by 'righteousness'. Although an uncommon word nowadays, 'righteousness' is used so many times in Scripture that it is clearly very important. We read in Proverbs 14:34: 'Righteousness exalts a nation, but sin is a reproach [or disgrace – NIV] to any people.' This is something that I am conscious of every day as I work in the fields of engineering and business.

Early years

I was blessed by being born into a Christian family with five generations of evangelical Christians on my father's side and six on my mother's. Unfortunately, the last few generations had been Exclusive Brethren (EB). I spent the first twenty years of my life as a member of the EBs, growing up in the east of England. This gave me a great knowledge of the Scriptures but some very confused thinking in terms of application to daily living; the '*apartheid*' practised by EBs in too many ways cocooned me from the realities of 'real life' in my early years.

My father and grandfather were Christian businessmen. Their example taught me from an early age not to separate my life into 'sacred' and 'secular' compartments. I later came to understand that such separation was unbiblical and 'Greek'; the Bible teaches a much more holistic 'Hebrew' viewpoint. I have always found it difficult to behave in a different way in my business/professional life from the way I do in the other aspects of my life.

One of my grandfather's maxims, which has been a guiding principle throughout my adult life, was: 'Righteousness is the first principle of the kingdom.' These exact words do not occur in Scripture but the principle is certainly consistent with Matthew 6:33. As I write, I am teaching a seven-week series at church on the Sermon on the Mount and have again been struck by the continual connections Matthew makes between 'the kingdom' and 'righteousness', not least in this verse.

Largely due to their increasing 'exclusiveness', it was tough to be a teenager (my teenage years happened to coincide with the 1960s – an era of unprecedented change) in the EB. It was particularly frustrating, for example, to know that, no matter how gifted I might be, I would never be allowed to go to University, as that would expose me to 'worldly' teaching and associations. In any case, my 'destiny' had long been marked out: I was to succeed my father in the family retail business, which I reluctantly entered at age sixteen. However, after a year of increasing frustration for me, EB 'rules' changed, forcing my father to close his shop on Saturdays, far and away his busiest day. The reduced income would never be able to support two families (never mind three, if my brother also came into the business), but having left school without any significant qualifications, there were few career opportunities available to me. Eventually, my father persuaded the Apprentice Supervisor of a local engineering/manufacturing company to take me on as a student apprentice on a trial basis. I started there in September 1967 and a completely new phase of my life began.

Always reasonably good at working with my hands, the various aspects of an apprentice's manual work came naturally to me, but I found as much satisfaction in the required study of engineering to National Certificate level in the local College. The company's main products were steam turbines and gas compressors and I personally assembled (at age 19!) a 1000 kW condensing steam turbine generator set for recovering waste heat from marine diesel engines on a merchant ship. All the vessel's electricity could be produced from waste heat in a 'combined-cycle' system – my first experience of maximizing what we would now call 'resource efficiency'. I have tried to apply this principle in my daily work ever since.

As my apprenticeship progressed, I realized how little the 'protection' of the EBs had equipped me for the real world of which I was becoming part. The unions in the company at that time were dominated by communist thinking, a world-view I found attractive; to an ideological teenager the concepts of 'wealth distribution' and 'fairness' were very appealing. Another attraction to me was atheism. I became increasingly convinced that no omniscient God would have subjected me to the horrors of being brought up as an EB. Although subsequent events were to change this viewpoint completely, I have been left with an all-pervading awareness of the need for 'social responsibility' and 'social justice' in everything that I do.

Of course, admitting this would have resulted in instant excommunication from the EBs. This would have meant leaving home and never having anything more to do with my family. Too young and unsure of myself for this, I lived a double life for the next few years, paying lip service to Brethren doctrine but believing none of it. Eventually my increasingly rebellious behaviour drove the local leadership to give me a 'last chance' to reform. This involved attending the EB 'summit' meeting in Aberdeen in July 1970, where I was an eyewitness of the cataclysmic events which exposed the evil lurking in the EB movement. This is not relevant here; suffice to say that I was exposed to the greatest manifestation of evil that I have ever known. During this experience, I believe I had a direct revelation from the God I thought I had shut out of my life: if the forces of evil were so real, then there must be an equal force for good in the world.

Jesus is Lord

This encounter with God, this personal epiphany, was followed by exciting months of learning how great and absolutely real God is. I realized that my problem with God was entirely of my own making – helped greatly by the EBs! I came to terms with the need to accept Jesus as Lord of my life. Perhaps because of this, I have never since had any doubts of the existence of God.

My subsequent experiences, good and bad, have only gone to strengthen my daily walk in communion with the One who is God of the Universe and the Lord of all Creation.

The years immediately following this experience were momentous ones: marriage, the completion of my apprenticeship (I received the Chairman's Award for the best student completing training in the company!), the birth of our two children, and a gradual liberation from Brethrenism. It was a time too when my wife Hannah and I, in a small evangelical church, were greatly blessed by wonderful Bible teaching from ex-brethren – they were some of the greatest Bible scholars I have ever known. It was a period when the Lord restored the Bible knowledge of my upbringing and took away the previous misapplications.

I still considered work a separate part of my life from church, although there were no particular conflicts between my beliefs and what I was required to do in my daily work. I was gaining experience in many aspects of engineering, one of the most significant, in the light of my subsequent career, being my first experience of 'renewable' energy. This involved designing turbines for cane-sugar factories where all process heat and power required to drive the crushing mills and other equipment was produced from steam raised by burning the cane waste or 'bagasse'. Although we did not then know the terms, what we were supplying was what would now be called a 'biomass-fired CHP (combined heat & power) plant'.

I moved on to a Dutch/American company in the Netherlands, where I worked on a number of significant power generation projects in different parts of Europe, including a large Energy-from-Waste (EfW) facility in Brussels which used its 'waste' heat in a District Heating system. Amazingly, we are only now starting to seriously consider such schemes in the UK, more than thirty years later. We found it incredibly mind-broadening to live in a different culture, especially one that was so much more environmentally aware than anything we had known before. I recalled hearing how the Dutch had resorted to not using their cars on Sundays during the 1973 oil crisis and wondering how they managed. A couple of years later we were living there and realized that cycling everywhere – particularly to church on Sunday – was absolutely normal. We were having our first real experience of living a sustainable lifestyle. Moving to the Netherlands also gave us our first experience of God specifically directing us to a particular church, which we later found was the one closest to our home. The pastor spoke no English but his long sermons and a Dutch/English Bible speeded up our language skills!

My career progressed, and I moved to work for a large German company in the Ruhr and broadened my experience into many different areas of power generation and process gas compression. As I look back, I can see how the Lord was building my knowledge/experience base for what he was leading me to. In those years, experience in the use of closed-cycle gas turbines for community power and heat supply, coal gasification, industrial CHP systems and a prototype wind turbine development would all prove significant later when my work and my faith became inseparable. Before long, we moved back to the UK, working in the German company's London office. I started to preach regularly and teach adult Bible classes in our local evangelical church, drawing on all my experiences to make my teaching as applicable to real life as I was able to.

When my company moved me to its New York City office, I had a new set of challenges for my faith. I still remember being 'wowed' by my new office – on the thirty-sixth floor of a Manhattan skyscraper, with a floor-to-ceiling window looking out over the Rockefeller Center. I really thought I had arrived and I was still only thirty years old! Culturally, there was an immense difference between continental Europe and the USA, with the UK sitting somewhere between the two. On the positive side, the US was a land of great opportunity and living there was exciting; on the negative side, we were astonished by the American attitude to waste: 'food waste', and to our eyes the profligate use of fossil fuels – poorly insulated homes, large 'gas-guzzling' automobiles, driving vast distances quite unnecessarily and so on.

Once again, we knew God's leading to a local church and a choice of house; by this time, we were accustomed to genuinely seeking the Lord's guidance about practical decisions. In due course I was ordained an Elder of the church and became its Director of Adult Education. It was a new church, experiencing enormous growth in numbers, and the adult education classes were essential to the spiritual growth of people joining the church from a large variety of backgrounds. I found this one of the most rewarding times of my life. Once again, I tried to live out what I taught on Sundays in my daily work – 'walking the walk, as well as talking the talk'. When we decided to return to the UK, I was asked to consider staying on as Pastor of the church. However, by then I was sure that God was calling me specifically to leadership in the business world.

I was appointed as Joint Managing Director of a large Scottish manufacturing company which had been making losses for many years. A week after I joined my co-Managing Director was tragically killed in a road accident. Having to add his responsibilities to my own new duties (particularly since finance and accounting are not my strong points), I was aware how completely unequipped I was. For the first time in my life I knew that I was in a classic 'make-or-break' situation; I was certainly unable to do the job in my own strength, but I felt a strong sense of the Lord's leading. I came to the realization that God was 'an ever-present help in times of trouble', as much in my call to the business world as to a church. This was one of the most important lessons of my life. Much of the learning from the first twenty years of my life came into play. My father's and grandfather's belief in righteousness being the first principle of kingdom living, and the folly of trying to separate my life into sacred and secular compartments, became guiding principles.

Through some literally miraculous interventions the hitherto struggling business flourished and became the most successful compressor manufacturing company in the world in 1990, supplying fuel gas compressors for industrial gas turbine generators to many of the USA's landfill sites. The parent company (of which I was also a director) was at that time one of the world's top three wind turbine manufacturers. As well as hundreds of 250–300kW wind turbines supplied to the Californian market, it was involved in the development of the first prototype 1 MW and 3 MW turbines for use in the UK. Also during this period I was responsible for setting up and ensuring the successful operation of two manufacturing joint venture companies, one in India and another in China. All these activities reflected what I believed to be my calling in God to maximize the efficiency of the resources God had given us and to help to feed the hungry and the helpless. To me, these were simply part of the practical outworking of the 'stewardship' to which we are called.

When people asked me how I had achieved the company's success, I would respond, 'I didn't!' – a reply which often enabled me to share my testimony. At the same time, I had the opportunity to start an adult education programme in our church, drawing on my American experience. This was unique in the area at that time, and saw immense blessing in terms of transformed lives.

Jesus Christ is Lord of all

The next stage of the adventure was involvement in a church plant, where I found I had to draw on all my spiritual and professional experience. Responsibility for the leadership was demanding, especially as the church's formation coincided with leaving my company, largely due to my overt adherence to biblical principles. This was also an immensely valuable lesson – I had found that no matter how successful I had been in turning around the company, doing 'Business by the Book' is not a popular concept.

As a result of all this, my wife and I started our own company, also in the fuel gas compressor business. We certainly had our hands full and our faith challenged. Once again, believing that our calling was to an integrated Christian life, we made no attempt to separate our lives into sacred and secular components. In the same period, we became involved with the International Christian Chamber of Commerce (ICCC) where we were able to share our experiences with other Christians around the world who felt that their calling was to the business world – the 'work of the church' rather than 'church work'. It was during this period that I came to the practical acceptance that Jesus is Lord of all and that everything in my life was subject to him. I realized that I had to relinquish all control over every aspect of my life and especially my business life. This eventually led us to sell the business before we would otherwise have been ready or willing to do so.

This commitment to Jesus as Lord of all was challenged to the full in the next stage of my career. I became a consultant, and one of the first clients the Lord sent my way was the company where I had served my apprenticeship, twenty-five years previously. Within six months I was asked to take over as

Managing Director! It was a tempting offer, from a worldly point of view, but was it right? After much prayer and soul-searching I accepted the offer and we moved back to the area where I grew up – something we had vowed we would never do. We felt the Lord's direction – but what exactly did he have in mind?

From the beginning I gave authority in the company to the Lord, and as before, we experienced many miraculous interventions. I instituted a weekly prayer meeting for the Christians in the company and saw multiple blessings and answers to prayer both among the people in the company and through seeing our machines sold into applications that would otherwise have been most improbable. To take one example of this, one day I was phoned on my way to work by one of my Christian colleagues who was in Australia negotiating for an industrial CHP plant order. We were looking increasingly unlikely to win the order against strong Japanese competition. My colleague had just come out of the meeting, having been told that we were out of the running unless he dropped his price below that of the main competitor. We were not in any position to do that, so I convened the prayer group at work and we prayed earnestly for the Lord's intervention. My colleague rang me later with the information that when he returned to his meeting, the customer's negotiators announced that they had had a change of mind while he was away and would give us the order anyway, without any price reduction. They also pointed out a small error in our spreadsheet that meant that we would actually receive more than we had expected!

My tenure as Managing Director saw the company return to significant profitability and become established as the UK's leading manufacturer of equipment for renewable and sustainable energy systems. However, the American owners decided that despite the success of the business, I appeared to have difficulty in 'separating the sacred from the secular' and that I was clearly 'taking my instructions from someone other than them'! This led to me leaving the company and returning to full-time consultancy. However, through this whole experience the Lord had clearly been teaching me strong principles of stewardship for the care of his creation, particularly in the field of energy supply and demand. I really understood that there had been a progression in my life from 'Jesus is Lord' to 'Jesus is Lord of all' and on to 'Jesus is Lord of all creation'.

Jesus is Lord of all creation

This growing belief that the Christian's role as a steward extended to all the resources of God's creation and not only to the businesses to which I was called, has largely determined the course of my subsequent career. There are three major resources in business: Human, Financial and Physical (the latter sub-divided into Natural and Manufactured). As a Christian, an engineer and a businessman, I deal with all three (or four) resources on a daily basis. None of them *belong* to me – I am bound to deal with them correctly as a steward. To me, the word which best describes how the steward does this is 'righteousness'. This scriptural word is not well understood nowadays and is sometimes confused with 'self-righteousness' – a completely different concept. Perhaps a better modern word would be 'integrity'.

This righteousness has two aspects: 'doing things right' and 'doing the right thing'. The first of these is well-understood territory for an engineer: if we 'do things wrong', the results can be catastrophic – the bridge collapses or the power station blows up. However, we cannot always claim to 'do the right thing'; more often than not, we do what is expedient – for example, selecting lowest cost rather than optimum efficiency. Since the pressure on businesses to make money above all other things tends to drive us to these 'expedient' decisions, I have seen it as a major part of my role to 'do the right thing' in the companies where I have had the authority to do this.

Another way in which I try to do the right thing is through the professional institutions with which I have become more involved over the years. I believe that this is an opportunity I have been given to disseminate the message of creation stewardship. After all, I am a steward of the knowledge I have been entrusted with, as much as anything material!

As a Fellow of both the UK's Institution of Mechanical Engineers (IMechE) and the American Society of Mechanical Engineers (ASME), I have served on various committees and lectured in many places in both the UK and around the world on subjects such as sustainability, energy conservation and efficiency, and climate change. For instance, in a response to the IPCC's 4th Assessment Climate Mitigation Technologies section, I gave a presentation in 2007 to the IMechE on 'Doing the Right Things Right – Energy and Climate Change'. I regarded this as a positive way of aligning my faith with my professional expertise. Through all of these roles and authoring/editing numerous Government consultation responses, I have been able to achieve high-level advocacy with both politicians and civil servants.

As a participant in the ASME's 'Distinguished Lecturers' program (the first European-based person to have received this honour), I have spoken on 'Renewable Energy & Sustainability' at numerous locations across the USA and elsewhere. Although I do not usually speak explicitly about my Christian faith during these lectures, I am often asked afterwards if I am a Christian, which has opened up some very interesting conversations. It has been very instructive how much the typical response in the USA to my lectures has changed over the past few years – from general 'denial' that we need to change the way we treat 'energy' to fairly widespread agreement with a sustainable approach.

Because, for the reasons explained earlier, I had missed out on any 'University experience' when I was young, I felt that it would be useful to understand my empirical knowledge, gained in both business and engineering, in an academic framework. This resulted in studying for and acquiring a Master's Degree in Business Administration (majoring in Corporate Governance, Strategy and Management of Change) at the University of Glasgow Business School in 1998 and a Master of Science Degree in 'Renewable Energy and the Environment' at Anglia Ruskin University, Cambridge, in 2002. These degrees have helped me understand the theory (the 'why') behind what I know instinctively through my experience. In all of this, I have found everything I have learned entirely consistent with my beliefs, ethical standards ('righteousness') and Christian role as a steward.

My involvement with various 'marketplace ministries' over the years has been very helpful in confirming my belief that a Christian's responsibility is to live his or her faith in the workplace. My hope is that more of these excellent ministries will extend their teaching emphasis to the biblical commandments regarding the care of creation, and support the many Christian engineers and scientists who take seriously their responsibility in this area.

In many ways, the culmination of all of these experiences came with my appointment as a Visiting Professor in Alternative Energy Systems at the University of Newcastle-upon-Tyne. Among other things, I teach a module on a REFLEX MSc course entitled 'Policies, Politics and Ethics of Renewable Energy'. This draws together many of the different strands of my experience; being able to teach this course has proved to be very rewarding.

I strongly believe that God is calling me to work out the Christian business principles to which I have adhered over many years, in the stewardship of God's creation. In 2006, we relocated our home and consultancy business to a former hill farm in South-West Scotland. This has given us the opportunity to live out all of our beliefs practically in *every* aspect of our lives. We are currently in the process of converting the farmhouse and yard into a Sustainable Energy Demonstration Centre, which will show how a typical farm can be self-sufficient in all of its energy needs from a combination of the property's natural resources and the things that can be grown/raised on the farm. This Centre will also be quite explicit in demonstrating how our faith and commitment to stewardship and 'kingdom living' are the drivers behind this venture.

The project follows the principles of the 'Energy Hierarchy' and focuses first on the conservation of energy, which is achieved by much better insulation of walls and roofs, eliminating air leakage paths (no mean feat in a 150-year-old building!), and employing passive solar design principles in rebuilding and extensions; we are also cutting down on the need for travel away from base by using tele-, cyber- and video-conferencing facilities. We are doing everything we can to improve demand-side efficiency by installing low-energy lighting and appliances and a highly efficient 'heat bank'.

The next step will be to install a range of renewable technologies for the supply of total energy (not just electricity), which will include: micro-wind, micro-hydro, solar thermal panels, a ground-source heat-pump, micro-CHP (fed with biogas from an anaerobic digester fuelled by animal dung and food waste) and very efficient wood-burning stoves.

We are now members of the Scottish Episcopal Church and active in our local congregation. I have been licensed by the Bishop to lead services, which enables me to regularly exercise any talents I have for preaching and teaching, which become ever more practical in their application as time goes by.

We regard our present situation as the opportunity to bring together in a practical and integrated way the spiritual, theological, societal, business, technological and environmental lessons we have learned over the years and to demonstrate that genuine 'kingdom living' embraces all of these aspects of our lives.

In all of this, we are confident that we are walking in the Lord's will and are in the place where he wants us to be. We are in no doubt that we are 'striving' to work out the principles of God's kingdom here on earth and to see his righteousness in practical operation.

CHAPTER 8

Real Psychological Science, Real Faith

David Myers

David Myers was born in Seattle in 1942, educated at Whitworth College and the University of Iowa (PhD in Social Psychology); he has been Professor of Psychology at Hope College in Holland, Michigan since 1967. He is the author of seventeen books, including three widely used textbooks, *Psychology* (9th edition, 2010), *Exploring Psychology* (7th edition, 2008) and *Social Psychology* (9th edition, 2008).

My life has unfolded as a series of surprises. While working as a teenager in my father's insurance agency in Seattle, I never imagined becoming a pre-med chemistry student at Whitworth University. While working summers in Seattle's county hospital, I never imagined that I would resist sending in my medical school applications, and instead become a psychology professor. While earning my PhD in social psychology and wanting only to teach, I never imagined I would become a National Science Foundation-funded researcher for a dozen years. When doing that research, I never imagined receiving unexpected invitations to write about the interplay of my science and my faith, and then to write textbooks for introductory and social psychology. And when shifting into reporting on psychological science, I never imagined extending that writing into magazine articles, newspaper essays, and general audience books.

I recount this unexpected journey as a simple illustration of the meandering vocational road that so many of us travel. My surest prediction of your future, I tell students, is that your story will be like mine: it will not be what you are now expecting. And that is why the best preparation for the unpredictable future is one that develops your basic knowledge of the world, your skills of critical thinking and effective communication, and a secure sense of overarching identity and values, out of which your life purpose and vocational mission will emerge.

My own peculiar mission has become to discern and communicate truth to college students and the educated public. My focus is on reading psychological science as it comes to me through the forty-eight periodicals and fourteen list servers from which I harvest most of my information (the most important of which is *Current Contents: Social and Behavioral Sciences*, which gives me access to essentially all English-language psychology and psychiatry periodicals).

My primary audience is the student readers of my introductory and social psychology textbooks. To be invited to assist the teaching of my humanly significant discipline to so many unseen people is a great privilege, but also a keenly felt burden of responsibility. Happily, I am surrounded by a team of colleagues – assistants, reviewers, and editors – who work collectively to produce a carefully checked teaching package that is better than anyone, working alone, would be capable of. And amassing all this information has occasionally inspired spin-off books and articles on topics such as happiness, intuition, hearing loss, sexual orientation, and the science–faith interface.

But where, you may be wondering, does my Christian faith enter into doing and reporting on psychological research? It enters first, as other contributors to this volume explain, in the Christian mandate for doing science. The scientist's religious mandate, wrote neuroscientist Donald MacKay, 'is to "tell it like it is", knowing that the Author is at our elbow, a silent judge of the accuracy with which we claim to describe the world He has created.' Disciplined, rigorous inquiry – checking our theories against reality – helps fulfil Jesus' great commandment to love God not just with our hearts but also with our minds. Copernicus had the same idea: 'To know the mighty works of God; to comprehend His wisdom and majesty and power; to appreciate, in degree, the wonderful working of His laws, surely all this must be a pleasant and acceptable mode of worship to the most High, to whom ignorance cannot be more grateful than knowledge.'

The science-fostering theology that gave birth to science went something like this: if nature is sacred – if it is animated with river goddesses and sun gods – then we ought not tamper with it; but if nature is instead God's intelligible creation, then let us, as rational creatures made in God's image, seek to discover the divine laws. We glimpse this idea in the Psalms ('The firmament proclaims his handiwork', Psalm 19:1) and in St Paul ('Ever since the creation of the world his eternal power and divine nature, invisible though they are, have been understood and seen through the things he has made', Romans 1:20). Thus we can do science not *despite* being people of faith, but *because* we are people of faith.

Science and faith jointly mandate humility. Humility is basic to the empirical spirit advocated long ago by Moses: 'If a prophet speaks in the name of the Lord and what he says does not come true, then it is not the Lord's message' (Deuteronomy 18:22). If our or anyone's ideas survive being put to the test, so much the better for them. If they crash against a wall of evidence, it is time to rethink. Thus reading and reporting on psychological science has changed my mind many times, leading me now to believe that:

- Newborns are not the blank slates I once presumed.

- Electroconvulsive therapy often alleviates intractable depression.

- Economic growth has not improved our morale.

- The automatic, unconscious mind dwarfs the controlled, conscious mind.

- Traumatic experiences rarely get repressed.

- Personality is unrelated to birth order.

- Most folks have high self-esteem (which sometimes causes problems).

- Opposites do not attract.

- Sexual orientation (most clearly, men's) is a natural, enduring disposition, not a choice.

When working at the science–faith boundary, my three aims have been:

- 1. To explain psychological science and its applications to people of faith.

- 2. To document links between faith and human flourishing.

- 3. To compare big ideas about human nature found in psychological science and in biblical and theological thinking.

I have spelt out these principles in *Psychology Through the Eyes of Faith* (Myers & Jeeves, 2002) and in *A Friendly Letter to Skeptics and Atheists* (Myers, 2008). To illustrate how real psychological science meets real faith, I suggest in what follows how psychological science and faith *affirm* and *challenge* one another.

Psychological science and Christian faith are mutually affirming

In many academic fields, the results of thousands of studies, the conclusions of hundreds of investigators, the insights of dozens of theorists, can often be boiled down to a few big ideas. Biology offers us principles such as natural selection and adaptation. Sociology builds upon concepts such as social structure, cultural relativity, and societal organization. Music exploits our ideas of rhythm, melody, and harmony.

My specialty – social psychology – offers four really big ideas about human nature that are rooted in science *and* are congenial with Judeo-Christian understandings. Each is a two-sided truth.

As Pascal reminded us 300 years ago, no single truth is ever sufficient, because the world is not simple. Any truth separated from its complementary truth is a half-truth.

Our cognitive capacities are enormous; but to err is human

Less than one and a half kilograms of tissue in our skulls – the size of a cabbage – enables us to process vast amounts of information automatically and unconsciously, to soak up vocabulary and effortlessly manipulate it with complex grammar, to make intuitive judgments, and much more. Of course, reply the theologians. We are made in the divine image. We are little less than angels, God's own children.

Yet our judgments are vulnerable to predictable error. Our preconceptions bias our responses. We 'see' relationships and causes. We are more swayed by anecdotes than statistical reality. Failing to recognize these and other common errors, we are prone to over-confidence. Well, yes, say the theologians: we are finite creatures of the one who declares, 'I am God, and there is none like me' and that 'as the heavens are higher than the earth, so are my ways higher than your ways and my thoughts than your thoughts.'

Self-serving pride is powerful and perilous, yet self-acceptance pays dividends

People routinely exhibit a 'self-serving bias', by viewing themselves as more ethical, socially skilled, tolerant, and so forth than their average peer. Nine in ten drivers, for example, judge themselves as a better-than-average driver. Moreover, we misremember and self-justify our past behaviours. That we experience life through a self-centred filter comes as no surprise to Christian thinkers, for whom self-righteous pride has long been considered the original sin. Thus the Psalmist could observe that 'no one can see his own errors' and the Pharisee could thank God 'that I am not like other men'. For individuals and for nations, such pride often goes before a fall.

Yet self-affirmation helps maintain confidence and minimize depression. For Christians, the ultimate self-affirmation comes by accepting God's acceptance. Divine grace is the Christian parallel to psychology's 'unconditional positive regard'.

Attitudes and beliefs influence behaviour... and they follow behaviour

Under certain conditions – when our attitudes are directly pertinent and brought to mind – they guide our behaviour. Thus our attitudes toward physical exercise influence whether we exercise. What we think on the inside affects how we act on the outside. Indeed, say biblical scholars, faith is a source of action. When Paul's mind was changed on the Damascus Road, his actions changed.

But the reverse is also true. As a mountain of research makes plain, we are as likely to act ourselves into a way of thinking as to think ourselves into action. Unless coerced in a way that leaves us no sense of choice, our attitudes follow our behaviour. Improved racial attitudes, for example, followed desegregation. Likewise, faith is a consequence of obedient action. Faith grows as people enact their faith. 'The proof of Christianity really consists in "following"', noted Søren Kierkegaard.

We are the creatures – and the creators – of our social worlds

Every psychology student encounters studies of conformity, persuasion, role playing, and group and cultural influence that teach an important lesson: we are the *creatures* of our social worlds. Put well-intentioned people in morally challenging situations and evil pressures often overwhelm good intentions. Nice people often don't behave nicely. This parallels the biblical idea of transcendent good and evil. Evil is not just individual sin, it also emerges from corrosive forces – 'principalities and powers' – the response to which emerges from a communal religious life.

Yet studies of leadership, of personal control, of achievement, of the influence of numerical minorities on majorities, of self-fulfilling beliefs, and much more, also testify to the complementary reality: We are the *creators* of our social worlds. Amen, echoes the faith tradition: We are morally responsible and accountable. What we decide matters. The stream of causation from past to future runs through our choices.

Psychological science affirms the functionality of faith

In their attack on religion, today's 'new atheists' all contend that religion is toxic. It is 'both false and dangerous', asserts Sam Harris in *Letter to a Christian Nation*. In *God is Not Great: How Religion Poisons Everything*, Christopher Hitchens views religion as 'violent, irrational, intolerant, allied to racism and tribalism and bigotry, invested in ignorance and hostile to free inquiry, contemptuous of women and coercive toward children.' 'What is really pernicious is the practice of teaching children that faith itself is a virtue,' adds Richard Dawkins in *The God Delusion*. 'Faith is an evil precisely because it requires no justification and brooks no argument... Faith can be very, very dangerous, and deliberately to implant it into the vulnerable mind of an innocent child is a grievous wrong.'

Mindful of the example of Jesus, a radical critic of the religion of his day, Christians can respond, first, by affirming many of the indictments of religion, which *has* often been associated with idiocy and evil. But we can also thank the behavioural sciences for a mountain of evidence that associates religion (at least in Western countries with a Judeo-Christian heritage) with *happiness*, *health* and *helpfulness*. Here are some quick examples of each (more information and documentation is found in my other writings, including, most recently, *A Friendly Letter to Skeptics and Atheists*).

Happiness
Sigmund Freud described religion as an 'obsessional neurosis' that breeds sexually repressed, guilt-laden misery. Christopher Hitchens concurs that religious belief does 'not make its adherents

happy'. But the accumulating evidence is much kinder to C. S. Lewis's presumption that 'Joy is the serious business of heaven.' National Opinion Research Center surveys of 43,000 Americans since 1972 confirm what many other surveys have found: 26 per cent of those seldom or never attending religious services are 'very happy', compared with 43 per cent of those attending weekly or more. People with an active religious faith also have been found to cope better with the loss of a spouse, a marriage, or a job. Explanations for this faith–happiness correlation range from the social support of faith communities to faith-bred feelings of purpose, self-acceptance, and hope.

Health

Several large epidemiological studies (which follow lives through time to explore what predicts ill-health and premature death) have identified a 'faith factor'. Even after controlling for age, gender, ethnicity, and education, religiously active people are less likely to die in any given year and enjoy longer life expectancy (much like non-smokers). Part of this faith–health correlation is attributable to the healthier lifestyles (for example, the lower smoking rate) of religious people, but faith-related social support and positive emotions also may be influencing stress levels and immune functioning.

Helpfulness

In history, Christianity has been associated with the founding of hospitals, orphanages, hospices, universities, and civil rights movements – and with Crusades, Inquisitions, and the justification of bigotry and genocide. Religion, as Jesus and the prophets often reminded us, *can* be toxic. But on balance is it more humane or heartless? This much is clear: volunteerism runs high among religiously active people. In one Gallup survey, 46 per cent of 'highly spiritually committed' Americans were volunteering with the infirm, poor, or elderly, compared with 22 per cent of those 'highly uncommitted'. Ditto charitable giving, where national US surveys for the Independent Sector reveal a strong faith–philanthropy correlation. (In one survey, the one in four people who attended worship weekly gave nearly half of all charitable contributions.)

Psychological science and faith challenge one another

If I am to be faithful to my mission of discerning and communicating truth – God's truth – as best I can, then I must be open to changing my mind even about cherished Christian ideas. As ecological findings have driven biblical scholars to reread the biblical mandates concerning our stewardship of the earth and its creatures, so psychological science has stimulated me to rethink some of my religious ideas. That can sound scary, even to those of us rooted in a 'Reformed and ever-reforming' tradition. But if you and I are not God, and if we therefore inevitably err in our thinking (our religious thinking, included), then we can relax and rethink. Science has challenged me to rethink my childhood understandings of three things: the *soul*, intercessory *prayer*, and *sexual orientation*.

The soul
The emerging (and massively documented) scientific view that we are unified mind–brain systems challenges the popular religious idea that we are body and soul. Actually, I was surprised to discover, that's a Platonic, not a biblical idea. 'Does not death mean that the body comes to exist by itself, separated from the soul?' asks Socrates in Plato's *Phaedo*. For Socrates, drinking the hemlock was the soul's liberation. It was fundamentally *not dying*.

This is quite unlike the Old Testament understanding that *nephesh* (soul) terminates at death. In the Hebrew view, we do not **have** a *nephesh*; we **are** *nephesh* (living beings). It's rather like saying, 'There wasn't a soul (person) in the room,' or 'I love you from the depths of my soul' (being). The New Testament similarly offers us whole persons – 'souls' who can eat and drink. Death is not the liberation of a soul, not mere 'passing away,' but in St Paul's words, 'the great enemy'. We are dust to dust, ashes to ashes. The Easter hope of life after death is not something intrinsic to our nature, but rather God-given.

Unlike the Platonic dualism which influenced the church's past theology, this biblical understanding is fundamentally congenial with the scientific understanding of human nature. Both agree that our minds are nothing apart from our bodies. We are now – and in eternity, the Christian hopes – bodies alive. The scientific and biblical worldviews both assume – in contrast to spiritualist claims of reincarnation, astral projection, and séances with the dead – that without our bodies we are nothing.

If indeed we are embodied minds and mind-ful bodies, then we should care about ourselves and others, living bodies and all. (No wonder Christians have been so active in establishing hospitals and dispensing medicine.) Our spirituality is rooted not in possessing a thing, but in deep feelings of connection and devotion to something much larger than self.

Intercessory prayer

Anecdotes of people attributing rescues, healings, and successes to the power of their prayers sometimes makes those of us in psychological science feel a bit uncomfortable. Such claims can seem a bit presumptuous. (Did God not care about those who died or failed, or did those praying for them have too little faith?) Moreover, intercessory and petitionary prayer seems like a ready-made venue for what psychologists call 'illusory thinking', as when people perceive expected but non-existent relationships or causal connections among coincidentally correlated events, and believe they control random events.

So, said some researchers from both the prayer sceptic and believer camps, why not put prayer to the test? After a widely publicized 1988 report of prayed-for coronary patients enjoying better outcomes (though only on six of twenty-six outcomes), others soon sought to replicate the result. As an advisor to the John Templeton Foundation, I learned of one Harvard-related experiment – the mother of all prayer experiments – which was to assign 1,800 cardiac bypass patients to one of three conditions:

- Those told they may or may not be prayed for (and who weren't).

- Those told they may or may not be prayed for (and who were).

- Those told they would be prayed for (and who were).

I was sceptical, and didn't want my reasoning to seem, after a null result, like after-the-fact rationalization. So before the experiment was conducted I filed a two-page explanation of 'Why People of Faith Can Expect Null Effects in the Harvard Prayer Experiment' (available at davidmyers.org/davidmyers/assets/prayer-letter. pdf). I suggested the prayer concept tested in prayer experiments is more akin to magic than to a biblical understanding of prayer to an omniscient and sovereign God. Moreover, even for those who believe that God intervenes in response to our prayer, there are practical reasons for expecting a null effect, such as all the genuine, heartfelt prayers offered by friends and family of those in the supposedly 'no-prayer' condition. Finally, the evidence of history indicates that the prayers of finite humans do not manipulate an infinite God, as if God is a celestial genie. If they could, how many droughts, floods, hurricanes, plagues, stillborn infants, children with disabilities, suicides, cancers – the endless list goes on – would have been averted?

While we awaited the published outcome of the massive prayer experiment, five other large prayer experiments were published – all with null results. (One exception turned out to be an apparent fraud.) And then the *coup de grace* to prayer experiments: intercessory prayer in the Harvard prayer experiment had no effect on recovery from bypass surgery.

Jesus' own model prayer, which I pray daily, does not attempt to control a God who withholds love unless cajoled. Rather it affirms our dependence upon God's nature and creation, even for our daily bread. Through prayer we express our praise and gratitude, confess our wrongdoing, voice our heart's concerns and desires (as a child to a benevolent parent, who already knows our needs), open ourselves to the Spirit, and seek the peace and grace to live as God's own people.

Sexual orientation

Finally, the accumulating scientific evidence has confirmed my prior understandings of the importance of marriage for human flourishing (married adults tend to be healthier and happier, and co-parented children likewise enjoy improved odds of happy, flourishing lives). This case for marriage is so solid, so important, and so under-appreciated that I have devoted much energy to articulating it, through talks and writings and through my support of my country's National Marriage Project. Simultaneously, my presumption that sexual orientation is a moral choice has been challenged and then overturned. This has come from converging evidence concerning:

- 1. Prenatal hormonal influences on sexual orientation.

- 2. Brain and other differences between straight and gay individuals.

- 3. The stubborn immutability of sexual orientation (especially for males) has persuaded most psychological scientists that sexual orientation is a natural and enduring disposition.

All this caused me to revisit the Scriptures. I discovered that the Bible has little if anything to say about an enduring sexual orientation (a modern concept) or about loving, long-term same-sex partnerships. Out of 31,103 Bible verses in the Protestant canon, only seven frequently quoted verses (none of them are the words of Jesus) speak directly of same-sex behaviour. These seven passages concern behaviours that mostly occur in the context of idolatry, temple prostitution, adultery, child exploitation, or violence. (To be fair, faithful biblical scholars continue debating the import of these passages.) For one scholar's biblical case against acceptance of homosexuality, readers might wish to read Robert Gagnon. See westernsem.edu/media/pub_article/rreview/autumn05 for Gagnon's view of the biblical witness, and my response, with links to other biblical scholars.)

Mindful of misinformation about sexual orientation I

reflected on my calling: to discern and communicate truth. Was I only to do this when the results were to be warmly received? With trepidation, I invited Letha Dawson Scanzoni, an evangelical writer and veteran in these matters, to join me in co-authoring *What God Has Joined Together: the Christian Case for Gay Marriage.* On publication, the immediate result was front-page newspaper stories in my area of the country, and a deluge of sometimes angry but more often encouraging e-mails and letters (with more angry comment being directed at my institution).

I am well aware that my conclusion about sexual orientation and gay marriage antagonizes many Bible-believers and may differ from most if not all of this volume's other contributors. My point here is not to promote my view of this difficult issue, but rather to illustrate how people of faith might deal with their disagreements. Throughout the controversy, I have sought to retain cordial conversation and public dialogues with those who differed with me. I believe the information that Scanzoni and I have offered into the public sphere will stand the test of time, though I must always be open to the possibility of being proved wrong. By the nature of science, all its conclusions are provisional, and while the Bible itself is definitive and authoritative for Christians, our interpretations of it must always be less certain. We are all fallible humans, and God's revelation is ongoing. Thus if we each, with our differing understandings and backgrounds, will contribute our information and conclusions into the free marketplace of ideas and expose ourselves to one another's critique, then out of that exchange will ultimately grow greater understanding and discernment.

So, psychological science has not only enabled my response to the new atheist contention that religion is toxic, it also has caused me to peel back the conventional religious understandings of an immortal soul, of manipulative prayer, and of sexual orientation being a moral choice. But in each case I have discovered a biblically rooted understanding that actually anticipates recent science.

My faith also has sensitized me to assumptions and values that are implicit in my field's teaching, writing, research, and practice. As feminist, Marxist, and Christian critics continually remind us, psychology is not value-free. When writing textbooks, values are embedded in my terminology. (Shall I describe compliant behaviour as 'conformist' or 'socially responsive'?) And they influence my emphasis on topics such as evil, pride, prejudice, peacemaking, sexuality, and altruism. When my textbook publishers pass along queries from potential adopters who are wary of a book that is authored by an out-of-the-closet Christian who occasionally includes a religion-related topic and is infused with values, I reply that authors' values seep into all psychology texts. In answer to one recent query, I responded that in writing the text I have three pertinent aims.

First, I am striving to report on the entirety of psychological science. Insofar as psychological researchers have related their science to contentious issues related to sex, race, and religion, I have not tried to evade the issues (even when doing so would spare criticism, though making for a blander book). Thus, although the research on sexual orientation displeases some on the religious right, I have reported the news, with the result that the book has been effectively banned from Psychology Advanced Placement classes for college places in the state of Alabama (where it is one of the only texts singled out for denial of the state funding that supports most high school text purchases). The book has also taken some flack for its assumption of evolution, but again that's part of today's science.

Second, I offer margin quotes and narrative examples that aim to relate psychological science to other spheres of student interest and study... to politics, history, literature, religion, economics, sports, and so on. Thus, there is among these quotes an occasional quote from the Bible as literature (mostly famous lines from the Old Testament, I believe). In addition to my liberal arts purpose, these very occasional quotes aim to support the teaching of psychology – by helping to diminish the initial wariness of psychology felt by some strongly religious students.

Third, I intend the book to be appropriate for students and faculty of any faith or none (and who reside in many countries and read the text in various languages). Thus if at any point it seems to become parochial (e.g. by going beyond reporting research from the psychological literature or by advocating or presuming any religion), then I welcome feedback on where that has happened. Also, the Preface guide to critical thinking can be used by anyone who wants to scrutinize the book's application of scientific thinking to topics on the borderlands of science.

To those who may fear swimming as an identified Christian in the shark pond of a sceptical, anti-religious intellectual culture – well, I can empathize with the anxiety. For me it has been part of the challenge of authoring introductory and social psychology texts. Such work requires honestly and openly reporting on my discipline (and being critiqued by publisher-commissioned reviews from hundreds of professional colleagues). And it requires me to be true to myself and my core convictions and values. Happily, there has rarely been tension between these two obligations (had I seen my faith as anti-science, I would not have undertaken to be a reporter of my science). Still, it does sometimes take a thick skin, with criticisms from all sides.

In the future I hope to see more Christians in psychology not just as helping professionals and not just as spectators and critics in the stands, but also on the psychological science playing-field. We need fresh minds who, by getting in the game – becoming leaven in the loaf – will become part of the larger intellectual community. As C. S. Lewis once declared, 'We do not need more Christian books; we need more books by Christians about everything with Christian values built in.'

And if we are accused of being biased, or wanting to persuade people to our point of view – well, yes. Most good writing, suggests the psychologist-writer Mary Pipher, is 'writing to change the world'. As the Stanford religion professor and peace activist Robert McAfee Brown reflected, 'Why do we write? I submit that beyond all rewards... *we write because we want to change things*. We write because we have this [conviction that] we can make a difference.' Such is what motivates my teaching-through-writing: my efforts to excite curiosity, to guide intuition with critical intelligence, to transform judgmentalism into compassion, to replace illusion with understanding, and to highlight the common ground between psychological science and Christian faith.

CHAPTER 9

The Laboratory of the Cross
Wilson C. K. Poon

Wilson Poon is Professor of Condensed Matter Physics in the
University of Edinburgh, where he researches into emergent
properties of colloidal suspensions and bacteria. He was born
in Hong Kong and came to boarding school in Britain in 1979
for A-Levels. He was appointed to Edinburgh after gaining an
undergraduate degree and a PhD at Cambridge and a brief
period as a Lecturer at Portsmouth Polytechnic. He is a Fellow
of the Royal Society of Edinburgh, and a member of the Doctrine
Committee of the Scottish Episcopal Church.

I became a Christian in 1978 and started training as a physicist
in 1981. So for most of my Christian journey, I have lived with
the challenge of relating science and faith. This essay tells 'the
story so far'.

Christian and scientific beginnings

When I was growing up in Hong Kong, neither of my parents were
Christians. But they sent me to an Anglican secondary school,
and before that, to its feeder primary school and kindergarten,
because of their academic reputation. Christianity was a low-key
affair throughout. In secondary school, we all learnt the outline
of the biblical narrative 'at face value', without ever discussing
whether it was 'really so'. There were morning assemblies with
hymns, prayers and short homilies with occasional Christian
content. No one, staff or pupil, had to be a Christian. I certainly
was not when I entered secondary school.

Here I began my formal education in science. We were

taught a 'classical' curriculum. Physics was about mechanics, heat, light and electricity; chemistry dealt with reactions in test tubes; and biology was mostly focused on 'higher' organisms (but without any evolution). Atoms and nuclei, the electron theory of bonding, and DNA only made brief appearances. There was little attempt at relating these sciences to each other. Such a curriculum would be considered very old-fashioned nowadays. But it taught me that there was a perfectly valid macroscopic level of description of phenomena *without* resorting to microscopic explanations, and it instilled an 'anti-reductionist streak' in my nascent philosophy of science, where each branch of science had its own autonomy, with its own concepts, forms of reasoning and experimental practice. Later in my research, I have worked successively at the boundary between physics and mineralogy, chemistry and biology. But I have never thought that these sciences could, or should, be 'reduced to physics'. Instead, I have learnt that I must steep myself in a branch of science *on its own terms* before I could hope to relate it to physics in non-superficial ways. The theology–science dialogue requires no less.

I was baptized and confirmed during my last year in Hong Kong. I think I started considering these matters because I wanted to study abroad. Since this meant either America or Britain, both apparently Christian countries, I seem to recall wondering whether I accepted Christianity for myself or not. I cannot remember precisely what form of conclusion I came to; but looking back, I think it was more that practical Christianity had become *meaningful* to me after prolonged exposure, rather than that I thought it was in some theoretical sense 'true'. And, somehow, I realized that if *this* stuff had become meaningful, it required an act of commitment.

In and out of creationism

I left Hong Kong for Rugby in 1979 to take my A-levels. There, I learnt much from the chemistry teacher who ran the Christian Union, including a love for the Bible (and for thick-cut marmalade on toast!). Hiding in his large attic library for many happy hours, I acquired a taste for theology books. I also found a number of volumes advocating creationism – my first encounter with literature that sought to relate science and faith. I do not know whether my friend the chemistry teacher was a creationist or not; but he certainly did not discourage me from exploring creationism. The upshot was that by the time I arrived in Cambridge two years later, I was a dyed-in-the-wool creationist.

I found a substantial minority of like-minded people in the Cambridge Inter-collegiate Christian Union (CICCU). It fascinates me that a majority of these were fellow scientists. Perhaps arts and humanities students simply had too much 'textual common sense' to do something as gross as taking Genesis 1 literally. Many, including the editor of this present volume, tried to dissuade me from creationism, to no avail. My total lack of exposure to evolutionary biology up to that point did not help. Before I explain how I got out of creationism, I should reflect on what attracted me to it in the first place.

In his first *Lecture on Physics*, the Nobel laureate Richard Feynman speculated about a world in which all but one piece of scientific knowledge had been wiped out. He asked, 'What item would be most helpful to the next generation starting from scratch?' His answer was, 'Matter is made up of atoms.' I agree. But history suggests that there is an equally important *meta*scientific principle that our hypothetical 'science-less' generation would need: the principle that they should be able to give mechanistic explanations of the universe *without* recourse to divine agency. It took humanity many millennia before the majority dared to believe that this was true. I will call this the 'Laplace principle', because Napoleon reputedly once asked Pierre Simon Laplace where God was to be found among his equations, getting the answer, 'Sire, I have no need of that hypothesis.' The historical context of this (possibly apocryphal) story is important. Just a generation before, the great Isaac Newton invoked occasional divine 'poking' to explain certain irregularities in planetary motion. Laplace, who was born and died a Catholic, showed that a thorough application of Newton's own laws sufficed, without appealing to a *deus ex machina*.

I think creationism was attractive to me because it evaded the Laplace principle, apparently offering a whole area of science where it was possible, perhaps even necessary, to invoke the 'God hypothesis'. It gave tangible security to a young Christian for whom the question of truth was just beginning to be felt. Applying Occam's razor in my first attempt to relate science and faith, I found in creationism an attractively simple hypothesis.

It was not science but philosophy that cured me of creationism during my PhD. When I started *doing* science for myself, it struck me that the creationist philosophy of science did *not* reflect how I actually made progress. A typical piece of creationist reasoning goes like this: here are some observations that conventional biology or geology cannot explain – and that would be true enough – *ergo*, these disciplines are wrong and need replacing by a creationist account. But finding observations that do not fit the current theoretical framework and trying to explain them *within the same framework* was the very stuff of everyday scientific research. Without such robustness, there will be no theoretical frameworks, and no science. Moreover, the creationist paradigm was unfruitful – it did not suggest a research programme; rather, it specialized in poking holes in an established framework. So I slowly jettisoned creationism during my PhD years. There is a moral here: we should teach scientists some philosophy!

I had nothing to replace creationism with, but simply stopped thinking about the subject. My research taught me that leaving difficult issues for a while could pay off. I did that with 'evolution and creation'. A few years later, I realized that the problem had vanished because my biblical hermeneutics had matured. Meanwhile, something else demanded attention.

Science: a Christian vocation?

Doing a PhD was a lonely struggle. I started to question why I as a Christian should be doing such work. But there was a deafening silence on this issue at CICCU meetings and the services at the church I attended. Instead, the powerful unspoken message was that I was a student first and foremost so that I could 'convert' other students. Moreover, full-time Christian service, narrowly defined, was the top career choice afterwards – those in it were the only ones who ever got prayed for! So why was I slogging away at studying minerals at high temperatures?

Around this time, I started attending St Barnabas Church. The vicar, the Revd Douglas Holt (now a canon at Bristol Cathedral), became a life-long friend. He introduced me gently to philosophy, which (amongst other things) eventually weaned me off creationism. But he also helped me begin to articulate an adequate theology of vocation. I remember clearly that when I was introduced to Douglas, he did *not* ask me to lead a Bible study group, but enquired about my physics. Once I ascertained that this was more than politeness on his part, I was profoundly shocked. Here was a clergyman *really* interested in my work!

With Douglas' help, I realized that, wonderfully, the Christian gospel promised the redemption of *the whole of creation*. Out of many biblical passages on this subject, Revelation 21:24 became particularly important to me at that time. In his vision of the heavenly city, St John saw that 'the kings of the earth will bring their glory into it.' Given clues from the rest of Scripture (especially Isaiah 60–66), I understood this as saying that *all* that was good and true and honourable in *this* creation would be redeemed and gathered into the new creation to add to its splendour. And, bravo, this included everything in my scientific research that fitted the bill! I began praying 'Thy will be done *on earth* as it is in heaven' with new conviction.

Admittedly, this is only one component of a full theology of science as a Christian vocation. But it was an emotionally important starting-point: I no longer felt a second-class citizen in God's kingdom. My story highlights an aspect of the pastoral task that churches in general rather neglect (so that I sometimes still feel a second-class citizen in church!), and which the burgeoning 'science and religion' literature barely touches upon. Now, living in Scotland, I find that a eucharistic prayer-and-response often used by Scottish Episcopalians expresses well my sense of vocational 'at-home-ness' as a Christian. These lines are reproduced in the first two stanzas of a poem I wrote recently on science as a Christian vocation:

Benedictus

Blessed are you: Lord God of all creation:
Through your goodness
We have this Bread to offer.
Which earth has given and human hands have made.
It will become for us the bread of life.

Blessed be God for ever.

Blessed are you: Lord God of all creation:
Through your goodness
We have this Wine to offer.
Fruit of the vine and work of human hands.
It will become the cup of our salvation.

Blessed be God for ever.

Blessed are you: Lord God of all invention:
Through your goodness
We have this Cure to offer.
Fruit of the lab and work of evolution.
It will improve for us the Quality of Life.

Blessed be God for ever.

Blessed are you: Lord God of all intuition:
Through your goodness
We have this Proof to offer.
Fruit of the brain and work of abstraction.
It is the Self-understanding of your Universe.

Blessed be God for ever.

Laboratory of the cross

The end of my PhD coincided with a painful and turbulent period in my personal relationships: God felt very distant, even absent altogether. I thought and read a lot about 'the problem of suffering'. The book of Job became a firm favourite in the Bible. Many modern authors also helped. Paul Fiddes taught me about the 'creative suffering of God'. W. H. Vanstone helped me appreciate the 'stature of waiting' by highlighting Jesus' startling passivity once he was 'handed over' to his enemies. Dietrich Bonhoeffer's *Letters and Papers from Prison* gave me much insight into the 'hidden God', the *Deus absconditus*, that Isaiah spoke of: 'Truly, you are a God who hides himself, O God of Israel, the Saviour' (45:15).

During this painful time, 'science and faith' was off my agenda. When this episode started to fade in the mid 1990s, I began reading the mainstream 'science and religion' literature. I was excited by what I found – if I had seen this stuff fifteen years earlier, I might not have become a creationist! And yet, something troubled me. I felt that the books I was reading spoke of God in the context of science rather too easily. As a scientist, I worked completely according to the Laplace principle. Thus, day in and day out, my research mediated to me a palpable sense of God's *absence*, and I needed to know how to deal with that. The literature that I was reading offered little help in this matter, because it essentially bypassed it. I hesitated in raising the issue with my Christian friends, especially the scientists, because it felt like 'letting the side down' – it was non-Christians who were meant to equate science with God's absence!

Today, when I do raise this point amongst Christians, the response I get is often some version of 'natural theology'. Some start from science: the Big Bang or some other discovery apparently provides fresh pointers to God. Others start from the Bible, often quoting Romans 1:20 – 'Ever since the creation of the world his eternal power and divine nature, invisible though they are, have been understood and seen through the things he has made. So they are without excuse.' But natural theology based on science has a short 'shelf life' – such discussion from barely one generation ago already reads dated nowadays, because science has moved on. On the other hand, the appeal to Romans ignores the context. In Paul's day, everyone saw signs of divine action everywhere; the issue was *what kind of god* was acting. In this context, Paul argued that idolatry was without excuse. That context no longer obtains today: a sense of divine absence is the prevalent mood. So, neither strategy helps. To make sense of my encounter with the *Deus absconditus* in my daily work, I had to look elsewhere.

Illumination came when I connected this issue with my earlier reading on 'God and suffering'. In both cases, the apparent *absence* of God was the issue. I already knew that the cross made some sense of my painful relationships; now I realized that the same was true for 'science and faith'. In particular, if the man on the cross was the only-begotten Son of the Creator and Sustainer of the universe, then something like the Laplace principle is just what we expect. *This* God is unlikely to have made a world in which explicit reference to Godself is needed at every explanatory juncture. Instead, we may expect God's presence in the universe, in the person of the Spirit, to be about as obvious as God's presence in a dying rabbi hanging on a Roman gibbet.

When that dying man was taunted by the onlookers, 'If you are the King of Israel, come down from the cross!' (Mark 15:32), he had no answer. Indeed, his cry of dereliction only confirmed to these onlookers that he was *not* God's Son – 'My God, my God, why have you forsaken me?' (Mark 15:34). I began to hear a parallel between the 2,000-year-old taunt thrown at Jesus and a taunt that I hear often today – 'If you are a scientist, why do you believe in God?' In other words, the Laplace principle works, so God is a delusion. I now realize that it is my Christian vocation as a scientist to inhabit prayerfully precisely this place of felt absence, 'drinking its cup fully' with Christian and non-Christian colleagues, and not be too quick in offering arguments for seeing God's footprints in the universe.

Of course, if *I* were God, I would have made the universe differently: everything would have to be explained always with reference to *me*. But Christians worship a different God, a God whose Son calls all to take up the cross and follow where he went on the first Good Friday. Importantly, the new life to which we are called is 'hidden with Christ in God' (Colossians 3:3). Of course, such waiting and bearing is not in vain, because Christ has been raised from the dead on that first Easter Sunday. But, this side of heaven, we inhabit 'Saturday space'.

Dietrich Bonhoeffer understood these matters profoundly. Interestingly, in his *Letters and Papers from Prison*, he told us that he was reading 'with great interest Weizäcker's book about "the world view of physics"… [and] hope to learn a great deal from it' (letter 24/5/1944; Weisäcker was a distinguished nuclear physicist). Later, he spells out the theological implication of what he has learnt (letter 16/7/1944), in language strikingly reminiscent of Laplace's supposed answer to Napoleon:

> God as a working hypothesis in morals, politics, or science has been surmounted and abolished… God would have us know that we must live as men [and women] who manage our lives without him. The God who is with us is the God who forsakes us (Mark 15:34). The God who lets us live in the world without the working hypothesis of God is the God before whom we stand continually. Before God and with God we live without God. God lets himself be pushed out of the world on to the cross. He is weak and powerless in the world, and that is precisely the way, the only way, in which he is with us and helps us. Matt. 8:17 makes it quite clear that Christ helps us, not by virtue of his omnipotence, but by virtue of his weakness and suffering.

The relevance to a scientist-believer working in the 'laboratory of the cross' is clear.

Science, faith and faiths

What I have said so far can be seen as an attempt to construct a 'theology of science' – making sense of the scientific enterprise in the light of Christian belief. Such 'God-talk' (theology!) is absolutely necessary for us 'scientists in pews': in order to pray and worship meaningfully, we have to know how our faith makes sense of our vocation and our daily experience. I have emphasized divine hiddenness, but have left out other themes. Thus, for example, I have found it fruitful to understand my own scientific vocation as 'giving voice to Creation', which is wordless on its own (cf. Psalm 19:3).[1] But this is not the place to construct a full theology of science.

Inevitably, 'God-talking' science starts from a position of faith – it is faith seeking understanding (to quote Anselm). But why should anyone be a Christian in the first place? This question is, of course, as old as Christianity. But nowadays, it is almost obscured by another, wider question: hasn't science made *any* sort of faith redundant? It is not just that the Laplace principle apparently renders 'God' unnecessary. It appears that scientific rationality has made *any* sort of belief irrational. All believing scientists have been confronted by this question multiple times from their colleagues. Richard Dawkins famously talks of 'a process of non-thinking called faith', which is 'evil precisely because it requires no justification, and brooks no argument'.

But this misunderstands the nature of faith. I often explain it to fellow scientists like this – faith is like the 'operating system' of a computer; it is needed before anything else can be done! We can choose between Windows and Mac OS (or whatever), but 'no operating system' is not an option. Similarly, humans must have *faith*, but we can choose between different *faiths*. The philosopher Mary Midgley puts it like this in her book *Science as Salvation*: '[Faith is] something that you must have before you can ask whether anything is true or not. It is basic trust. It is the acceptance of a map, a perspective, a set of standards and assumptions, an enclosing vision within which facts are placed.'

Faith is needed to do science. Thomas Huxley understood this when he said (in *Darwin's Life and Letters, Volume 2*) that 'the one act of faith in the convert to science is the confession of the universality of order and of the absolute validity, in all time and under all circumstances, of the law of causation' – that is, the Laplace principle holds true. Huxley explains: 'This confession is an act of faith, because, by the nature of the case, the truth of such propositions is not susceptible of proof.' In fact, the proof of the pudding is in the eating – science works!

This act of faith itself is inevitably situated in a wider faith context, whether acknowledged or not. Some believe that the success of the Laplace principle means that there is no God, and order and causality are just brute facts. Others believe that these reflect the character of a Creator God. The choice between these faith positions is not, or should not be, arbitrary. Defensibly, the Christian faith has greater explanatory power than scientism (Dawkins's faith) – for a start, it answers the question, 'Whence order and causality?'[2] Compared to other religious faiths, it also has a unique resource (the cross) for understanding the success of the Laplace principle. Moreover, I believe that Jesus is who he claimed to be because that makes best sense of a corpus of historical documents (the New Testament). And so on.

But armchair rationality can only go so far. In the end, one has to decide whether to accept the invitation to taste the pudding. As Philip said to Nathanael concerning Jesus, 'Come and see!' (John 1:46).

Concluding musings

When I first started to articulate my thoughts on science and God's hiddenness, I asked many friends whether they had come across similar ideas in their reading. The Revd Canon Ian Paton, Rector of Old St Paul's, Edinburgh, pointed me to the poetry of R. S. Thomas. Thomas (1913–2000) was a rural parish priest in the Church of Wales. His poetry profoundly explores divine hiddenness. Fascinatingly, Thomas repeatedly mused on this theme in the context of science and technology. Here, for example, is his poem that inspired the title of this essay:

Emerging[3]

Not as in the old days I pray,
God. My life is not what it was.
Yours, too, accepts the presence of
the machine? Once I would have asked
Healing. I go now to be doctored,
To drink sinlessly of the blood
of my brother, to lend my flesh
As manuscript of the great poem
of the scalpel. I would have knelt
long, wrestling with you, wearing
you down. Hear my prayer, Lord, hear
my prayer. As though you were deaf, myriads
of mortals have kept up their shrill
cry, explaining your silence by
their unfitness.

It begins to appear
this is not what prayer is about.
It is the annihilation of difference,
The consciousness of myself in you,
of you in me; the emerging
from the adolescence of nature
into the adult geometry
of the mind. I begin to recognise
you anew, God of form and number.
There are questions we are the solution
to, others whose echoes we must expand
to contain. Circular as our way
is, it leads not back to that snake-haunted
garden, but onward to the tall city
of glass that is the laboratory of the spirit.

Thomas and other poets who have profoundly explored Isaiah's
Deus absconditus, from John Donne to Gerard Manley Hopkins,
are now constant companions in my exploration of the theology

of science: poetry reaches places that other *genres* cannot reach!
Indeed, after reading Stephen Fry's guide to 'DIY poetry', *The
Ode Less Travelled*, I started to write poetry myself. The poem
'Benedictus' has already appeared above. By way of conclusion,
here is another poem, written during Advent season 2007, which
encapsulates much of what I want to say:

Discerning Divinity

'The heav'ns declare the glory of the Lord':
Proof of his greatness, wisdom these afford.
All creatures great and small we see on earth
The love of God has brought them all to birth.
'Magna opera Domini' we read
In Free School Lane engraved on oaken creed.[4]

But Nature can be read in other ways
That do not flatter so the Ancient of Days.
'The heav'ns' eternal silence frightens me.'
This was the cry of Pascal's libertine.
We need no 'God hypothesis' to prove
Laplace's result that orbits stably evolve.
Some say that Nature's red in tooth and claw,
'Survival of the fittest', rather raw.
The microscope since Hooke has sore revealed
Sundry infectious agents to harm our weal.
Magna opera Domini? We face
A suffering globe in aeons of silent space!

If God is there, then old Isaiah is right,
'You are a God who's hidden from our plight.'
The 'glory' spoken of in Psalm nineteen
Must be a different kind from what we deem
Appropriate for God enthroned in heaven
Remote and far away from all our leaven.
Perhaps our thoughts on God are sore in error
Dissociating him from all our horror.

In fact, the Roman soldier hit the mark:
'This man is truly son of God,' he remarked
Hearing the cry of Jesus on the tree
'My God, My God why'st thou forsaken me?'

Saint John called this the Son of Man's own hour
Of glory, subverting human modes of power.
The presence of this God is truly hidden.
T'is 'glory', but not the kind that we'd have bidden.
The Cross and empty tomb together yield
A paradigm how God will be revealed.
Discarded grave clothes interpret Golgotha
That God is present in th'anathema.
The 'glory' spoken of in Psalm nineteen
Must be interpreted afresh to mean
The glory of the only begotten Son
Whose death has not the love of God undone.

The Cross of Christ our university
For learning to discern divinity.
The hidden God of Christ did not create
A world where explanations must relate
To God at every step along the way,
Giving the 'God hypothesis' a say.

A 'cruciform epistemology'
Is Paul's Corinthian theology:
Jewry and Gentiles, they did not dispute
The Cross for both a place of ill repute:
Those seeking after God should not look here,
Divinity was likely found elsewhere!
But at this most unlikely place to meet
God chose here all humanity to greet.
The Cross thus authorizes us to look
For God where God's own presence wears a cloak.
Faith is enjoined to tarry at those places
Where absence, pain and pointlessness it faces.

Discerning hidden presence cruciform,
Boldly we learn to take this as the norm
For revelation of divinity
While on this time-bound side of Eternity,
Where matter cannot yet bear the full weight
Of glory undimmed. For that we must wait.
For now, the pinnacle of matter bearing
Divinity: a body scarred and bleeding,
In Eucharistic Bread and Wine remembered
A suffering divinity en-mattered.
Thus 'Nature red in tooth and claw' may witness
To glory cruciform with Godly likeness.

'I am the resurrection and the life,'
The Crucified One says to all who strive
To take the Cross and follow on this way
While waiting for the final Easter Day.
Corruption will then put on incorruption
When space-bound matter undergoes transition
To bear the full weight of divinity.
Then hiddenness will yield to clarity.
Meanwhile, we dwell in Holy Saturday.
O Risen Jesus, teach us how to pray
And how to love you, heart and soul and mind,
Your hidden presence everywhere to find.

ACKNOWLEDGMENT
I thank the Revd Dr Patrick Richmond (Christ Church, Norwich)
for commenting on earlier drafts of this chapter.

NOTES
1. Interestingly, Jesus repeatedly gave voice to the voiceless (the dumb and
   the marginalized).
2. Note that this is not inferring divinity from 'order' (a design argument
   from which God emerges), but claiming that if the Judeo-Christian God
   exists, then 'order' is explicable (starting from God to see what follows).

3. First published in R. S. Thomas, *Laboratories of the Spirit*, London: Macmillan, 1975, © Kunjana Thomas 2001, used with permission. A convenient source of this and other relevant poems is R. S. Thomas, *Collected Poems*, Phoenix (2000).

4. 'Great are the works of the Lord, studied by all who delight in them' (Psalm 111:2) – engraved in Latin (*Magna opera domini...*) on top of oak doors in Free School Lane, Cambridge, guarding the entrance to the (old) Cavendish Laboratory.

CHAPTER 10

Earthquakes, Volcanoes and Other Catastrophes[1]
Robert White

Bob White graduated in Geology from the University of
Cambridge in 1974 and was awarded a PhD in Marine
Geophysics in 1977. After spells as a postdoc, he was appointed
to the academic staff at Cambridge in 1981 and to the Chair of
Geophysics in 1989. He was elected a Fellow of the Royal Society
in 1994. He runs a research group in the university investigating
the dynamic earth and has published over 200 academic papers.
In 2006 he founded with Denis Alexander the Faraday Institute
for Science and Religion at St Edmund's College, Cambridge
(where he has also been a Fellow since 1988). He is married to
Helen and has two (now adult) children.

All children are born scientists. Any parent knows the perpetual
refrain of 'Why does this happen, why that, why the other; why,
why, why?' Though many distractions, and what is laughingly
called 'growing up', tend to submerge those childish enquiries,
some of us are fortunate enough to have spent our lives indulging
our natural curiosity and have been able to make a living out
of it to boot. A life as a scientist is in some ways to live out
a protracted childhood – fifteen minutes listening to a group
discussing the latest controversial ideas at a conference might
well reinforce that impression.

How does Christian faith affect one's scientific endeavours
– and vice-versa? To a first order (as a physicist might say), a
Christian faith has no greater and no lesser influence on how one
behaves as a scientist than any other activity. I was asked recently
what advice I would give to a Christian politician about how to

deal (in this case) with the prospect of global climate change. My answer was that it would be much the same whether they were a politician or a policeman, an office cleaner or a managing director, a parent bringing up children at home or a professor in the academy: it would be along the lines that they continually remind themselves before speaking or acting that one day they will have to account to God for everything they have done, and for their use of the opportunities and talents they have been given (Luke 8:17–18). Are there things we should have done, but didn't? Would we be ashamed to say those words or to do those things if Jesus were standing beside us in the room watching? Because, of course, in reality he is.

Our work, the attitudes we bring to it and the way we do it should be as much part of our worship of God as is the hour or two we spend in church on a Sunday. Of course, as fallen humans we continually fail to reach the standards of behaviour towards God and to others that Christ sets before us. Certainly I do. But as Christians we are a 'work in progress', a work which will only be perfected in the new creation. In the meantime we are called to be salt and light in a fallen and lost world, a task in which we can take the first faltering steps only by the grace given us by God and through the promptings of the Holy Spirit.

There are some activities which are beyond the pale: quite clearly we should not knowingly do anything immoral or illegal. Nor, in the same vein, can the ends ever justify the means. As an academic, I have the luxury of freedom to choose what research I do, so I do not often find myself in a position where I am asked by my employer to do something I don't think I should do. Nor is the pursuit of excessive monetary gain normally the main temptation faced by academics.

For academics there are perhaps rather different but equally insidious temptations. One of them is the pursuit of a 'reputation': the wish to be recognized above others as a pre-eminent authority. This is not to say that you shouldn't do your work as well as possible, and publish cutting-edge papers in the best international journals if that is within your reach. But if it segues into doing others down in an attempt to enhance yourself, then it has undoubtedly crossed a line. If it turns from healthy competition about better understanding how the world works to unseemly rivalry with others, then how can that be worthy of God's calling? How would that square with the fact that all people are created in God's image? Speaking to a Christian community, the apostle Paul wrote: 'Do nothing from rivalry or conceit, but in humility count others more significant than yourselves. Let each of you look not only to his own interests, but also to the interests of others' (Philippians 2:3–4).

Another temptation faced by academic scientists is that the pursuit of new ideas, of new experiments can be so exciting, so heady that it unbalances one's priorities. That temptation is not, of course, unique to scientists: businessmen, city traders, all face the same pressures. But for academics the temptations are perhaps more easily indulged: there are few constraints on how you spend your time, no specified working hours (and usually no specified holidays). Yet if this leads us to neglect our families, our responsibilities to the communities in which we live, our friends, and indeed our God, then it is at root selfishness, which, to call a spade a spade, is no less than sinfulness.

What follows is my personal story as a scientist and a Christian believer, and how these have interacted in my own life.

School and university

My memories of school in the 1960s are of spending a lot of time outdoors: bicycles were our passport to freedom and I spent many happy hours cycling around the quintessentially English countryside of Leicestershire and Nottinghamshire where I grew up. The Scout movement gave me an enduring love for the outdoors. Together with the Duke of Edinburgh's award scheme, the confidence and self-reliance we developed from many camping and hiking expeditions opened up vistas for travel into remote places. A lightweight hiking tent was one of the first things I bought with money I earned during a year off before going to university. It is still going strong today, though at twenty pounds, lightweight is a strictly relative term...

The other thing I remember was continually making things: with a huge box of Meccano parts, from old cardboard boxes, scraps of wood and the like. Jumble sales were a great source of old radios and gramophones which could be cannibalized for their motors and electronic components. I built crystal radios and amplifiers, aeroplanes, biscuit-tin ovens and a rather wonky go-cart. All this stood me in good stead when I eventually started doing scientific research, because many of the instruments we used for marine geophysical studies are home built. And once you are on a research ship at sea for four or five weeks, if something went wrong you had to fix it with whatever you had available.

My father worked for the Ordnance Survey making maps. Strangely, I ended up making maps too, though of the seafloor rather than the land, and in areas that no one had mapped before. I loved science at school, and applied to do Physics at university. My application to Cambridge University was initially turned down and I accepted a place at Imperial College London. But my A-level results led to me being accepted at Cambridge, and I have never properly left since.

My parents were (and are) faithful churchgoers, and I progressed through all the years of Sunday school. I remember being fascinated by the formulae in the *Book of Common Prayer* which enable you to calculate the date of Easter for decades – indeed for centuries – ahead. Many a sermon was spent trying to fathom it out. I suppose that was my first introduction to science and religion, because the date of Easter is based on astronomical calculations of the phase of the moon.

At Cambridge I automatically and without much thought joined the two organizations in which I had already been involved for much of my youth. But this time they both changed the course of my life. In the Scout & Guide club I met Helen, who is now my wife of over thirty years; and in the Christian Union I met Jesus, whom I have also followed for well over thirty years.

On the academic front, I discovered Geology. One of the unique features of Cambridge is that in the sciences you are accepted for a general course in Natural Sciences. Though I had come expecting to do Physics, it was necessary to take at least one new subject. Geology had field trips, and because it was a smaller subject with trips led by academic staff, it had a camaraderie missing in the huge undergraduate classes of the subjects like Physics and Chemistry. And it rapidly became clear to me that whereas in Geology we were (and undergraduates still are) learning about and critiquing current research papers and ideas (and not infrequently learning about them from the very people who had developed the theories), in Physics you never got much past work done in the 1950s. So I switched to Geology and eventually ended up working in Geophysics, effectively getting the best of both worlds. Geology of course offered plenty of opportunities for outdoor work. One year I estimated that I probably spent more time under canvas than sleeping indoors – not as difficult as it might sound, since Cambridge terms only occupy twenty-four weeks of the year.

All the time I was growing as a Christian on a wonderful diet of teaching in the Christian Union at central meetings and in small groups, and through membership of the Round Church. The central churches of Cambridge do an amazing work with students – year after year they have to start afresh from the beginning, yet generations of students leave with a sound Christian grounding to all corners of the world, often to positions of influence in both secular and Christian work. It wasn't until my wife and I spent sabbaticals away from Cambridge that we fully appreciated what a privilege it is to sit under such consistent, godly teaching week in, week out.

Research

I moved into PhD research under the supervision of Drum Matthews, who, with his student Fred Vine, had postulated the theory of seafloor spreading, which led directly to plate tectonics. He was an inspiring leader (White, 1999), and much of what I have learnt about how to do research came from him. My research was in marine geophysics, seeking to understand the earth from observations made at sea. Since 70 per cent of the world is covered by water and the structure and development of the seafloor is much simpler than that of the continents (because it is much younger and therefore not complicated by hundreds or thousands of millions of years of geological history), it was to prove a fruitful endeavour.

In the mid 1970s, much of the seafloor was completely unknown and unexplored. So I had the privilege of investigating hitherto unknown areas and discovering many new features and indeed a new plate boundary. They were heady times and scientific progress was rapid. I went to sea on research cruises most years. The flip-side to this was leaving my wife and two children for five weeks or more at a time, usually out of contact in those days before emails and satellite phones. As is often the case, during these periods my wife bore a heavy load in supporting me in my work.

In my department at Cambridge there was a small group of extremely able and committed technicians who built amazingly innovative and effective seabed instruments which enabled us to measure things that no one had measured before: a sure way to make progress. They were matched by a succession of outstanding research students who used new analytical techniques as computer power burgeoned, and applied new theories to move scientific understanding forward. One of the joys of my career has been working with such talented young people doing PhDs, over forty to date, and seeing them develop skills far in advance of my own and move on to professional positions in industry, government, academia and indeed in full-time Christian work.

During all this time, it never crossed my mind that there was any conflict between what I was learning scientifically and my Christian faith. Nor do I remember there being any particular problems in this area in the minds of my Christian friends who were scientists. We were busy simply getting on with the job of doing science and living out Christian lives. I don't want to give the impression that this was without difficulty. Wresting information scientifically is long, often tedious and frequently hard, grinding work – in my case, I struggled with equipment failures or losses, with weather that sometimes curtailed our work at sea, with computer programs that never quite behaved as one wanted, with continually raising grants for what is very expensive research, and retaining enthusiasm and commitment in the light of the almost inevitable grant rejections and delays along the way.

Yet the long days and nights, the blind alleys and disappointments are forgotten in those (rare) moments of finally understanding something new, of seeing how a range of disparate data fits into place. Living a consistent Christian life is a continual battle in a not dissimilar way, as any veteran Christian will testify. Yet I can say with certainty that over the years, as my Christian understanding has grown, it has done nothing but fill me with greater certainty that the Christian gospel is truth, truth that all the world needs desperately to hear, and that I am completely unworthy of the grace God has shown me. The more I learn, the more I see of the consistency and depth of what the Bible says about the human condition and our relationship with both the cosmos and the sovereign creator God.

Geology and Christian belief

Science is a secular activity insofar as its very strength lies in not appealing to any external causes (such as divine activity). So scientific theories can be understood in the same way by atheists, Buddhists or Christians and work equally well in Beijing, Birmingham or Budapest. This is not to claim that some cultures may not be more conducive to the development of science than others, or that science cannot offer any insights that colour and give added depth to one's religious beliefs. All life's experiences bear on one's beliefs and vice-versa. Indeed, I have often thought that scientists are particularly privileged in their studies because their underlying beliefs are so consonant with Christian tenets: both scientists and Christians believe that there is an underlying reality to be found; that some things are true and others palpably untrue; and that we can distinguish between them in statements that apply to all people and for all time. Scientists, and most particularly geologists, have the added bonus of studying God's creation directly in a way which is not the case for our arts and humanities colleagues: in a milieu of relativism and post-modernism where things mean what you want them to mean, the latter have fewer and less-certain anchors. It does not surprise me that the city centre churches in Cambridge consistently have many more students studying science than humanities.

One of the insights of geology for me is the amazing providence of God in creating a home just right for humans to inhabit. Geologists get used to thinking in terms of timescales of millions of years. The Earth, for example, has been here for 4,566 million years, give or take a few million years. The best estimate of the age of the universe is that it is about three times older, around 13,700 million years. Life has been present on Earth since almost as soon as it was possible. Isotopic evidence for life dates from 3,800 million years ago, and the oldest known fossils are about 3,500 million years old. One of the amazing facts about the Earth is that throughout that time it has maintained a temperature between 0°C (when water would freeze) and 100°C (when all the water would evaporate), despite the sun getting 30 per cent hotter over the same period and the earth's rotation having slowed four- or five-fold. Without that consistency of surface temperature, life as we know it could not have survived. Furthermore, over the past 50 million years the earth's average surface temperature hasn't changed by more than 10°C from the present, making it possible for mammals, and eventually for humans, to flourish.

These immense timescales are sometimes difficult to comprehend. A helpful way to get them into perspective is to think of the age of the Earth as one year. On that scale, the oldest known microbial fossils date from around Easter, the first multicellular animals from mid-November, the dinosaurs went extinct on Boxing Day, early *Homo sapiens* came on the scene less than half an hour before midnight on New Year's Eve, Adam and Eve appeared a minute before midnight, and Jesus was born just fourteen seconds before midnight.

All this could be taken as meaning that humans have occupied such an infinitesimal part of the history of the universe that we really aren't anything special; that we are just an accidental happenstance. That is the view of reductionist atheists. There is no question that we are animals and share through our evolutionary history our genetic fabric with all other living organisms on Earth. But another way of looking at the evidence is that God has made an immensely fertile universe in which those 13,700 million years preceding our appearance were used in getting conditions just right for humans. This has involved progress from the evolution of stars where the very atoms of which our bodies are constructed were synthesized in nuclear reactions, through the growth of our solar system, and finally to the development of an oxygenated atmosphere in which mammals could survive on earth. The biblical view is that humans are special – we are made in the image of God, which means, amongst other things, that we can relate to God and he to us in an interpersonal way (Genesis 1:26–31; Psalm 8).

It is almost inevitable that I repeatedly have to spend time responding to Young Earth Creationists (YEC), who have an unwavering confidence in their own interpretations of the early chapters of Genesis, believing that the earth cannot be more than about 10,000 years old. My respect for the Bible as the word of God is as high as theirs, but we part company over the exegesis of the early chapters of Genesis and over scientific evidence for the age of the earth. The scientific evidence for an old earth is overwhelming and is based on numerous independent lines of evidence (see White, 2007 for a summary). Indeed, the evidence that Adam and Eve, the first hominids into whom God breathed spiritual life so as to make them humans in his image rather than just animals, lived about 8,000–10,000 years ago is consistent with both biblical evidence and archaeological findings. The only part of the timescale on which I part company from YECs is in the extent of the pre-human period, when of course there were no human observers anyway. There is not space here to discuss the reasons why the YEC claims for a young Earth lack scientific credibility, but well-argued secular and Christian point-by-point rebuttals are widely available (e.g. Wiens, 2002).

The most fruitful approaches take seriously both the scientific evidence and the literary genre of the Genesis passages dealing with the six days of creation. Since specialized scientific writing did not emerge until the founding of the first scientific journals in the seventeenth century, it is anachronistic to press scientific meanings on to Genesis. In any case Augustine, Origen and other early Church Fathers were already interpreting Genesis figuratively in the early centuries AD (for discussions of the interpretation of origins in Genesis and the evidence from science see Kidner, 1967; Alexander, 2001; Lucas, 2001; Wilkinson, 2002). The central aim of the Genesis text is theological: to explain God's purposes in his creation and his own relationship to it. The early Genesis narratives proclaim that the universe was created by a loving, personal God in an orderly fashion, that he was pleased with it, and that one of his main objectives was to make it a place in which humans could live fruitful lives and have loving relationships with himself. The biblical evidence of a purposely created universe, taken together with the scientific evidence for its evolution over billions of years into a place fit for human habitation, reinforce the message that humankind is not the accidental product of a meaningless universe.

My sadness about the debate within Christian circles over the age of the Earth is that it is sometimes elevated by the YEC community almost to an article of faith. It can also provide a barrier to reaching out to other scientists if they are told that they need to accept something so obviously contrary to scientific understanding of the world. The age of the Earth is not a salvation issue. That it need not be divisive is illustrated in my own experience: our home group in Cambridge included for many years one of the most prominent YEC proponents in Britain and his wife. We agreed to differ on the age of the Earth but were one in fellowship and friendship as we studied the Bible together and sought to apply its teachings to our lives.

Education and outreach

Although science and Christian faith have never presented any major intellectual conflicts for me, it is clear that in our culture there is an often unspoken assumption that they are in fact opposed to each another. This is certainly proclaimed stridently by atheists such as Richard Dawkins, and fostered by a media preferring conflict to consensus. Sometimes Christians contribute to this distrust of science and retreat into statements that the Bible as interpreted literally is the only truth. The implication is that the science must be wrong – or worse, that some of its theories, such as those dealing with evolution or conclusions regarding the age of the Earth, are part of an anti-religion conspiracy. This generally creates more heat than light as well as being a rather poor evangelistic strategy, with scientists at least.

If our worship of God is to be meaningful and authentic, it has to embrace *all* of our endeavours, including insights from science. Anyone receiving a British government grant to do research now is required to explain the results to the wider public as part of accepting that funding. This seems quite proper, since the public paid for it. It seems to me that scientists who are Christians have a similar duty to explain their science to fellow believers and to educate them so that they are equipped to grapple with some of the hard ethical and practical issues that face folk in the world today. It is for that reason that Denis Alexander and I wrote a book together 'for the thinking person in the pew' to discuss scientific understanding of the world and how that impacts on Christian faith (Alexander & White, 2004). Denis is a biological scientist and I am a physical scientist, so we reckon we cover much of the range of science between us.

The collaboration between Denis and I expanded when we gained funding to set up the Faraday Institute for Science and Religion in Cambridge at the beginning of 2006. Our objective was to reach working scientists via weekend and week-long courses in science and religion, and to do high-quality academic research in science and religion, organizing regular seminars and lectures and producing material at both an academic and a popular level. Most science–religion enterprises are based in theological departments. So as not to put off scientists, we purposely located the Faraday Institute in a neutral setting at St Edmund's College, Cambridge University. Our lectures and seminars are posted on a website (www.faraday-institute.org) and have become a well-used resource internationally. Another important aspect of our work is to show the reasonableness of the Christian faith to those who are not Christians, by allowing them to engage at lectures and dinners (easy to arrange in a Cambridge College!) with well-known scientists at the peak of their particular disciplines who are also Christians.

There is no shortage of ways for Christians to bring their faith to bear upon current issues in the world. In my case, this is largely in the environmental arena, where global climate change is one of the great uncertainties and challenges facing humankind (Spencer & White, 2007). This is a particularly apposite issue for Christians because it is the poor and marginalized living in low-income parts of the world such as sub-Saharan Africa and parts of Asia and South America who will suffer most from climate change, whereas it is the largely Christianized high-income countries of Europe and North America who have created the problem. Because our high standards of living have been purchased through the selfish and unsustainable use of natural resources, we have a particular responsibility to care for those affected by global climate change.

Another area in which my academic expertise and my Christian faith converge is in so-called 'natural' disasters. The name itself is misleading, because God is sovereign over all of the cosmos, including what we call 'nature', so there should be no sense in which a massive earthquake, tsunami, flood or volcanic eruption is outside God's purview. But it remains the case that such catastrophes cause great loss of life in a world that has an exponentially growing population (three times more people are alive today than when I started school), with an increasing proportion living in mega-cities in locations particularly susceptible to natural disasters. It is likely that sooner rather than later there will be a catastrophe that causes over a million deaths. Historically floods are the world's main killer; by 2020 it is estimated that half the world's population will be at risk from this cause. And again, it is the poor in low-income countries who invariably suffer by far the most in natural disasters.

Although the secular world wrings its hands about the problems and consequences of natural disasters and global climate change (and often enough shies away from the hard decisions required to address them because they usually entail changes in lifestyles), Christianity brings a radical new approach. The Christian perspective is that the resources of this Earth are only on loan from God, and that they are to be used for the worship of God and the good of all. Christians are called to live counter-culturally.[2] It is a profoundly Christian response to be prepared to give up some of our privileges for the sake of others, modelling in a small way Christ's ultimate sacrifice for us (Philippians 2:1–11). Christians should care for the stranger and the foreigner even if they live out of sight on the other side of the world. And where the secular world has no answer to the evident injustices and suffering in the world, the Christian has the assurance that sin and injustice have already been dealt with for all time on the cross, and the certain hope for the future that in due course the whole cosmos will be renewed in the new heavens and new earth.

God has created an orderly, consistent universe where it is possible not only to do science, but also to use understanding from it to help others. Medical advances such as the eradication of smallpox and improved healthcare are obvious examples, but there are myriads of others. In my own area of research they include understanding better the causes of natural disasters and global climate change. This provides the means to educate people about them and to facilitate suitable mitigation and adaptation policies – part of what it means to fulfil God's very first commandment to humankind to have dominion and to rule over the world. The commandment was linked to blessing in Genesis 1:28. I consider myself fortunate to have been able to spend my career in science, playing a very small part in that process.

NOTES

1. My title is taken from the epithet with which my friend and colleague Denis Alexander often introduces me when I give talks at the Faraday Institute.

2. John Stott's volume on *The Message of the Sermon on the Mount* in 'The Bible Speaks Today' series was originally entitled *Christian Counter-Culture: the Message of the Sermon on the Mount* (Stott, 1978).

CHAPTER 11

Reflections of a Christian Working in Science and Conservation
Simon Stuart

Simon Stuart is a conservation biologist with undergraduate and doctoral degrees at Cambridge and ornithological fieldwork experience in Tanzania and Cameroon. Since 1985, he has worked as a scientist with the International Union for Conservation of Nature (IUCN), focusing on measuring species extinction risks with a particular emphasis in recent years on amphibian declines. His work has a global focus, and he also serves as an International Trustee of A Rocha – Christians in Conservation.

Prologue

One July morning in 2007 I was sitting on the veranda of my hotel room in the Philippines reflecting on the state of creation. It was a beautiful view over the Verde Island Passage, between the islands of Luzon and Mindoro, a stretch of water which (according to my good friend, the ichthyologist Kent Carpenter – and he should know) contains more species of fish per unit area than any comparable area in the world, including areas in the so-called 'mega-diverse' countries of Indonesia and Malaysia. It has been called 'the centre of the centre of marine shore-fish biodiversity' (Carpenter and Springer, 2005). It is an incredible area. The sea is teeming with what seems like an endless diversity of fishes, corals and other forms of life. And unlike so many other places, this exceptional ecosystem still seems to be more or less intact.

I was in the Philippines to attend a workshop reviewing the status of every species of reef-building coral in the Indo-Pacific – over 90 per cent of the 845 species of reef-building corals in the world. Our findings were, to put it mildly, sobering. The leading world experts on corals went through each species, one by one, to assess its level of extinction risk (IUCN, 2008; Mace *et al.* not in press). We concluded that, of the species for which there was enough information to assess their status, nearly one third were at risk of extinction. Of even greater concern were these findings:

- 1. The driving force in the decline of coral species is coral bleaching caused by elevated ocean temperatures.

- 2. Before the massive bleaching episode of 1998, less than 2 per cent of the reef-building corals qualified as threatened with extinction.

In less than a decade, the number of globally threatened coral species has increased fifteen-fold, and the situation continues to deteriorate. If this was not enough, decreased ocean alkalinity caused by the rapid build-up of greenhouse gases in the atmosphere, is reducing ocean carbonate ion concentrations and the ability of corals to build their skeletons (Cooper *et al.*, 2007). This could have a devastating effect on reef ecosystems in the coming decades, and we hardly factored it into our species-by-species threat assessments. In short, the gloomy results of the workshop were probably over-optimistic.

As I sat pondering these disturbing trends, and feeling the sadness of the ongoing loss of beautiful ecosystems and species, I felt God say to me that I should write a lament on the status of his creation. This alarmed me. I had no idea how to write a lament. But the invitation to contribute to *Real Scientists, Real Faith* has given me the opportunity to be obedient to God's clear message. This chapter is not a lament, but I hope it may be a precursor for it.

A young naturalist

I cannot remember a time when I was not fascinated by animals. I now believe that this is how God made me. It is part of how I tick. I was extremely fortunate to grow up in Dorset with an abundance of wildlife around me. I developed a fascination for birds, and had a number of rare species on my doorstep – Dartford Warblers, Nightjars and Hobbies. From early on I was also very interested in reptiles and amphibians, and two species very rare in Britain – the Sand Lizard and the Smooth Snake – occurred close to my home. All sorts of weird and wonderful animals found their way into our house. My parents, apparently unfazed, did everything they could to foster my passion, and I was surrounded by a vast array of natural history books which I read avidly. Later on, my mother enjoyed recalling how I used to write lists of threatened species even when I was very small. When I was sorting through her papers after her death ten years ago, I found some of these early writings! As someone who went on to work for many years on the *IUCN Red List of Threatened Species*, I was struck by how little my interests have changed! Looking back on it, my career path seems to have been pretty inevitable.

My good fortune continued. At the age of thirteen I started at Canford School where an amazing biology teacher named Tim Hooker took me under his wing. He taught me an enormous number of things (in addition to the regular biology curriculum), including how to count birds, how to identify them by their songs, how to catch reptiles and amphibians, how to identify fungi and which ones were edible, and how to cook the latter! It did not stop there. Tim organized a friend and I to spend part of a summer on the Shetland island of Foula, where we learned to ring seabirds. I remember climbing down into a foul-smelling cave, and passing young Shags out to the ringing team at the entrance to the cave. They would then return the ringed Shag for me to replace carefully on its nest before passing out the next one. I loved it. After this, Tim arranged for me to visit Tanzania, beginning a love affair with Africa. He was a friend of chimpanzee-expert Jane Goodall who was working in the Gombe

Stream National Park on the shores of Lake Tanganyika. She needed someone to help teach her young son. I don't think I was much good at that, but teaching only took a few hours a day. The rest of the time was mine to watch birds, look for chimpanzees, baboons, red colobus and other monkeys, and swim in the lake and experience being nibbled by a huge diversity of cichlid fish.

So thanks to my parents and Tim Hooker, by the time I went to Cambridge University, I had an impressive knowledge of the natural world. Then two most important things happened. In my first year at Cambridge I met Ann, another biologist in my year, who, ten years later, became my wife. Second, I became a Christian (as did Ann a few months before me). It was not that I had been anti-Christian before. As a small boy, I had been in the choir at Wimborne Minster and also attended a very Victorian prep school that closed soon after I left. I was taught the Bible there by an octogenarian teacher by the name of Mr Swell. Most people hated his lessons, but I loved them and benefited a great deal from them. Later on at Canford, a number of overtly Christian teachers impressed me with their sincerity and care for their pupils. But despite my interest in all things Christian, none of it made particular sense until I arrived in Cambridge. I was most attracted by the authenticity in the relationships among the Christian undergraduates, something that seemed amazing to me, as hitherto I had lived in the insecure teenage world of seeking to perform and impress in order to gain acceptance and significance. It was the uncomplicated love that the Christians had for each other, and above all for Jesus, that won me over. I suppose that my conversion was thoroughly postmodern in that I met Jesus, and welcomed him into my life, before I came to understand the gospel in more conventional terms. But he welcomed me nonetheless, and life has never been the same. It is the most important decision that I ever took, and one that I have never regretted.

My interest in the natural world continued to develop during my time in Cambridge. Looking back, I do not think that my science and Christianity intersected much. I always had the feeling that a career in conservation biology was God's calling, but it was many years before I came to understand that science and conservation could actually be God's work and part of my worship of him. While at Cambridge, my interest in Africa grew. I came under the influence of two academics, Con Benson (who was curator of ornithology in the University Museum of Zoology) and Keith Eltringham (who studied large mammal ecology and wildlife management in East Africa). Con was an old man when I met him, but for the few years that I knew him I had the privilege to be taught by the most knowledgeable expert on the avifauna of Africa. While still an undergraduate, I led two university expeditions to study the rare, endemic birds of the Eastern Arc Mountain range of Tanzania. Through these experiences I learnt something about leadership and managing people – as well as developing an abiding interest in African birds. I then went on to do a PhD on the biogeography and conservation biology of the Eastern Arc avifauna. Keith became my supervisor (and an excellent one he was) and Con was a key scientific advisor (though, sadly, he died shortly before I finished). I spent three years in the field in Tanzania before returning to Cambridge to write up my thesis.

A scientist in conservation

After my doctorate (in fact before it was completed) in 1983, I was recruited by the International Council for Bird Preservation (ICBP – now BirdLife International) to work on the African Bird Red Data Book. My boss was Nigel Collar, one of the great characters in conservation at both a personal and intellectual level. It took us about two years to complete the book (Collar and Stuart, 1985), and I think it is fair to say that it set a new standard in the documentation of threatened species. When we started we wondered if enough information could ever be found to say anything meaningful about most of the species, but through extensive networking with a large number of ornithologists we were swamped in data, much of it previously unpublished. I learnt something then that I've found to be true time and time again. When one asks how much is known about a particular species, the usual answer is 'nothing'. But as one digs deeper, one discovers much more information than most people expect. There is a wealth of information out there to support conservation and to guide decision-makers, but most of it is not in forms that can be readily accessed or used. Much of my subsequent career has been devoted to making information available in such a way that it can be used to advance conservation (in other words, making lists again!).

While I was at ICBP I organized and led an expedition to Cameroon to learn about the rare forest birds, amphibians and mammals in the mountains in the west of the country. From this, ICBP developed its conservation programme in Cameroon, which continues to this day. In late 1985 I was recruited by the International Union for Conservation of Nature and Natural Resources (IUCN) and moved to Switzerland, where Ann already had a job teaching biology in the International School at Geneva. We married the following year and started our life together by exploring the beautiful scenery and natural history of the Alps and the Jura. It was a wonderful start to married life. My particular job involved working for the IUCN Species Survival Commission (SSC). I have been with them ever since, in various roles which have taken me into an ever broader array of activities. I worked with many outstanding people, too many to name here, though George Rabb, the visionary Chair of the SSC from 1989 to 1996, stands out as a true leader. I had to learn about all sorts of things, such as fundraising, project management, staff management, office politics and the like.

For much of the time I seemed to be drifting further and further away from science. I became heavily involved in the process to develop the new IUCN Red List Categories and Criteria. The IUCN Red List of Threatened Species is the world's official listing of globally threatened animals and plants, and was the brainchild of Sir Peter Scott, who chaired the SSC for many years, up until 1979. However, the Red List in the 1980s was, to say the least, a haphazard affair. There were no hard-and-fast criteria for deciding what was, and what was not, allowed on to the list, and politics and personalities played a big role in decisions. The IUCN's scientific credibility and impartiality were seriously at risk. Previous attempts to rectify the situation had failed for various reasons. The turning-point came in 1989 when a young scientist at the Institute of Zoology in London, Georgina Mace, was asked to come up with a new proposal for deciding whether, and how much, a species was threatened. Her proposals, made jointly with Russell Lande, broke new ground and provided the first quantitative criteria for assessing extinction risk (Mace and Lande, 1991). I was given the task of being Georgina's link in the IUCN Secretariat, with the job of facilitating the development of an agreed set of rules to govern the IUCN Red List. The rules had to be scientifically robust but also acceptable to an essentially conservative SSC. Georgina and I ran numerous consultations involving scientists covering a wide variety of skills and experience (botanists and zoologists, marine, terrestrial and freshwater scientists, etc.) before coming up with a finally agreed approach. We learnt workshop facilitation the hard way by being thrown in the deep end. But in 1994 the IUCN Red List Categories and Criteria were adopted. We upset some people, especially in government departments dealing with fisheries when they found that cod and bluefin tuna were listed as threatened. This led to further workshops and consultations, resulting in the not hugely changed version that exists today (IUCN, 2001).

Over the years I became more senior in the IUCN Secretariat, and spent a lot of time on management and running meetings. I even ended up as Acting Director General at one point. But I was becoming increasingly separated from real conservation issues. Then a new opportunity arose. In 2001 I was given the chance to set up a new Biodiversity Assessment Unit, based in Washington DC, as a shared initiative of IUCN and the United States-based charity Conservation International (CI). Russ Mittermeier and Gustavo Fonseca at CI, both leading figures in the SSC, encouraged me to make this move, and after prayer Ann and I felt that it was the right thing to do. So shortly before 9/11, we moved to Washington with our two daughters, Claire and Jyoti. This became another exciting place for us to explore natural history (the salamanders of eastern North America are special, as are the warblers on their annual migration northward each spring).

My first task in my new role was to run the Global Amphibian Assessment (GAA) – the first ever review of the conservation status of all the world's 6,000+ amphibian species. Having spent years working on how to determine whether or not a species is threatened, we now actually had to put our system into practice. This was a fantastic project to work on, and I had an excellent team who did most of the leg work. We ran 16 workshops, worked with 550 scientists, and the results were launched in 2004 to worldwide media attention. We found that one third of the world's amphibians were at risk of extinction, that the situation was rapidly deteriorating, and that as well as familiar threats like habitat loss, amphibian extinctions were taking place because of a 'new' fungal disease, chytridiomycosis, the incidence of which appears to be linked to climate change (Stuart *et al.*, 2004). The GAA is currently being updated, and we now have four other major ongoing assessment projects on mammals, reptiles, and marine and freshwater species. It was because of our marine project (the Global Marine Species Assessment) that I found myself in the Philippines in July 2007.

Integrating science and Christian faith

As mentioned above, my professional and Christian lives did not much interact. For sure, I knew other Christians working in conservation. But I lacked an over-arching theology to give me a holistic view of the world I inhabited. Looking back on it, I don't understand how I tolerated such a compartmentalized life, but I suspect that I was not atypical. However, in 1999, Ann and I met Peter and Miranda Harris, the founders of A Rocha – Christians in Conservation. A Rocha is a family of Christian conservation organizations operating now in eighteen countries on all continents, and finding exciting and innovative means to demonstrate God's love for all that he has made (see www.arocha. org). Ann and I became friends with Peter and Miranda, and I became an International Trustee of A Rocha. After we moved to Washington, Ann became A Rocha USA's first Education Director. It was through Peter and Miranda that we learnt what now seems blindingly obvious – that the gospel is about more than personal salvation (though obviously it includes that). We saw that the doctrine of creation is not something buried away in the early chapters of Genesis, but actually permeates the entire Bible. Not only did God make everything, and make it very good, but creation was affected negatively by the fall (Genesis 3:17; Jeremiah 12:4), and is encompassed positively by God's plans for redemption (Romans 8:19–22; Colossians 1:19–20). We started to see that the ecological crisis has a spiritual root. But God has not given up on his creation – he owns it and sustains it (Psalm 24:1–2l; Leviticus 25:23). Indeed, creation exists with the purpose of displaying God's glory – as it most surely does (Romans 1:18–20; Revelation 5:13). The doctrines of creation and salvation are complementary; in a sense, salvation is in fact re-creation (2 Corinthians 5:17). Peter and Miranda taught us that our work in conservation is an integral part of our Christian calling, and part of our worship of the Creator God.

Gradually I started to see all my supposedly secular conservation work as part of my Christian walk. Although I would probably always have claimed this, it now started to make sense theologically. I could now see the Global Amphibian Assessment, for example, as God's work. It was something that he wanted me to undertake, and the results enabled us to understand what is happening in God's world more clearly. Moreover, as I felt the pain and sadness of the decline and disappearance of some remarkable species, I now understood that this was in fact God's pain arising from his own deep love and care for all that he has made.

Creation in jeopardy

My work on the assessment of the threatened species (what is now called 'biodiversity assessment') has enabled me to gain a privileged overview of what is really going on in creation today. When I started out in conservation, we operated under a very simple paradigm. Species were threatened by definable threats. All we had to do was to identify the threatened species, find out what threatened them, and then design conservation programmes to alleviate these threats. When we spoke of threats, we meant things like habitat loss, over-harvesting, pollution and invasive species – all readily identifiable, and in principle resolvable through tried and tested means, such as protected area establishment and management, sustainable development programmes (often designed to provide local human communities with alternative livelihoods to the over-use of species), control programmes for invasive species, environmental education projects, and conservation legislation. All these things remain important, of course, but they are no longer anything like sufficient to stem ongoing extinctions.

Our biodiversity assessment work has, especially over the last ten years, shown that species are increasingly impacted by pressures that have no immediate remedy. One of the first indications that we are on uncharted territory was increasingly severe and frequent coral bleaching due to the warming of the oceans. Even if the world had the political will to take truly radical measures to address climate change, it would take decades to stabilize carbon dioxide levels, and consequently ocean temperatures and acidity can be expected to rise for the foreseeable future. In short, we have no immediate remedy for coral bleaching. The consequences of the widespread loss and degradation of coral ecosystems will no doubt have huge impacts on other species, and we are only just starting to look at the implications for coral reef-dependent fishes. The impacts on the human communities that depend on fisheries in coral reefs could also be extremely severe and lead to the loss of livelihoods among the poorest of the poor.

Another early sign that something new and disturbing was happening to the world's species came from the amphibians. Two particular stories caught public attention. In Australia, the two species of Gastric-brooding Frog – the only frogs that incubated their young in their stomachs – died out suddenly, one in 1981, the other in 1985. The disappearance of the Golden Toad in Costa Rica in 1989 attracted even more publicity. However, the Global Amphibian Assessment showed that these were far from isolated instances. We documented over 120 species worldwide which had experienced unexplained, dramatic declines. Many species could no longer be found. The disappearances had one thing in common – the species vanished from places that seemed to be well protected. There were no obvious, identifiable threats. The old paradigm wasn't working. We now know that these amphibian extinctions are mostly caused by the fungal disease chytridiomycosis, interacting with climate change. There is no known remedy for this disease in the wild – another threat for which we do not have a solution.

Sometimes, even apparently identifiable pressures that ought to have a solution seem to defy our best attempts at conservation. Our Global Mammal Assessment has highlighted the disastrous state of large mammal populations in East and Southeast Asia. Hunting for meat and traditional Chinese medicine has severely reduced numbers in species that were abundant only a few decades ago. This has affected not only the species we expect to be threatened, such as tigers and rhinos, but also most Asian species of deer, cattle and monkeys – in fact anything bigger than a rabbit. 'Traditional' means of protection – legislation, law enforcement and education are simply not working. All this holds a bitter memory for me personally. In the late 1980s and early 1990s I devoted a lot of time to developing a conservation programme for the Kouprey – a large species of wild ox from Cambodia, Vietnam and Laos. Our efforts were too little and too late. The Kouprey is now almost certainly extinct due to hunting.

I could go on, but the message is clear. If we look at the global picture from a detached, secular, scientific perspective, there are very few grounds for hope. All the trends are downwards, and we lack the means to reverse many of the threats, even if we had the political will. But as a Christian, I now see things differently. We live in a creation that is cared for and owned by a Father God who has made a covenant with 'all living creatures of every kind on earth' (Genesis 9:8–17). He is the God to whom we can sing:

> How many are your works, O Lord!
> In wisdom you made them all;
> the earth is full of your creatures.
> There is the sea, vast and spacious,
> teeming with creatures beyond number –
> living things both large and small.
> There the ships go to and fro,
> and the leviathan, which you formed to frolic there.
> These all look to you
> to give them their food at the proper time.
> When you give it to them,
> they gather it up;
> when you open your hand,
> they are satisfied with good things.
> When you hide your face,
> they are terrified;
> when you take away their breath,
> they die and return to the dust.
> When you send your Spirit,
> they are created,
> and you renew the face of the earth.

PSALM 104:24–30

I believe that God laments over the sorry state to which we have brought his creation through our own selfishness, self-indulgence, greed, neglect and ignorance. He also holds us accountable:

> Because of this [i.e., the sin of the people] the land mourns, and all who live in it waste away; the beasts of the field and the birds of the air and the fish of the sea are dying.

HOSEA 4:3

How long will the land lie parched and the grass in every field withered? Because those who live in it are wicked, the animals and birds have perished.

JEREMIAH 12:4

As for my flock, this is what the Sovereign Lord says: I will judge between one sheep and another, and between rams and goats. Is it not enough for you to feed on the good pasture? Must you trample the rest of the pasture with your feet? Is it not enough for you to drink clear water? Must you also muddy the rest with your feet? Must my flock feed on what you have trampled and drink what you have muddied with your feet?

EZEKIEL 34:17–19

The time has come for… destroying those who destroy the earth.

REVELATION 11:18

Hope

Yet God does not leave us entirely with lament and judgement. He is also the God of hope – indeed, without him there is no hope for his creation. We learn this from passages such as Romans 8:19–23 and Colossians 1:15–20, teaching us that 'the Creation itself will be liberated from its bondage to decay and brought to the glorious freedom of the children of God', and that 'God was pleased to have all his fullness dwell in him [i.e., Jesus], and through him to reconcile to himself all things, whether things on earth or things in heaven, by making peace through his blood, shed on the cross.'

However, God also gives us hope in the present time, not just in the future. Stuart *et al.* (2005) put it this way:

Perhaps of greatest importance [in terms of reasons for dialogue between evangelicals and secular conservationists] are the resources that authentically Christian theology can bring to an otherwise bleak environmental situation by establishing the grounds for hope. By this we mean something more than simply the belief that at the end of time God will restore his creation and that the loss of the dodo from Mauritius and the golden toad from the Monteverde Cloud Forest in Costa Rica is therefore not the end of the story. Of course this future hope is an important one, but when we say 'grounds for hope,' we are referring to our present situation as well. Evangelical Christians are committed by their biblical beliefs not only to the conviction that God himself cares for His universe in a daily and ongoing way but also that He helps and guides people in their conservation efforts. We are therefore not on our own against the relentless forces of unsustainable development and rapacious materialism. Every time we celebrate a conservation success story such as the recovery of the white rhinoceros in southern Africa, we are strengthened in this present hope that God is working with us to redeem his creation. Furthermore, these present successes are a very real foretaste of even greater things to come on that day when God will fully restore all that He has made.

It is easy to recount a catalogue of conservation failures. Looking back over the conservation initiatives with which I have been involved, a few have been complete failures (as in the case of the Kouprey), many are still ongoing and cannot yet be called successes (but without them things would probably have been worse), but a few are certainly successes. One in particular comes to mind.

In 1984 I led an expedition to Mount Kilum in western Cameroon. What we found there was most disturbing. The area has a unique fauna and flora, quite different from those on the other mountains in the region, with a number of species being found nowhere else in the world. But deforestation was rampant, and no effective conservation measures were in place at all. We reported on the situation to BirdLife International. To their great credit, they started a major conservation initiative on Mount Kilum which continues to this day, working with the local human communities. The most recent data show that the forest extent on the mountain is actually increasing, an incredible success given the strongly negative trends elsewhere in this region. I had no further involvement with the project after writing the report of our expedition (Stuart, 1986), although some members of our team returned to Cameroon to continue conservation work there.

I believe the Lord is looking after his world. During our 1984 visit, I took a day off to climb a peak overlooking Lake Oku, a stunningly beautiful crater lake on Mount Kilum, to spend a day in solitude with God. And these are the words that came to me as I contemplated the ongoing destruction of this very special place:

> 'For my thoughts are not your thoughts,
> neither are your ways my ways,'
> declares the Lord.
> 'As the heavens are higher than the earth,
> so are my ways higher than your ways
> and my thoughts than your thoughts.
> As the rain and the snow
> come down from heaven,
> and do not return to it
> without watering the earth
> and making it bud and flourish,
> so that it yields seed for the sower and bread for the eater,
> so is my word that goes out from my mouth:
> It will not return to me empty,
> but will accomplish what I desire
> and achieve the purpose for which I sent it.
> You will go out in joy
> and be led forth in peace;
> the mountains and hills
> will burst into song before you,
> and all the trees of the field

will clap their hands.
Instead of the thornbush will grow the pine tree,
and instead of briers the myrtle will grow.
This will be for the Lord's renown,
for an everlasting sign,
which will not be destroyed.

ISAIAH 55:8–13

I could almost feel the trees clapping their hands. But I had no idea back then that this was God's prophecy for Mount Kilum. To believe that the conservation situation on the mountain could be turned round would have seemed ridiculous – the pressures causing the destruction of the forest were so great. My faith was not strong enough to believe that anything could be done about it. But God had his own plans for this place that he made and loved. He is indeed a God of hope.

ACKNOWLEDGMENTS

I thank Ann Stuart, Sam Berry and Peter Harris for their helpful comments on an earlier draft of this chapter.

CHAPTER 12

Surprise and the Value of Life
Andrew G. Gosler

Andrew G. Gosler is Research Lecturer, Edward Grey Institute of Field Ornithology; Human Sciences Lecturer in Biological Conservation, Oxford University; Chair of the Institute of Human Sciences, Oxford University (2008–2011); Supernumerary Fellow, Mansfield College, Oxford. Educated at Aberystwyth, Reading and Oxford Universities. Chair, British Ringing Committee of British Trust for Ornithology (1995–98). Editor, *Ibis* (British Ornithologists' Union) (1998–2006). Tucker Medal of British Trust for Ornithology (1998). Member of International Ornithological Committee of International Ornithological Congress.

I doubt that there can be any surprise greater or more personally significant than that of the non-believer who finds faith in middle age. But when that dawning comes from within a lifetime's study of (indeed passion for) evolution, others might share in that surprise. The issue of surprise is a major theme that I shall return to, but I should give some outline of my history, as much for me as for you, to try to understand how I came to faith. In retrospect, I see that my personal search for truth through science has also been a search for personal truth, to find myself, so that ultimately science and faith have become intimately interwoven.

Home life

Some of my earliest recollections are of sitting on our kitchen table drawing horses: horse after horse, in walk, trot, canter and gallop and from every angle my young mind and hand could manage. I must have been about four, and I had discovered amongst my father's books a slim volume entitled *How to Draw Horses*; I was captivated. I was captivated by the elegant lines, the agility and the movement I found in the simple sketches within that book; but there was more, because the book also had some simple anatomical drawings showing how the final form depended on the underlying skeleton and muscles. I was fascinated by the anatomy and by the transformation of skeletal articulation through the astonishing complexity of musculature into the beauty of the whole animal that had so captured my attention. *How to Draw Horses* was one in a series of *How to Draw…* books from which my father had several titles including hands, ships, children, planes, trees and portraits, but none so touched me as did *Horses*. I think it is from that spark that my interest in biology, and more specifically in the relationship between biological form and function, began. It probably also explains why, thirty-five years later, I learned to ride, but that is another story.

Horses were not all that fascinated me at the age of four. I remember giving my poor mother a hard time with a stream of rather metaphysical questions. As I recall, these did not centre so much around the obvious 'Where did I come from?' as around the idea of eternity. I think I had been asking about stars and the answer had involved space and that it went on for ever without end. Having learned to count, I was also aware that numbers must go on forever, as should time (or so we thought then). It may be because these things all demanded my attention at such a young age that they have been at the centre of my personal search throughout my life. Whatever the answers turned out to be, they would have to satisfy an interest in anatomy and eternity.

Looking back, with regard to religion I see my childhood to have been a confusion of issues, a fact which undoubtedly reflects my parents' own positions. I came from a Liberal Jewish family in West London, for whom Jewish identity had validity and value independently of any understanding (profound or otherwise) of God. That identity was about whom we were and where were our roots, an issue that might have had particular significance for Jews living in the long shadow of the Holocaust (my own grandfather had lost a sister in Bergen-Belsen just a month before the end of the war). I rarely spoke to my mother about God, but I believe she felt his presence strongly in her life. My father's Judaism is more social and cultural; he has for many years considered himself an atheist, partly because of what he perceived as bigotry and hypocrisy within religion, two things about which he warned us children (I am the second of three sons). Despite all the inconsistencies that I might have experienced through all this in my childhood, I now regard the open-mindedness that I inherited from my parents, which has now allowed me to find faith, as one of the greatest tributes to them. My brothers and I were nurtured in a free-thinking, loving, atmosphere for which I shall always be grateful.

To be raised simultaneously both within a faith (for example, we attended Sunday school where we learned about Jewish history, the festivals, and to read Hebrew) and also in a generally secular household, was confusing enough, but from the age of five morning prayers at school included the Lord's Prayer, and while we were not allowed to go carol-singing with our school-friends, we did have a Christmas tree, and received Christmas cards and presents, because my parents didn't want us to feel left out. And so I learned about Jesus at school, but was told at home that Jews considered him to be a prophet. It would be many years before I would think about this independently for myself. My early attempts to reconcile all this, especially in the light of my rapidly growing interest in evolution, dinosaurs and then birds, were too confused to be of value to me and so, after Bar' Mitzvah, it was probably inevitable that I would lapse into a slightly restless agnosticism (actually apathy would be a better description). From then until my awakening of faith in the late 1990s, I was simply uninterested in religious matters; indeed I would have regarded it as too strong a *commitment* to have labelled myself an atheist!

Birds

An interest in dinosaurs, which developed from my close attention to a colouring book on the subject bought during an early visit to the Natural History Museum at South Kensington, gave way at the age of ten to the interest in birds that has sustained me ever since. Birds, bird-watching and ornithology ruled my teens. I think my parents were quite concerned because it wasn't obvious to them (or to me, for that matter) how one might make a living from birds: the opportunities then were far scarcer than they are now. At that time, living in Ealing, the routes and timetables of the London buses and Underground dictated my travels. Favourite haunts included Richmond Park, where I saw many birds that were uncommon nearer home, including my first woodpeckers, owls, kingfisher, warblers, flycatchers, redstart and unexpected waterfowl including, on one occasion, a red-throated diver. At Osterley Park I saw my first tree sparrows and bramblings, and at Perivale Wood (owned by the Selborne Society) I helped with a Common Bird Census and was invited to join the Management Committee as a Junior Representative. Through the Selborne Society I also learned about the Revd Gilbert White and his *Natural History of Selborne* and by implication that a significant interest in natural history, albeit pre-Darwin, could be compatible with a devotion to God.

I must admit that at that time my interest in birds was so exclusive that I didn't much notice other forms of life. I learned to identify all the common trees, shrubs and more significant herbs, but this was more because they were essential components of habitat, or provided food, for birds than because they interested me for their own sake. Likewise for invertebrates: if they weren't bird food, they didn't exist to me. Despite this, perhaps extreme, focus on birds, although I enjoyed seeing new species, adding them to my life-list was never a goal. I was a frequent visitor to the Bird Gallery of the Natural History Museum, where I learned a great deal about form and function, evolution, ecology and systematics – that is, not just how to distinguish one species from another. In addition to a delight in evolution that developed from my museum visits, my feeling that this place, with its shrine-like monuments to Darwin, Huxley and Owen, was itself a cathedral to natural history developed in me a sense of relationship between biology and spirituality. But it was not a sense that this science, which revealed so much about the history of life, had replaced

God. Rather, it was that God was more powerfully present, more real, *here* than anywhere I had known. I think this sense is also captured by the final paragraph of Darwin's *Origin of Species*,[1] and perhaps this reveals something of his own spirituality (see also Wilson, 2006: 7). As I have probably indicated, the inspiration that I felt from evolution presented no great threat to any position of faith that I had; indeed quite the reverse. I had, for example, been taught (consistently on this point) at school, home and in synagogue, that the Genesis text was not to be taken literally: its meaning and value lay in the relationships between God, humanity and the natural order that it revealed through allegory. It therefore came as a shock in later life to discover, probably from reading Richard Dawkins' *The Blind Watchmaker*, that some people regarded Genesis as historical fact (Dawkins, 1986).

Value and values – intrinsic and contingent

There was another side to my avian obsession, which was significant in my personal development. I came to regard birds – each species – as precious, uniquely evolved, irreplaceable and therefore of inestimable value, a view which has been the ground for my personal conservation ethic ever since. Furthermore, I felt that if the value of each species arises through its being a unique evolutionary 'event' (as indeed is each individual life), then that value is independent of my valuing of it as a human observer – that is, its value is intrinsic, and not contingent. It followed that extinction was the greatest loss imaginable, and the fact that we humans were the cause of most, if not all, extinctions in recorded history, meant that there must be something seriously wrong with my own species. I came at this time to regard humans (as I still do) as the most destructive force on the planet; and the fact that most people I met, including friends and family, seemed oblivious of the damage we were causing, and seemed to regard extinctions as nothing more than an occupational but inevitable hazard of human progress, seemed to reinforce my view that humanity was irredeemable. It also seemed clear that religion, with its apparent anthropocentricity, was simply part of the problem: it could have nothing to offer for the solution.

It was through reading Environmental Biology at Aberystwyth University that I began to see the world beyond birds, even though while there I did train and qualify as a bird ringer (a 'bander', in US terminology). Studying ecology, I began to see a unity in nature that my avicentric perception had hidden from me and, more significantly, that all organisms exist in relationship to every other – be they mates, prey, predators, parasites, or indeed habitats. With the wider perspective of ecology, I began to appreciate that while *I* might perceive birds as distinct entities of seemingly greater value than anything else (including humans), that perception could not reflect reality. There was no rational ground for believing that birds had any greater value than any other organism. In other words, I realized that my view of the natural world was unsustainable and it gradually changed, but it was replaced not by an atheistic nihilism, but by a perception of the grandeur of *all* life.

In the process of asking whether birds have any greater value than any other organism, the question inevitably arises as to whether they have any less, and in particular where human beings fit in. Although humans routinely assume that they have greater value than any other animal, isn't that anthropocentrism precisely *the* problem? The question then arises of whether life itself has any value. As an undergraduate, I read *The Selfish Gene* (Dawkins, 1976), which argued that nothing had any absolute value from an evolutionary point of view: either value was anthropogenic or anthropocentric, in which case a life's value could only ever be what humans ascribed to it; or contingent upon some ecological role (for example, pandas might value bamboo). Whilst I might accept this as an intellectual exercise (even though it contradicted my own relating of value to evolutionary uniqueness), I was deeply troubled by it at a practical level, because my personal experience told me that most humans *didn't* value nature. If we couldn't argue for nature conservation from the ethical standpoint of its intrinsic value, this left only utilitarian arguments. It was already clear to me that alone, utilitarian arguments for conservation were inadequate because they implied that if no human use were found for a particular species, its extinction could be considered no loss. Of course, we now see that extinctions do not happen like this, via the filter of human scrutiny, since in the biological holocaust of anthropogenic deforestation, pollution and climate change that is now underway most losses will in fact be of species that won't even have been described when they are snuffed out of existence.

So *The Selfish Gene* troubled me, not because it robbed me of God, but because it robbed life itself of any value: Dawkins argues that the origin of genes preceded life, in the sense that life arose only as a means to perpetuate genes – lifeless, unthinking, uncaring chemistry. Furthermore, it suggests that a sign of maturity is being able to recognize one's anthropocentric valuing of life for the 'mistake' that it really is. But hang on – life *is* wonderful *and* amazing. It depends heavily on co-operation at higher levels of organization than that of the gene (Noble, 2006), a fact which is all the more wonderful if it truly arose in the manner that Dawkins describes, and life exists in all its glorious fullness (love, joy, pain, suffering, warts and all) only at the level of the whole organism, the individual, and not at that of the gene (chemistry). Moulded by selection through the lives and deaths of organisms, the *value* of a gene lies in its contribution to, or potential for, life. Dawkins' attempt to reverse the natural view that *life* gives *genes* value is an aspect of *The Selfish Gene* that I could never accept. Indeed, I could not help feeling that any biologist who argues that life has no value has lost the plot. But how does one reconcile these issues? Dawkins' view is that if the facts trouble your worldview, that's unfortunate, but your worldview was wrong. This is a plausible intellectual standpoint, but it ignores the possibility that *the facts* considered by Dawkins were not, in fact, the whole truth.

Oxford and atheism

After taking a Master's degree in plant taxonomy at Reading University, I came to Oxford to work as a field assistant in the Edward Grey Institute of Field Ornithology (EGI). Shortly afterwards, I was awarded a studentship, and so had fees to work for my doctorate in ornithology; at last I was making a living from birds. I was surprised at Oxford to find that most people, even in the EGI, were not as passionate about birds as I was, and the issue of the *value* of life soon emerged for me as a material one. It did so because bird welfare seemed to be a more significant issue for me than for some of the zoologists around me. Whether or not my perception was correct, it seemed that they had accepted the *Selfish Gene* view of life so thoroughly that they had extrapolated it to their working relationships with animals.

Because of my bird-ringing qualification, I soon found myself with sole responsibility within the department for training students in ringing techniques. This enabled me to instil in them from the outset that the welfare of a wild bird in their hands was a matter of significant responsibility (a bird is more than just a data point on a graph). The coming of the Animals (Scientific Procedures) Act in 1986 raised ethical issues much more sharply than before for everyone engaged in animal-related work, including ecological studies. Despite its shortcomings, it is largely thanks to this that it is no longer possible to pay mere lip-service to ethical issues in animal research, and my appointment in the 1990s to the Ethical Review Committee of the Zoology Department brought the issue of value strongly into focus.

Through the 1980s and 1990s I became increasingly dissatisfied with the arguments for atheism that I found promoted gratuitously in my biology reading. Hitherto I had been content to ignore God, but I was now being forced to think about the issue. For example, having read a surprisingly strong scientific argument *for* the existence of God in Peter Medawar's *The Limits of Science* (1984), the best argument for demolition that he could muster in the next chapter was that it 'defied common sense'! I had long held the view, based on my rudimentary understanding of quantum mechanics, that for a scientist 'common sense' was the last refuge of the desperate. Furthermore, in the opening to *The Problems of Evolution*, Mark Ridley (1985) had pointed out that the very notion that species were not immutable (i.e. that they evolved), itself, defied common sense. So common sense gets us nowhere. Indeed, since my view that life has value was part of *my* common sense, it must at least be as valid a position as Medawar's, even if it proved not to be scientifically sustainable. I began to realize that the conclusion that God did not exist did not come inexorably from any real science, but from the systematic annihilation of straw men − from simplistic literal readings of Genesis, 'common sense', and an absolute confidence in the 'meaning' of the *Selfish Gene* model, which itself might be wrong − as argued by philosophers (Sober & Wilson, 1999; Ruse, 2001, 2004; Haught, 2004) and increasingly by biologists (Sober & Wilson, 1999; Miller, 1999; Ruse, 2004; Jablonka & Lamb, 2006; Noble, 2006). In other words, whilst I had (I thought) been content not to consider God in my life in any way, shape or form, through reading standard biology texts I was being made to consider the evidence for atheism, and frankly I wasn't impressed. The thought dawned then that if the best arguments for atheism were so weak, it must follow that God really might exist. Browsing in a second-hand bookshop in Oxford one day, I came across a book entitled *Believing in God* by a Dominican priest, Gareth Moore (1996). I was delighted by its sanity, and its humility, and it fascinated me. I started to read books at the interface between science, philosophy and faith (e.g. Ward, 1996; Polkinghorne, 1996, 1998a,b; Jeeves & Berry, 1998; McGrath, 1998; Clark, 1998; Ruse, 2004). A new perception opened.

Theology, biological conservation and information

Through the 1990s I also immersed myself increasingly in the scientific literature associated with biological conservation, and here crystallized, at last, the ethical paradox to which I had become sensitized. In addition to the (to me unsatisfying) utilitarian arguments for conservation (along the lines that somewhere in the rainforest may exist a cure for cancer), I read time and again the explicit statement that a valid ground for conservation was that life had '*intrinsic value*' (Gaston & Spicer, 1998; Hambler, 2004; Norton, 2005) – that is, value by virtue simply of its existence and independent of any human (or other organic) valuer. The authors never elaborated on this, perhaps because they were aware of the metaphysical nature of this claim (and its biblical roots). However, it often became clear elsewhere that they personally (or culturally) subscribed to a *Selfish Gene* worldview – that life could have no value beyond the relative and contingent value that humans placed on it. It was as if the authors didn't believe their own statement intellectually but nevertheless felt it so strongly to be their personal motivation as conservationists (as did I) that they should sneak it in under the reader's radar and hope nobody questioned it too deeply. So forcibly has the inconsistency struck me that I have made a point of asking colleagues whether they believe that life has 'intrinsic value'. Invariably (so far) they answer yes, but when questioned further as to where this value originates, I simply get blank expressions and shrugs. This is important. Because of it, I have witnessed the distressing spectacle in a seminar of a committed and dedicated (judged by his own work) conservationist arguing himself out of his own sense of commitment because he suddenly recognized the contradiction in his own philosophy. Thankfully, this was not a permanent injury, but the point is highlighted: we have to explore the notion of intrinsic value.

I must make clear here that my coming to faith in Christ did not rest on a single issue such as the value of life. It was a holistic redefining of perspectives that came together through every aspect of my life: relationships with people and animals, science, teaching, art, music, philosophy, birdwatching, horse-riding, everything. Indeed the views presented here on intrinsic value developed after my acceptance of Christ (I was baptized in 2000), and I regard them as some of the fruits of my new life in him. I shall argue that intrinsic value is real, and that it is reflected in the information content of existence. Important in developing this view has been the recognition of an association between value and rarity (think of antiques) or irreplaceability, and the fact that ecologists often measure bio-diversity using a statistic derived from Information Theory.[2]

Materialists argue that nothing exists but matter and energy. Yet clearly there is another, essential, phenomenon: information. What is information, and where in the matter–energy realm does it exist? Even for the materialist to argue that only matter and energy really exist, information is necessary, a fact which causes the statement itself to implode (Byl, 2004). We tend to think of information essentially as a mathematical concept, but it is more than this. For example, we accept that DNA 'carries' information, yet it cannot be observed directly (it must be interpreted). There is therefore a sense in which information seems to be transcendent, independent of the matter and energy with which it is associated. Yet even more than this: it is intimately involved with dynamic process as well as material existence. It can be said that everything that exists, in both the energy–material and mental realms, is inseparably associated with, or exists simultaneously as, information.

Information is of course associated with the concept of a 'signal', which is distinct from 'noise'. For this insight we owe a great debt to Claude Shannon, a mathematician and engineer working for the Bell Telephone Laboratories in the 1940s. Shannon recognized that information (the signal) is the antithesis of entropy (noise), and that entropy declines as information increases. Hence we can argue that since, within this universe, everything that exists, either realized or potential, is a manifestation of information, we might regard information as the signal of existence, as opposed to the noise of chaos: information is the very light in the darkness.

The mathematical formulation of information, which measures the quantity of information in a signal, and from which ecologists derive their diversity index, was also developed by Shannon, and is known as the Information Statistic. This statistic is based on the quantity p, which represents the probability of an event. Shannon described this quantity as its 'surprise' because rare, or less probable, events are more surprising (Aleksander, 2002). As Shannon's statistic is regarded as the essential mathematical definition of information, the concept of surprise is seen to be inherent to our understanding of information itself.

So information is intimately bound up with the rare event, the improbable. Now, considering a (broadly evolutionary) biological series such as bacterium, fish, frog, mouse, chimpanzee, human, suggests that what essentially has been going on through organic evolution has been an increase in surprisingness, in information, as well as (as it happens) an increase in the relative ability to manipulate information itself (i.e. cognitive ability). It may be that the order of this series also matches your instinctive order of valuing these organisms (unless you are an ornithologist), and I suggest that this might reflect an innate ability to recognize information content, which tends to lead us to value the rare, the improbable, the surprising.

It is clear, however, that we do not value things only because they are rare; our sense of value involves a further component. Further insight here might be found from the analogy with antiques, suggested earlier, for which provenance is also important. As my anthropologist friend John Paull pointed out, a chipboard desk is still a chipboard desk irrespective of how old or rare it is, but if it had been James Cook's chipboard desk (John is Australian), we might view it differently. Provenance then is an important component of the information associated with an item contributing to its rarity, and our appreciation of value. In the special case of life too, I suggest we must consider provenance.

Wonder and surprise

The point is that existence, all that exists, exists *as* information. This means that it appears to us, within this universe, to be improbable, and therefore surprising. Since we equate value with rarity, and improbability (surprise and information content) is simply the rarity of an event, in equating information with value we recognize an important congruence, which most of us might accept (indeed, we might even argue from common sense in this regard):

- existence is more surprising (in the sense that it has more value) than non-existence;

- life is more surprising (has more value) than non-life;

- complex life is more surprising (has more value) than simple life;

- conscious life is more surprising (has more value) than non-conscious life;

- self-aware life is more surprising (has more value) than non-aware life; and,

- perhaps most surprising, then, is life that contemplates its very existence.

We must be very clear what we mean here by 'intrinsic value', because our very existence is endangered by hubris if we misunderstand it. We know that the Earth's biosphere can function (indeed it did so for millions of years) without humans, but it cannot function at all without microbes. Thus in terms of value to the planet's ecological functioning, microbes are demonstrably more valuable than humans. However, this is not *intrinsic* value, it is value for a specific purpose (Gaia),[3] it is *contingent* value. But this demonstrates forcibly that *we* should not value organisms differently by virtue of differences in their intrinsic value: all have their utilitarian value to the functioning of the whole. The significance for conservationists of defining intrinsic value lies in terms of recognizing a value that exists metaphysically and independent of our being.

In recognizing the need for a metaphysical perspective in defining intrinsic value, I was struck by the fact that John's Gospel tells us that in the beginning was the Word – that is, before all things, was the signal: information; nothing was ever made except by the Word. Furthermore, as I came to know God,

I also came to associate him with surprise. This became clear to me not only from the many references to surprise found in texts of Christian testimony: C. S. Lewis (1955) – *Surprised by Joy*; Gerard Hughes (1985) – *God of Surprises*; Colin Russell (1991) – *Surprised by science*; and Tom Wright (2007) – *Surprised by Hope*, but also from the numerous wonderful 'coincidences' that have attended my own coming to faith. William Temple wrote: 'When I pray, coincidences happen, and when I don't, they don't.' Non-believers may say that coincidence is just that – it is noise and carries no information, and thus has no value: it is certainly not evidence of God's immanence. But I had forty-two years in which to assess the 'background rate' of coincidence in my life, and the last eight years stand out for me: the coincidences *have* had value for me, and by implication they carried information, they were not noise. I will give a brief taste.

In 1999 my wife and I had to put our books into temporary storage. In packing them I found myself holding a Bible. Partly because I had never made much sense of the Old Testament, and partly because the atheist writers had made me curious about Christianity, I started to read the Gospels. What I found was a Jesus who sounded like my father: hot on the issues of religious bigotry and hypocrisy, and not at all what I'd been led by the atheists to expect. That Christmas Eve I attended midnight service at our parish church (Holy Trinity, Headington Quarry), supported by my wife Caroline for whom (unlike me) this was not alien territory. Caroline had come from an Anglican family, but had lost her faith years earlier, and indeed I should like to dedicate this testimony to her for so wonderfully supporting my own faith while still lacking belief in God herself.

The preacher at that service was Tom Honey (now a Canon at Exeter Cathedral) whom I already knew as a birdwatcher and who had been at the same school as me in Ealing (where he had known my older brother). His sermon was precisely what I needed at that time. I started going regularly to the church and, having decided to accept baptism in the autumn, worried about how to tell my parents. A friend wisely counselled me to write and tell them, giving them the reasons for my decision as best I could – and to invite them to the baptism service. I was baptized by the Bishop of Oxford. My parents accepted my invitation and were delighted by their warm welcome in our church. They were even more delighted by the Bishop's very sympathetic sermon on the relationship between Christianity and Judaism. And when my mother and I asked the Bishop if he had been aware of my background and he replied that he had not, he too was moved to learn of the surprise value to us of his address.

God, creation and improbability

The argument I have presented suggests that exploring the nature of information more fully may provide deeper insights into the true nature of reality. Information exists most powerfully in the mental realm; it is surely the very stuff of consciousness and of relationship, whether mathematical, ecological or personal. If all 'things' (material and spiritual) exist as information, while some also exist, or are 'realized', as matter–energy, then might we consider the soul as the information 'image' of the living being, including the consciousness of that being as well as the information associated with physical form, function and process? If this is in any sense correct, perhaps we might gain further insight into what is meant by being created in the 'image' of God.

Space does not permit me to elaborate on the value of the support that I have received for my Christian journey from friends, family and indeed colleagues (though they are probably unaware of this), but the value I have come to see in humans through these relationships, gives me hope that our species might be redeemable after all. I have come to recognize that while humans are indeed the most destructive species on the planet, this is because of the broken relationship with God described allegorically in Genesis, which results in the perception of *Homo sapiens* as the centre of all things. The irony of this is palpable since, for example, an evolutionary argument for atheism is that religion is irrational precisely because of its anthropocentricity.

But it is this broken relationship that has resulted in the distorted judgments that result from utilitarian ethics, and the inability to recognize the value, indeed sanctity, of life. The crucifixion gives the lie to the notion that God delights in the suffering of creation (Dawkins, 1986, 2006); the resurrection shows the potential value of surprise. The present environmental crisis is ultimately a consequence of human greed, of selfishness, of the poverty and criminality that arise from these, and of ignorance. Consequently, and contrary to the assumptions of my youth, I have found that Christ's teachings have much to offer us by way of salvation from this crisis.

Two final points. First, while the very fact of existence appears surprising to us as we contemplate it from within a universe where the occurrence of events is contingent on probability, it seems unlikely that this should be so for God; if he created the universe, it cannot surprise him that it exists. While this says nothing about the nature of God's interaction with the extant universe, it does suggest that the value which God places on creation is related not to its information content, but to something else: an act of divine grace consistent with the continuing act of creation (MacKay, 1960). The second point is that if value is coupled with improbability within this creation, it follows that God should appear to us to be both of inestimable value, and also highly implausible. In God's apparent improbability, then, I agree, in the end, with Richard Dawkins (2006).

NOTES

1. 'From the war of nature, from famine and death, the most exalted object of which we are capable of conceiving, namely the production of the higher animals directly follows. There is a grandeur in this view of life, with it several powers, having been originally breathed into a few forms or into one; and that, while this planet has gone cycling on according to the fixed law of gravity, from so simple a beginning endless forms most beautiful and most wonderful have been and are being evolved' (the ending of Charles Darwin's *The Origin of Species*, 1st edn).

2. The information statistic from which ecologists derive the diversity index H-bar, is $p.\log_2 p$ where p is the probability of an event (where $0 \leq p \leq 1$). In ecology, p_i is taken as the probability that an individual organism

drawn at random from a community belongs to species 'i', and the values are summed across species to give the statistic H-bar. This allows one to include in a single quantity both the number of species present in an ecological community and the distribution (or equitability) of individuals amongst those species.

3. Gaia: a theoretical global cybernetic system whereby living and non-living components interact *via* dynamic feedback which results, for example, in a stabilizing of the planet's atmospheric composition, marine salinity etc., and thus also climate, over millions of years to the benefit of life itself. Evidence for Gaia has grown steadily since James Lovelock first proposed its existence in the early 1970s, although it remains controversial. See Lovelock, J. (1995), *The Ages of Gaia: A Biography of Our Living Earth*, London: Norton.

CHAPTER 13

A Passion for Science and a Passion for God
Joan Centrella

Joan Centrella is an astrophysicist at NASA's Goddard
Space Flight Center, where she is head of the Gravitational
Astrophysics Laboratory. Her research interests include black
hole mergers, gravitational waves, numerical relativity, cosmic
structure formation, and cosmology. She is a Fellow of the
American Physical Society. In May 2007, she was awarded the
NASA Exceptional Scientific Achievement Medal for ground-
breaking work in the simulation of gravitational wave signals
from merging black holes. She wrote this article in her personal
capacity, and not in her official NASA capacity, and the views she
expresses here are her own, and not necessarily those of NASA
or the US government.

I am a practising scientist and a practising Christian. As a
scientist, I enjoy the excitement of astrophysics, contributing to
our knowledge of exotic cosmic phenomena such as black holes
and gravitational waves; as a Christian, I am blessed with faith in
God and the grace of living in his presence every day.

Claiming to be both a scientist and a Christian may seem
contradictory, or even oxymoronic, to some. After all, we have
the popular stereotypes of scientists as naturalistic atheists and
of Christians fearful of a science that they think undermines
faith. The media frequently regale us with tales of 'culture wars'
in which science and religion – particularly Christianity – are
presented as being irreconcilable enemies.

This is completely different to my experience. Of course, I
have had to work through various challenges, and in this article

I share my journey and some of the issues I have faced. At the outset, I must make it clear that I am neither a philosopher nor a theologian. While some of the issues I discuss have led me into these arenas, I'll be speaking here primarily about how I experience my life as both a scientist and a Christian.

Exciting astronomy

I first discovered astronomy when I was a child, in the fourth grade of elementary school. After I finished my homework, I would browse through the later chapters of my school books. The science book was especially interesting. Towards the end of it, I encountered amazing chapters about the Sun and solar system, the stars and galaxies. My eyes were opened wide at the astonishing beauty and grandeur of the universe. Later, as I investigated various college programmes and careers, I made the incredible discovery that one could actually make astronomy and astrophysics a life's work! That settled it for me – I knew I must be a part of this amazing adventure. I have never seriously looked back; I am now a professional astrophysicist.

We know that near its centre, every galaxy has a black hole with a mass exceeding a million or even a billion times the mass of our Sun. When two galaxies merge, their black holes come together and start orbiting around each other, gradually getting closer and closer until they merge into a single massive black hole. Einstein's General Theory of Relativity predicts that these orbiting black holes cause waves in the curvature of space-time, much like ripples on the surface of a pond after you throw in a rock. These space-time ripples are called 'gravitational waves' and travel outwards at the speed of light. Scientists around the world are building instruments designed to detect these waves, which will test a key prediction of Einstein's General Relativity and give us a new type of signal with which to probe the universe. However, these waves are very elusive and detecting them requires high-precision measurements. Knowing the pattern these waves make is thus an important ingredient in making these detections.

My research is about trying to understand something about these exotic phenomena, and specifically to calculate the wave patterns that result when two massive black holes spiral together and merge.

When I was young, I also began to learn about God. Most of my understanding came through attending church with my family and catechism classes for children. In particular, I learned that God created everything, including the heavens and the earth. As I learned about science and that I, too, could be a scientist, it seemed quite natural to me that I could study all that God had created. The intertwining of these two threads – that God created the universe and that I would learn about what God created – has stayed with me throughout my life.

Being a woman in science – and in the church

As my understanding of and interest in science expanded, I began to experience some challenges. In particular, my aspirations to be a scientist were questioned and occasionally ridiculed by peers and even some adults. I was frequently told that such things were 'for boys'. As you might imagine, this caused me – a young woman – considerable pain and turmoil as I grew up. Nevertheless, my deep passion for science drove me on.

I also began to experience some conflicts with the church. In my case, science was not the issue; rather, the focus was on the value and role of women. In addition, I began to question Christian moral values and the restrictions they seemed to impose on my life. As a young adult my response was to walk away from the church. I never became an atheist, but I did set out to live my life without God.

After more than fifteen years, I returned to the Christian faith. Like the prodigal son, I had come to some very large difficulties in my life that I recognized were beyond my own ability to handle. At the same time, I was spiritually hungry. I knew I needed a spiritual focus in my life, but I wanted to choose my own spiritual path and not just follow the one I learned as a child.

I investigated and explored various different spiritual approaches and options. After all of this I chose to follow Christ, because his words in the Gospels impressed me as being true in a very deep and fundamental way. From my previous experiences I knew that following Christ meant agreeing to live as a Christian, and I struggled seriously with this issue. In the end I decided that the truth of Christ was paramount, and I accepted his lordship over my life. This led me to begin to take Christian discipleship quite seriously.

Facing Conflicts

When I returned to the church and the Christian community, I found that conflicts and problems – some old and some new – were still present. The landscape now was somewhat different from what I had experienced as a child; in particular, science and faith were being more stridently proclaimed as antagonists by people on both sides. My belief that, as a scientist, I was studying all that God had created was still deep and strong, and I never really engaged in this type of warfare. However, I did face other conflicts, and here I want to focus on two that played primary roles in my life: being a woman scientist in Christianity, and the importance of my work as a scientist to God and to the Christian community.

As an astrophysicist, I am a woman in a field that is dominated by men. While this posed a number of challenges in my professional life, I persisted and eventually succeeded. When I returned to the church, I was already a successful scientist, with publications, students, and research grants. I entered a world of Christianity in which it was said that women were not allowed to lead. Yet there I was, a woman, leading. It is sad to report that I was marginalized by Christians because I am a woman. And it was very distressing and even painful to be told that my being a leader was displeasing and even unacceptable to God.

Being a scientist and carrying out research at the frontiers of knowledge requires discipline and dedication, as well as considerable time, energy, and effort. It was therefore quite disconcerting to be told that the primary value of my work was to obtain money, which I could then give to people who were in 'full-time Christian service'. Now please don't get me wrong! I do get paid as a scientist, and I gladly contribute to the church, missionary work, relief efforts, and the like. The problem I had was the implication that my work as a scientist did not count as serving God.

Along the same vein, I was also told that being a woman leader in science was not the real problem. Rather, what really counted was the work done in the church, and the effort I was leading was not in the church. Piled on top of this was the problem that many Christians actually believe that science is an unholy enterprise and undermines faith in God. As I strove to integrate my new understandings of what it meant to follow Jesus Christ with my passion and profession as a scientist, the conflicts and rejection I experienced in the Christian community were very painful.

But God is very gracious to me, and through prayer and perseverance some resolution of these issues has come. Over the years I have explored various Christian churches and traditions. This exploration has helped me to see the issues more clearly, separating wheat from chaff. I have come to understand that all gifts, whether in science, leadership or other arenas, are given by God to both women and men. In addition, I now understand that my passion for astrophysics is a hallmark of my calling in life to be a scientist, and that the work I do as a scientist is both important and pleasing to God. I see that science is, first of all, for the glory of God, in discovering what God has created. And science is also for the greater good, as the knowledge that science brings – even about rather esoteric subjects such as black holes and gravitational waves – is valuable to humanity. These perspectives have provided a foundation of peace and confidence, allowing me to focus on the work God has indeed called me to do and meet the very real and important challenges I face as a disciple of Christ.

Today, I lead a research group of talented younger people in a very competitive field. Over the past several years, our computer simulations of merging binary black holes and the gravitational waves they produce have put us at the forefront of major research breakthroughs in gravitational astrophysics. In addition, I am the head of a department comprising about ten faculty-level scientists with their own research efforts, post-doctoral fellows and students. As a scientist who takes her Christian faith seriously, I often find this road to be difficult, keeping me humble and on my knees in prayer. With this in mind, let me give you a few examples of how being a disciple of Jesus Christ provides the framework for my professional life.

Christian calling and witness

Jesus gave us two great commandments. In the first, he tells us that we are to love the Lord our God with all our heart, with all our soul, with all our mind, and with all our strength. Now, this sounds to me a lot like the type of intensity I bring to science – but I know it goes beyond that. In particular, this commandment draws my focus back to God, who is at the centre of my life. Whatever I am doing, wherever I am, God is with me and I can know his presence.

Jesus' second commandment is to love your neighbour as yourself. I confess that I often find this more challenging than the first. Now, Jesus is speaking here of *agape* love, which the New Testament defines as incorporating patience and kindness, not boasting or being rude, and not keeping a record of wrongs. But who are my neighbours? Certainly the people I work with, especially the members of my research team, count as neighbours. But it is also clear from the parable of the Good Samaritan that the idea of 'neighbour' extends way farther than this – even to our competitors. I admit that this can be a real struggle for me, especially in a fast-paced environment with the pressure to be first with new results, to obtain grants, and so forth.

Jesus also teaches that to whom much is given, much will

be required. I find this a very sobering statement, for I am one to whom much indeed has been given. In particular, I am grateful to God for giving me not only the ability to do science and lead others, but also considerable resources for my research group. I am a senior member of the scientific community, and the younger people in my group depend on me for their resources and their careers. At the same time, I have a responsibility to lead in such a way that the community as a whole benefits, even as my group is empowered.

Another aspect of Christianity that resonates deeply with me is the metaphor of the body of Christ. The New Testament talks about all the members of the church as being part of the body of Christ. In particular, it stresses that one part of the body (say, the eye) cannot do without the other parts (say, the hand). Instead, all the parts are needed to compose the body, and those parts that may seem weaker are actually indispensable.

Science today is often done by teams of researchers. This is particularly true in my field of work, for a team is needed to build and run the large, complex computer codes with which we carry out numerical simulations and obtain new scientific results. As the leader, I am frequently out in front – giving the talks, getting the grants, and often receiving the honours. The younger scientists spend much time in the background, doing the hard and often frustrating work of developing the computer programs and carrying out the simulations.

While I recognize that a team of scientists is not the same as the church, I find the body-of-Christ metaphor to be very helpful to me as a scientist. All members of our team must receive appropriate credit as well as opportunities to be creative and to have fulfilling careers. Each member is essential, and we cannot do this work without each other.

Today, I find that the real challenges I face as a practising scientist and a practising Christian come from striving to live my life consistently as a disciple of Christ. My hope is to lead with a sense of stewardship, in the pursuit of excellence. I truly love astrophysics and the excitement of helping to open new frontiers in our knowledge of the universe. At the same time, I see that my work and particularly my leadership is primarily service to others: to God first, and then to my neighbours. My vision of who these 'neighbours' are has grown to include not only the members of my research group and the department I head, but also our competitors, the larger scientific community, and even the world as a whole.

I do not pretend that living such a consistent life is easy. In particular, success brings many temptations; I often fail. God's standards are much higher than those of the society around us, both inside and outside of science. Fortunately, as Christians we are blessed with the grace of prayer and the presence of the Holy Spirit. In all of this, Christ's sacrifice on the cross and the forgiveness that it brings day by day have profound significance for me. I am deeply grateful for this forgiveness, and for the resulting hope that encourages me to try again.

CHAPTER 14

No Easy Answers
John Wyatt

John Wyatt is Professor of Neonatal Paediatrics and Consultant Neonatologist at University College London Hospital. He is a Fellow of the Royal College of Physicians and of the Royal College of Paediatrics and Child Health. He chairs the Christian Medical Fellowship Study Group. He is the author of *Matters of Life and Death* (1998).

At high school my abiding passion was physics and I had a rather romanticized ideal of becoming a research scientist. I gained a place to read physics at Oxford University and started the course with great enthusiasm. But my first year of university was a time of spiritual crisis and challenge. Although I had been raised in a Christian home, I had profound doubts about the intellectual credibility of orthodox, biblical Christianity. At university I was able for the first time to test the truth claims of Christianity and the rational evidence for belief in the God of the Bible. Over that first year I had a steadily increasing conviction that the Christian faith did stand up to the most fundamental questions I could come up with. And if this faith was true, then it had radical implications for the way I should live. My decision to change direction and study medicine was bound up with my growing Christian commitment. I sensed a new vocation – to use the scientific abilities I had been given for the benefit of people whom God loved.

After medical training and junior hospital posts in London, I was increasingly drawn into paediatrics and then into neonatology, the medical care of newborn infants. In the 1980s this was a new and rapidly growing medical specialty. It combined the human challenge of caring for the most vulnerable

of human beings with the technical and scientific demands of
novel intensive care methodologies.

Clinical care: problems with newborn babies

Intensive care for newborn babies had made great strides since
its first experimental introduction in the 1960s and 1970s.
Survival rates had improved markedly, but the great unsolved
problem of neonatology was (and remains) that of brain damage
leading to long-term disability such as cerebral palsy or learning
difficulties. I had the remarkable opportunity of joining a
multidisciplinary research team at University College London
(UCL) which was developing sophisticated new brain imaging
techniques (magnetic resonance and near infrared spectroscopy)
to investigate the mechanisms underlying brain damage and
search for preventative strategies.

As part of the clinical team we were caring for babies and
their families whose lives were devastated by the consequences of
brain damage. This gave a powerful drive to our research efforts.
There must be something we could do to find how to prevent or
treat this terrible problem. Over a period spanning more than
twenty years we made slow but steady progress. The sequence
of metabolic events in the infant brain following exposure to
damaging oxygen lack was elucidated. Then we demonstrated
that moderate brain cooling had a powerful protective effect,
provided it was started within a few hours of the start of the
oxygen deprivation. This was highly controversial, since the
ruling orthodoxy had always been that it was essential to keep
all newborn babies warm! However, other research groups
around the world were coming to similar conclusions. To my
surprise, I found myself acting as co-Principal Investigator for
the first international randomized trial of neonatal hypothermia
treatment, involving major centres in the UK, the US, Canada
and New Zealand. Although much work still needs to be done,
it seems that hypothermia treatment when used appropriately

does lead to a significant reduction in death and long-term disability and that it will find a role in treating vulnerable babies across the world.

My personal experience, like that of so many other research scientists, is that the fundamental Christian understanding of the cosmos, the Christian world-view, supports and motivates scientific exploration. The profound conviction that the universe is built on rational principles, and even more remarkably, that it is possible for the human brain to uncover and understand those principles, lies at the heart of the research enterprise. It is the Christian understanding of creation order, and of human beings made in God's image, which underpins and illuminates these convictions. In addition, in the search for new and effective medical therapies, the Christian understanding of creation supports the idea of the remarkable healing potential locked within the human body and of the fundamental link between the natural world and humanity itself.

As a practising doctor caring for newborn babies and confronting the painful realities of disease, disability and suffering, there is the constant challenge of building a bridge between my Christian faith and the highly technological and scientific world of modern neonatology. At the heart is the need to develop a more profound understanding of what it means to be a human being. Christian ethics (understanding what is right and wrong) comes from Christian anthropology (understanding how we are made).

Precious dust

In biblical thinking human beings are made out of dust, like the rest of the natural creation. This is seen both in Hebrew, where the name 'Adam' is derived from *adamah*, 'the ground', and also in English where the word 'human' is derived from *humus*, 'the soil'. We have a profound solidarity with the rest of creation. Biblical Christians should not be surprised at the recent findings of remarkable similarities between the human genome and that of other species on the planet. We are made out of the same stuff as everything else. It seems to me that this ancient understanding illuminates the amazing ability of molecular and genetic research in rodent and other animal models to be translated into medical applications for humans. We belong together. We share the vulnerability, dependence and contingency of the biological world.

But at the same time biblical thinking stresses that human beings are unique amongst all the living organisms on the planet. We alone are made as God's image. In some mysterious way we reflect the profundities of God's character and nature. It has been well said that 'A human life is not just a gift of God's grace, it is a reflection of his being.' The dignity of our humanity is fundamentally derivative; it comes from him whose image we bear.

This implies that human beings are not self-explanatory. We derive our meaning from outside ourselves. Much scientific research on human beings is driven by an understandable desire to achieve an ultimate explanation of what it means to be human. It is the desire to understand ourselves – to achieve self-transcendence. There has been a great deal of interest in comparisons between the human and chimpanzee genome. If we can understand the role of the comparatively small amount of DNA which is unique to human beings, perhaps we will finally understand what makes us different from the great apes. But it seems to me that the quest for self-transcendence is doomed to failure. Indeed from a Christian perspective it can be seen as a form of idolatry – to make the human form itself the ultimate source of meaning in the cosmos. We will never understand what it means to be a human being by advances in human genomics or by neuroscientific breakthroughs. In part this is because the quest is self-referential and ultimately circular. Can the human brain ever fully understand the workings of the human brain? Can an evolved being fully understand the mechanisms and consequences of its evolution? But more importantly, the quest for self-transcendence is doomed to failure because the ultimate nature of human beings is derived from outside ourselves, from a different order of reality completely, from the nature of God himself.

Imagine a super-intelligent alien civilization in the Andromeda galaxy. They have picked up a distorted image which appears to have been transmitted from a small planet in an outer arm of the Milky Way. The image consists of coloured lines in a mysterious pattern. The alien intelligences analyze every aspect of the image. Each pixel is dissected in terms of frequency, intensity, saturation, relationship to neighbouring pixels, and so on. However detailed the analysis, the aliens will never understand what they are looking at, unless they realize that the image is a map. In fact it is a distorted image of the London Underground map. The collection of coloured pixels represents another sort of reality completely, a series of metal tubes set into the ground in a particular location on a particular planet.

The analogy is obviously limited, but perhaps it illustrates the way in which the unique and multifaceted structure of our humanity represents, maps onto, another reality – the mysterious being and character of God.

The challenge for biblical Christians is to keep these twin understandings together, without emphasizing one at the expense of the other. Human beings are made out of the same stuff as everything else. We are simply an unlikely combination of trace elements, genomic transcription, biochemical engineering, and neuronal processing. And yet at the same time each one of us is a mysterious and unique reflection of God's unseen reality – each one is a being of infinite value and eternal significance. In the literal Hebrew of Psalm 8, each human life is described as 'lacking a very little of God...'

The materialist says that human beings are *really* sophisticated self-replicating survival machines who happen to have achieved self-consciousness. On the other hand the philosophical dualist says that human beings are *really* spiritual beings who happen to be attached to a body for a period of their existence. Biblical anthropology has to resist both of these alternatives. Human beings are, at one and the same time, fully physical and fully spiritual beings. We hold the physical and immaterial realities in tension, a tension which is familiar to biblical theology. We see it in the doctrine of the incarnation – Jesus was at one and the same time completely human and completely divine. We see it in the doctrine of inspiration – the words of the Bible are at one and the same time the words of human writers and the words of God. We see it in the doctrine of God's providence in history – events in history are contingent, dependent on multiple causal factors, and yet they are the outworking of God's hidden purposes.

This twin perspective on human life can illuminate the mysterious process of the development of a human person from an embryo, a single totipotent cell. At one level this is 'just' a cell. It has all the usual components of a mammalian cell: a bilipid membrane, a nucleus, mitochondria, organelles. The cells of the embryo multiply in an ordered and predictable fashion. And yet at the same time as the embryo develops, God is calling into existence a unique and wonderful being. At one level the embryo is just biology, a collection of genetic information and cellular machinery. But at the same time it is a physical sign of an immaterial or spiritual reality, even a sacrament of a hidden covenant of creation. A sign that God is bringing forth a new being, a god-like being, a unique reflection of his character, a being to whom he is locked in covenant commitment. At the same time that the biological mechanisms are ticking away, the divine artist is creating a unique masterpiece. So we cannot treat the human embryo with contempt because it is 'just' a minute blob of jelly, any more than we can treat the written words of the Bible with contempt because they are 'just' human words. These particular physical words are special, they have a unique spiritual significance; this particular physical blob is special, it is a sign of God's creative covenant.

In my view the way of thinking that stresses the distinction between the embryo and the later person, tends towards a form of philosophical dualism. It implies that the embryo or foetus is merely a physical entity and of little consequence until the spiritual bit, the soul, or the responsive mind enters. Since it is the spiritual bit of humanity that really matters, the argument is that the purely physical stuff of which the embryo is constructed may be regarded as disposable or used for research. To me, this way of thinking splits the indissoluble biblical link between the physical and immaterial realities of human existence.

Of course, we have to recognize that not every embryo is destined to develop into a person. More than 50 per cent of all human embryos fail to implant in the uterus or miscarry at an early stage of pregnancy. Studies indicate that the majority of these embryos have major chromosomal anomalies which are incompatible with life. We cannot always know in advance what the future of an individual embryo will be. But it is equally true that as we trace our own personal history back into our mother's womb, we recognize that there is no stage in human development at which we can confidently say, 'I was not there.' When you were a one-cell embryo, God knew you and loved you and was calling the unique you into existence. Moreover, some people reading this will have been conceived by *in vitro* fertilization. If the embryologist who selected you for reimplantation into the uterus when you were an eight-cell bundle, had instead decided to use that particular embryo for research, you would not be here reading these words.

Limits

This form of reflection leads me to the somewhat controversial view that embryos should not be deliberately created or destroyed, even for the laudable purpose of developing new medical treatments, for instance in the creation of embryonic stem cells. Of course I understand and respect the position of other Christians who have come to a different conclusion, believing that the unique value and significance of a human life commences at some stage after fertilization – at the development of the central nervous system, for example. But my own belief is that it is a mistake to use biology to determine the point at which God's unique covenant with an individual person commences. You cannot use electron microscopy or DNA probes to meet people. It is what philosophers call a 'category mistake'. You discover the personhood of the other when you reach out to them in love, protection and commitment. So it seems to me that we should reach out to embryonic humans, with protection, care and commitment, in the hope that their personhood will subsequently become revealed to us.

A Christian understanding of humanity has particular implications for those caring for newborn babies, because the philosophical status and value of the newborn has become an increasingly controversial and difficult area. A number of influential philosophers and ethicists have even raised the question as to whether newborn babies, especially those who are premature or malformed, should be regarded as full members of the human community. Some have argued that a newborn baby, like a foetus, should be regarded as just a 'potential person', without the full human rights and privileges of older children and adults.

This is based on the argument that some form of self-awareness is central to what we understand by our 'personhood'. Closely related to this is the concept of autonomy – a person is a being who is able to determine their own path, to make choices; the word 'autonomy' literally means 'self-rule' or 'self-governance'.

The philosopher Peter Singer puts it like this, 'When I think of myself as the person I now am, I realise that I did not come into existence until some time *after* birth' (Kuhse & Singer, 1985: 133). Since the newborn baby shows no sign of awareness of its own existence, then it can't be said to have any interests in its own life or future, unlike you and me. This means that to end the life of a newborn baby because it is severely malformed or suffering from brain injury, or indeed for any reason, cannot be said to be ending the life of a person. It is merely preventing a potential person from coming into existence. In fact some have argued that there is a moral equivalence between contraception, abortion and infanticide. All are acts intended to prevent a potential person from coming into existence!

It has also been argued that there are non-human beings who meet the criteria of persons, including at least chimpanzees, gorillas, monkeys and dolphins. In fact it has even been proposed that within the foreseeable future some supercomputers may have the essential properties to be regarded as persons. Some years ago I had a public debate with a distinguished professor of medical ethics who argued that if a computer became self-aware, it would be a greater moral evil to switch off its power supply, than to kill a newborn baby which was unwanted. (I subsequently learnt that the wife of the said professor was less than enamoured with his views on newborn babies – describing them as 'the ethics of Herod'!)

It is tempting to dismiss this kind of argument as self-evident nonsense, but I think that Peter Singer and similar thinkers are both insightful and helpful, since they illustrate the logical consequences of their materialist and utilitarian presuppositions. If conscious self-awareness and autonomous choice are the ultimate values, then some members of the human species must be regarded as having less value and significance than others. The most fragile and vulnerable members of the species should give way and serve the needs of the more fully developed and valuable members of society.

But the biblical perspective turns this way of thinking on its head. In the Deuteronomic law, the mighty Yahweh describes himself in striking terms:

> Yahweh your God is God of gods and Lord of lords, the great God mighty and awesome, who shows no partiality and accepts no bribes. He defends the cause of the fatherless and the widow, and loves the alien, giving him food and clothing. And you are to love those who are aliens, for you yourselves were aliens in Egypt.
>
> DEUTERONOMY 10:17–18

There is a striking contrast in this passage between the person of Yahweh in his absolute power, and his gracious concern to defend the nobodies of society. The significant triad of widows, orphans and aliens, recurs many times throughout the scriptures. They symbolize those who were most *vulnerable* in the social structures of ancient Israel. The widow had no husband to defend her from abuse and hardship, the orphan had no parent, the alien or immigrant had no community, no religious or family structures to fall back on. Yahweh's people had a responsibility to act according to his character and to develop social structures which protected the most vulnerable.

So I see that a central aspect of my role as a neonatologist is to defend the interests and concerns of these most vulnerable members of society. Paradoxically, it is precisely because of their vulnerability and dependence, that newborn babies deserve the greatest level of protection from abuse and manipulation.

This is especially important when planning medical research which involves the newborn. Some have argued that because newborn babies cannot give valid consent to research, then no experimental research procedures should be carried out in this age group. But this policy would mean that no progress was possible in medical care at the beginning of life. So it has become generally accepted that research in newborns can be carried out under stringently controlled circumstances: that parents are fully informed and involved if research is contemplated, and that it is only carried out with their free consent. In addition, clinical research in newborn babies must ensure that any possible risk or adverse outcome is minimized. It is for this reason that our research group at UCL, in collaboration with colleagues in the Department of Medical Physics, decided to employ methods of newborn brain imaging which did not involve ionizing radiation and hence avoided tissue damage. Cranial ultrasound, magnetic resonance spectroscopy and imaging, near infrared spectroscopy and electrical impedance tomography are all methods of interrogating the newborn brain without any identifiable risk, and these methods have the potential to provide new information about the mechanisms and prevention of brain injury.

To a neonatologist, the Christian doctrine of the incarnation has special resonance. When God broke into human history as an actor in the human drama, how did he come? What character did he adopt? He came not as the imperial Caesar, the world president, the Olympic athlete. He came as a pathetic, vulnerable and totally defenceless newborn baby. A baby who can do absolutely nothing for himself, who depends on human breasts for milk and human hands to wipe his bottom. No wonder this was the aspect of Christian theology which the Greek philosophers found most scandalous and frankly laughable.

I have come to realize that I am called to treat every newborn baby in my care, even the pathetic little scrap in the corner with tubes coming out of every orifice, with the same sense of wonder, tenderness and respect that Mary and Joseph had towards their little bundle all those years ago. Because Jesus was a baby, all babies are special. Because Jesus was a dying man, all dying people are special. And in this strange and wonderful story of the incarnation we discover that dependence does not demean or diminish our human dignity. In fact it seems to me that we are designed to be dependent on others, we are designed to be a burden to one another. Truly human existence is one of 'mutual burdensomeness'.

To the secular philosopher dependence is a terrible threat because it robs us of autonomy – the essential defining characteristic of personhood. But in Christian thinking dependence is part of the narrative of a human life. You came into the world totally dependent on the love and care of others. The very fact that you are reading this is only because someone loved you, fed you, and protected you when you were a defenceless newborn baby. After this we go through a phase of life when others depend on us. And most of us will end our life totally dependent on the love and care of others. But this does not rob us of our humanity. No, it is part of the common narrative of human life. It is an essential aspect of the human nature which God in Christ has vindicated and authenticated.

Treating babies with respect and protection does not mean that we have a duty to provide every possible medical treatment in every possible circumstance. There are tragic situations in which intensive medical care can become abusive and damaging. It is possible for modern technological medicine to change from a source of healing and restoration and instead become a strange monster, even an institutionalized form of child abuse. Treating babies with respect means that sometimes we must learn to let go, to recognize the point where medical treatment becomes futile and abusive, where the burdens of treatment exceed any possible benefit. But this is not because we estimate one life as less valuable or less morally significant than another. Each human being deserves our wonder, respect and compassionate care. I believe our role as clinicians is not to make 'value of life' judgments, to evaluate one life as fundamentally more worthwhile, more significant when compared with another. But we can and must make 'value of *treatment*' judgments, to evaluate the relative benefits and burdens of treatments and to stop treatment if it is excessively burdensome, futile or abusive.

It has been my painful privilege over the years to care for many dying babies, and to try to support parents and families devastated by the loss of a precious and irreplaceable life. Strangely, as I look back, it is often the dying babies and their parents who stand out in my memory. Despite the emotional trauma and intensity of the experience, there is a genuine sense of privilege in providing respectful and loving care to a dying person. To a doctor who is a consistent materialist, death must always represent a form of failure – the triumph of disease and disorder over technological solutions. I know that feeling. I have held the body of a dead baby in my arms and wept together with the parents at an overwhelming sense of helplessness, of failure, of outrage, at this cruel, untimely death. But to a Christian believer, although death is an evil against which we struggle with all our skill and courage, it is also a mysterious reality which can become, by God's grace, even a strange form of healing, or in C. S. Lewis's words, 'a severe mercy'. There are some medical situations which are so intractable, the problems so profound, that only death can provide a form of healing, a gateway into a new reality.

Isaiah wrote this description of the coming age:

Be glad and rejoice for ever in what I will create, for I will create Jerusalem to be a delight. I will rejoice over Jerusalem and take delight in my people... The sound of weeping and of crying will be heard in it no more. Never again will there be in it an infant who lives but a few days, or an old man who does not live out his years.

ISAIAH 65:20

God himself recognizes the peculiar outrage of an infant death. That is the Christian hope, and it is what this particular neonatologist longs for. The day that is coming. The day when never again will there be an infant who lives but a few days.

CHAPTER 15

One Impossible Thing Before Breakfast: Evolution and Christianity

Simon Conway Morris

Simon Conway Morris is Professor in Evolutionary Palaeobiology
at the University of Cambridge. He is a Fellow of St John's
College and of the Royal Society. He took his first degree at
the University of Bristol, and apart from four years at the
Open University, his career has been spent in Cambridge.
His research interests include the study of Burgess Shale-
type faunas, the first appearance of fossils, and the Cambrian
'explosion'. Some of this work was reported in *The Crucible of
Creation* (1998) while more recently his *Life's Solution: Inevitable
Humans in a Lonely Universe* (2003) addressed the importance of
evolutionary convergence. His interests extend to the science/
religion debate and the public understanding of science. He gave
the Royal Institution Christmas Lectures in 1996. If undisturbed
he can often be found reading G. K. Chesterton, with a glass of
wine nearby.

One doesn't have to look very far (dear me, I almost wrote 'lift a
stone') to find colleagues who regard any religious perspective as
grievously skewed, a terrible distortion of reality, of interest only
to those involved with the most arcane areas of anthropology. And
should one meet somebody who professes, well, *actually believes*,
that can only point to a lamentable softness of mind. Nor is this
an area of murmured regrets, of quiet condolences, in shadowy
rooms with heavy curtains blocking the outside sunshine. On
the contrary, the disagreement is strident, often vitriolic. Let
me give you two examples. Here is what an Australian, David

Oldroyd, wrote in the opening paragraph of his chapter in a collection of essays on *Darwinism & Philosophy*: 'I should first state my metaphysical position. I am an atheist. The arguments for theism appear so preposterous that their finding any favor can be accounted for, in my view, only by sociological means' (p. 30). The merits of his chapter as a whole I will leave for others to judge, but what I found intriguing is that his dramatic, no-prisoners-taken proclamation has no obvious bearing on the rest of his thesis which broadly addresses the question of stratigraphy and evolutionary trends. Why the outburst?

Nearer home and nearer the bone: alluding to my own views on directionality in evolution (to which I return below), Jürgen Brosius in an article in the journal *Paleobiology* has a footnote in the form of what can only charitably be called an 'amplification'. Its reference was to a section broadly addressing the role of contingency in the history of life. He wrote (p. 11):

> Although it is highly beneficial to occasionally challenge entrenched concepts [and here Brosius is referring to Conway Morris 1998 and 2003], I wonder whether this is a poorly disguised attempt to let religion participate in evolutionary thought: if you can't fight evolution – join it? Instead of catering to the ultra-naïve creationists, Conway Morris (2003) appeared to target a more intelligent segment of our non-rationalist population, perhaps those who should know better but cannot liberate themselves from infantile imprinting and religious indoctrination.

The relevance of the attack is more obvious than Oldroyd's, but once again one wonders what this little barb is meant to achieve. We can pass by the presumed tacit compliance of the editors, who are charged with the control of a scientific article as against mere polemic in a very well-respected journal. All one can say is that it certainly takes a very strange view of religious belief. It is perhaps regrettable that Brosius did not care to enquire of me what my own view of 'ultra-naïve creationists' might be, let alone bother to quote me on this issue, but that I suspect was hardly the point.

Well, no matter. We all know that when it comes to religious belief the world is as sharply divided as it ever was, yet now it seems as if there is something new in the air. The belligerence, contempt, loathing, derision, condescension, arrogance and sheer bad manners of some exponents is stifling. Not, of course, that these traits are unknown elsewhere. Plenty of Christians, for example, are belligerent and so on, but one hopes that on reflection they would be deeply ashamed of such behaviour, however recurrent. But secularists' anger seems to be something different. Their point is not that gods are anthropological manikins, but that religious types are manifestations of extreme wickedness, engaging in activities that are almost indistinguishable from, for example, child abuse. Indeed, in extreme circumstances their warped and bizarre beliefs may well require the imposition of drastic remedies. Clearly we have touched a rather raw nerve.

It certainly is not my intention to attempt any 'dialogue'. If the aforementioned Brosius chooses to regard my stance as being no more than 'infantile imprinting and religious indoctrination', then it is difficult to see how any sensible exchange of views will be possible, given that my opponent's mental image seems to be one of nurseries full of cooing babies patrolled by crafty priests. But it is noteworthy that despite torrents of diatribe, remarkably little emerges in any concrete way. Indeed, my sense is that the secular agents have run out of things to say; why else the shrillness and (more interestingly) a reluctance to familiarize themselves with the subject area? In their oxymoronic attempt at novelty, they seldom refer to their predecessors, perhaps because the comparisons are telling. Think of Thomas Carlyle's existential horror of a 'Universe all void of Life, of Purpose, of Volition, even of Hostility… one huge immeasurable Steam engine rolling on in dead indifference', or in some ways even more terrible when George Eliot spoke of 'God, Immortality, Duty, [so she] pronounced with terrible earnestness how inconceivable was the *first*, how unbelievable the *second* and yet how peremptory and absolute the *third*' (quoted by Haynes, 1982: 2).

Ironically, Victorian perspectives of deep, existential despair are much closer than imagined to some religious belief.

While we admire the pillars of faith, their interior world is often far less rosy and secure than popularly supposed. Indeed, if a lifetime commitment hinges on a moment of insight about the numinous revelation that unrolls as the abysses of creation reveal their infinite depth, the fact remains that for many of a religious inclination (if not conviction), their faith is hedged by doubt and uncertainty. This should not be regarded as a confession of weakness: it is because of the unknowability of God, the paradox of being involved in an intimate engagement with a Person but still remaining as but a straw that is tossed in a howling maelstrom of existential doubt.

Sticking to the truth

So am I about to abandon Christianity? Will I finally have my limpet-like attachment to utter absurdities prised from my pathetic grasp? Will I finally submit my letter of resignation to Brosius' 'non-rationalist population', assuming of course I can find an address? No, not at all. Of course, I will continue to doubt, but I trust I will also continue to learn. I will not try to persuade you that Christianity is true; others can do that much more effectively, although, like me, they will ask for the courtesy of an open mind. Rather, I will propose that the gibe of 'non-rationalism' comprehensively misses the point and reflects the very closing of the scientific mind. Indeed, you may discover that there is rather more to reality than meets the eye if you want to follow this path.

To help to explain how I got to where I am, and more importantly why I now sense that our adventure has scarcely begun, I begin with myself.

I was born in London and decided to become a palaeontologist at the age most children are still determined to succeed as train drivers. My parents were Christian to a degree, but my father only returned fully to the fold not long before his untimely death from cancer. I studied geology at Bristol and was fortunate with both my teachers (especially an irascible Scot, one Crosbie Matthews) and small classes. Thence I went to Cambridge with more than a hunch that the famous fossil deposit known as the Burgess Shale, located in western Canada would be very special. I was exceedingly lucky to be supervised by Harry Whittington. It was he who also encouraged me subsequently to apply for research fellowships at various Colleges; by a whisker I was accepted by St John's in 1975. The electors were probably baffled by the title of my essay that began 'Interesting fossil worms…', based of course on the rich assemblages from the Burgess Shale.

This deposit is located near to the small town of Field, in the Canadian Rockies of British Columbia and hosts a quite remarkable fossil biota, approximately 510 million years (Ma) old. The diversity and exquisite preservation in this fossil fauna give us a privileged glimpse into one of the most important evolutionary events, the Cambrian 'explosion'. In a relatively short period of geological time, perhaps equivalent to about 40 Ma, the pace of evolution shifted from an exceedingly lethargic mode to pell-mell; animal evolution greatly accelerated and body-plans were spewed out of a Darwinian furnace. Unsurprisingly, this extraordinary explosion has attracted attention; indeed Darwin himself was puzzled by it. Attempts have been made to explain it away, most commonly by treating it as an artefact that simply represents the earliest possibility for fossils to form abundantly. However, the general view now is that the Cambrian 'explosion' is real, although the trigger is still hotly debated. A rise in atmospheric oxygen is perhaps the most plausible explanation.

As it happens, I am writing these words in China, where for a number of years I have had a very fruitful collaboration with Professor Degan Shu on the Chengjiang deposits in Yunnan province. The fossils there beautifully complement those of the Burgess Shale, but are somewhat older. They have yielded a number of new forms, including the earliest known fish. On this visit I have just had what appears to be a lucky escape: some very rare fossils, which I had studied earlier, seemed to throw new light on a particular evolutionary question. But only two specimens were known. A third specimen turned up, and some niggling doubts that had been carefully swept under my researcher's carpet suddenly became relevant. A brilliant idea is brilliantly wrong. Fortunately, there is no publication and so no chasing of wild hares. There is still an interesting story to be told, but it is less dramatic and certainly these fossils have not revealed all their secrets.

So it was too with my work on the Burgess Shale: it had some glorious mistakes, glaringly obvious in hindsight. They mostly involved the minutiae of interpretation of unfamiliar forms, preserved like 'squashéd slugges', as a French colleague called them. There was, however, a more pervasive error which was less forgivable, but here's my excuse. Imagine you have an ocean trawler that also conveniently is capable of time travel. Off we go, but owing to the Manton Conjecture ('Surely you remember? You know, when the zeta function intrudes on the third derivative, that's right…'), only a very short visit is possible. So working like a maniac, you grab everything in sight, sometimes in shoals, sometimes as a handful of slithering worms, at times perhaps only a unique specimen. Time to depart! But as the time-travelling trawler climbs upwards and through the cloud bank, before temporarily de-materializing (here, happily, the Manton Conjecture has never been shown to fail), you know that your fleeting visit has hardly scraped the surface of the Cambrian ocean. So too with the Burgess Shale: it is a remarkable sample, but still only one small scoop into the past.

Because in that period of geological time evolution was moving at such a rate and changes were rapid. As a result, you quite often find a fossil that is quite clearly some sort of animal but one with only a vague similarity to any known group. It's bizarre, it's a 'weird wonder'. One option is to say, 'Well, here's a new body-plan, a new phylum', an experiment in evolution that evidently failed. Why? Because it is extinct. One can then speculate what might have happened if this design had survived and others that ultimately populated the world around us (including, of course, ourselves) had gone to the wall. For all we know, the choice was on a knife-edge. This idea, which I mentioned in passing in a technical monograph (Conway Morris, 1985) and more fully in a popular article (Conway Morris, 1987), was seized upon by the late Stephen Jay Gould and turned into a best-seller, *Wonderful Life* (Gould, 1989). Gould was generous in his praise of the work carried out in Cambridge, but it is clear that his enthusiasm was because he saw it as another nail in the coffin of the idea that evolution is either directional or, in his view even worse, shows progress. This interpretation was central to his ideology – that the emergence of humans was evolutionarily entirely fortuitous.

Gould certainly had a number of heterodox strands in his evolutionary thinking, but the view that humans (or indeed any other species) are effectively accidental is a belief that is almost universal amongst neo-Darwinians. Such luminaries as George Gaylord Simpson (1994) and Jared Diamond (1995) have been equally insistent that humans are fortuitous, with an important corollary that any extraterrestrial analogue to ourselves is exceedingly unlikely. Simpson and Diamond are both, of course, outstanding exponents of Darwinian evolution, but it seems fair to say that so far as popularization is concerned, they are outclassed by Gould. Indeed, his effectiveness as a communicator was because he constantly strayed beyond the science itself, but repeatedly dragged in evolution as a chorus. He argued that since humans are a product of chance, we are unconstrained by outmoded moral systems embedded in credulous, pre-scientific minds by non-existent agencies. Consequently we are at liberty to make the world the best of all possible places, free of mythical hocus-pocus, including undeniably malign influences such as racism. Ironically, many of Gould's scientific opponents also subscribe to similar scientistic utopias, where science will transport us to the heights of unparalleled happiness and beauty, leaving the stagnant marshes of religious obscurantism behind, emptying the nurseries of the cooing babies and leaving those crafty priests to their fiendishly futile devices.

The manifest failure of this scientistic agenda hardly needs emphasis, nor, if Richard Dawkins' utterly lamentable 'Ten Commandments' are any guide (Dawkins, 2006: 263–64), can we expect any insights into our existential predicament to be other than childish. But for Gould the work on the Burgess Shale came (so to speak) as a god-send: real facts, real conclusions and a firm mandate to dethrone man and thus liberate him. Unfortunately, things began to unravel rather quickly so far as the fossils which underpinned the thesis of *Wonderful Life* were concerned: supposedly bizarre animals turned out to be misinterpreted or, just as important, new forms turned up that suddenly began to fill in the jigsaw of evolution. A more coherent story started to emerge, with the net result that the wonderful fossils of the Burgess Shale, Chengjiang, and other localities such as those from Greenland, turned out to be instrumental in allowing us to see how bodyplans are actually constructed. The discussion is redolent with unfamiliar names like halwaxiids and vetulicolians, and there is still very active debate, but the idea that the Cambrian was awash with failed body-plans can now be abandoned.

Evolution and convergence

Around the same time that I was re-assessing the Burgess Shale, I became interested in the evolutionary phenomenon known as convergence. This is actually an unremarkable observation that certain biological 'designs' work very well, so unsurprisingly are arrived at independently. In other words, different starting-points end up with much the same solution. Perhaps the best-known examples are the camera-eyes of ourselves (and other vertebrates) and the octopus (and other cephalopods, a group of molluscs), or the sabre-tooth carnivores, which evolved at least three times in the cats and independently in the marsupials (thylacosmilids). My interest was surely provoked by Gould's famous metaphorical articulation of the re-running of the tape of life. If, as he insisted, the Burgess Shale animal *Pikaia* (our putative ancestor) had been knocked on its tiny head, then our lineage would have been forever denied its place in the sun. True but trivial, because evolutionary convergence demonstrates that the same solution would emerge, come what may. When did I stumble to this view? Certainly by the time I reviewed Gould's set of essays bound together as *Bully for Brontosaurus* (Conway Morris, 1991), I was busy pointing out that Gould's own examples supported the thesis for convergence.

Since then my interest has blossomed and I am quite happy to bore any passer-by for hours with tales of convergence in enzymes (e.g. carbonic anhydrase), echolocation (as in birds), or response to death (in elephants). To find convergence in molecular systems might be unexpected, to find it in sensory systems is a clue to the universality of mental states, whilst to find it in an awareness of death touches on the unknown. Perhaps convergence has a wider implication than often thought? Moreover, there are intriguing insights even in the classic cases. Take the case of the camera-eye. Whilst there is no doubt that cephalopods such as the octopus and squid have excellent vision, the received wisdom is that the vertebrate eye is superior because a degree of visual processing takes place in the retina before the signal goes to the optic lobes. This does not happen in the cephalopods. However, less well known is that immediately behind the retina of (at least) the octopus an area of nervous tissue achieves the same processing. The reason for the differences is that the respective retinas have different embryological origins, and thus the footprints of evolutionary history are readily discernible; the crucial point is, it doesn't make any difference. Consider now the thylacosmilids, the extinct marsupials that lived in South America and are strikingly similar to the sabre-tooth cats. Again an important point is sometimes overlooked. The thylacosmilids belong to a group known as the borhyaenids, which as the name hints are mostly rather dog-like. The thylacosmilid is an extraordinary morphological excursion, quite unlike any other borhyaenid (Argot, 2004). It is as if there is a sabre-tooth 'space', waiting to be occupied. Not only that, but amongst the placental sabre-tooth cats, the method of hunting is broadly divisible into runners and ambush predators, and each type has its own characteristic adaptations. The thylacosmilids fall into the ambush variety.

Convergence is, of course, widely acknowledged and uncontroversial in itself. So what else is there to say? It is all very well giving examples, however fascinating they might be. I suggest some things that may point to some more interesting general principles. First, convergence is ubiquitous: insect milk, lizard placentas, fish agriculture, elastic proteins; I'll be happy to supply the details. Second, and tellingly, the adjectives employed in describing convergence are nearly always ones of surprise: 'remarkable', 'unexpected', 'astonishing', 'stunning', even 'uncanny'. For descriptions of what is Darwinian adaptation, this seems a little odd. Third, given the combinatorial immensity of biological hyperspace (typically the number of possible alternatives is c. 10^{50} to 10^{250}), then it is self-evident that only an infinitesimally tiny fraction of this space can ever be occupied; a far, far smaller 'space' than is, for example, represented by the size of an atom in proportion to that of the visible universe (these are separated by approximately 37 orders of magnitude). Doubtless, this is why it is generally thought that any other fraction of biological hyperspace can be as easily occupied, and presumably at an entirely different point. The ubiquity of convergence, however, suggests that our point of occupation may be specially favoured. Contrary to the received opinion that most things in evolution will work, the reality may be that practically nothing works.

There are several metaphors that try to capture this idea. One is to extrapolate the argument just given, and to think of stable positions – attractors if you will – that act as irresistible 'magnets'. An alternative metaphor, which I prefer, is to imagine a map across which life must navigate. The landscape, however, is extremely precipitous and it is only by the narrowest of roads that life can thread its way through inaccessible mountains and past impossible chasms. However, both descriptions beg the question of what defines the 'attractors' or the 'map'. There are two other aspects that I find intriguing. For the first time we can begin to confer a predictability to evolution because stable solutions must recur, not only here, but everywhere. Second, and in a way related, we might start to identify some general biological properties, much as physicists and chemists do. The adaptive immune system (which incidentally is convergent) is one example. It employs a remarkably versatile molecular system to respond to almost any pathogenic challenge. 'Decisions' have to be made extremely rapidly, the appropriate antigen identified and then massively produced before the bacteria 'wins'. Now think of the brain. It is far too complex to be encoded directly by the genes. A key process in its early development is an immense number of 'decisions', effectively how to wire the brain. If the brain is to function effectively, there is no time for hesitation. Obviously there is an analogy to the immune system, but much more interestingly, some of the same molecules are used. Indeed it is most likely that these molecules first evolved for brain development and were only later co-opted for the immune system (Blalock, 1994). Here we have stumbled on a similar design system. And whilst speaking of nervous systems, it is interesting that the proliferation of nerves finds striking parallels to the growth of blood vessels (Carmeliet & Tessier-Lavigne, 2005).

Mention of the brain is doubly relevant because it is evident that advanced cognition is convergent and has evolved independently at least three times (apes, crows and octopus), and more likely at least three more times (dolphins, elephants, parrots, and maybe bees) (see Conway Morris, 2003). If this is true, then it is not just mammals *per se* but at least three groups (apes, dolphins, elephants, and actually a fourth instance with the New World monkeys) have each arrived at the same solution. The contrast, however, between birds and mammals, and even more so octopus, is particularly intriguing because the structure of their respective brains is markedly different. So how does the same cognitive map emerge? At what level of brain organization should we look? Cellular? Chemical? Atomic?

Consciousness

We are actually touching here on one of the only two real scientific mysteries: how was the Universe instantiated and how are we conscious? So far as consciousness is concerned, no matter how much convergence we identify within and between sensory systems and no matter what is the structure of the brain, we seem not a whit closer to explaining how it is that my neural porridge is gripped by sounds of the Good Friday music from Wagner's *Parsifal*, the sight of a new Moon, or the remembered taste of a Madeleine cake. And I would suggest that the materialist perspective on these questions of qualia has not so much broken down but was never particularly relevant. Of course, claims for the former (that somehow consciousness has been 'explained') appear with monotonous regularity, but strangely none convince. Nowhere do I read in neurobiology: 'Well, that's that, chaps, all solved, consciousness is simply due to x; time to shut up shop, what?'

In trying, oxymoronically, to think through this area, a vital clue for me came from a stimulating essay on music, especially animal music, written by Patricia Gray and colleagues (2001). They point out that this music is patently convergent, but to explain it simply in terms of vibrating columns of air seems inadequate. We are talking about music we can not only listen to but enjoy, with its harmonies, melody and invention. Moreover, there are plenty of anecdotes of musicians and birds combining instrument and song. So this similarity can be approached in quite a different way, not by denying the physics of sound production, but by transcending it. Let us suppose, they argue, that there is a universal music 'out there', so the reason the music is the same is because it is discovering the same source. This is familiar as a Platonic argument but it casts evolution in quite a different light. It is in marked contrast to the received orthodoxy that looks to 'emergence': from simple starting-points things become successively more complex. Quite why this emergence occurs is obscure; while much is made of the mantra of self-organizing systems, their relevance to biological systems remains rather tenuous.

This is not to deny that emergence is real and evolution is very largely a reflection of this process. The point I am making is somewhat different and more general. Thus, the properties of emergence may well be built into the universe, but one senses there are still more fundamental principles at work. When it comes to consciousness, if one adheres to a notion of bottom-up causation then of course mind can only be the result of chemistry and aggregating neurons. Whilst this is the standard evolutionary response, it seems incoherent to me: the sheer intractability of how matter comes to understand anything remains insoluble. Materialists will insist, of course, that the senses somehow guarantee mind. But unless the world is deeply rational, which they must deny because of their belief (*sic*) that all is the product of blind and meaningless forces, then we can find no explanation for the is-ness, the 'hiccity', of the world, its qualia of experience, let alone the chariots of thought that allow us to formulate extraordinary abstractions. An alternative view that has, I think, rather more to recommend it is to propose that evolution is more like a search-engine, so that the universe does not become conscious, does not boot-strap mind, but like the universal music, discovers mind as a pre-existent reality. This is, of course, a familiar trope, captured by Eddington's remark as to how in his view the universe was looking more and more like a great thought.

And this applies with equal force to the 'origin' of language. A colleague once said in my hearing that in the last billion years only two things of any importance had happened: the Cambrian 'explosion' and language. In their different ways, both transformed the world. Here too the usual appeal is to an emergence, as is evident in the fascination for purported genes for language. This is not to say that with either language (or the mind) the material world is, well, immaterial, but simply to insist that a materialist explanation *in toto* will fail. Now a particular curiosity about language, in contrast to the evolutionary convergence of intelligence and cognitive maps, is that many animals elaborately vocalize and have learnt to do so independently. In the case of vervet monkeys at least they convey specific information, whilst dolphins are semantically and syntactically competent to decipher different human messages. But neither they nor any other animal asks their friend to pass the gin and adds, 'No, thank you, quite enough tonic, indeed a splash more if you'd be so kind…' If evolution is a search-engine, then maybe language is also 'out there', like music and mind, even though we articulate it by material means.

Here I am greatly influenced by the thinking of Owen Barfield (e.g. 1952), an extraordinarily underestimated man, although not by his close friends C. S. Lewis and J. R. R. Tolkien. His ideas are heterodox and wide-ranging, but so far as language is concerned he made two related claims. First, in earlier stages of human development a particular word could have an immense burden of meanings, so that apparently mundane words like 'wind' or 'iron' actually carried a whole series of deep and abstract concepts. Subsequently, language almost literally splintered (Flieger, 2002), to the benefit of ever more precise meanings in highly specific circumstances (most notably in the sciences), but with the loss of a unique grasp of reality. Second, words that were once literal have tended to become metaphorical (think of the term 'scruple': it is used today to imply moral hesitation but was once an obstruction in a shoe). The specific becomes rather vaguely abstract, while, as mentioned, the abstract disintegrates. There is an echo here of both the *logos*, the transcendent Word, and also the naming of animals in the Garden of Eden, followed by the Fall and, more particularly, the Tower of Babel – a sense that what was once whole and mythopoeic has now become hopelessly fractured.

Obviously, this discussion is merely superficial in the case of consciousness and language, but I am struck by the deep theological resonances such possibilities may present. In a way familiar to philosophers and mathematicians, the suspicion is that the world is considerably more interesting and complex than meets the mundane eye. I find it decidedly odd that many scientists declare that the only route to understanding anything is *via* their method alone. How on earth can they be so sure? Certainly science tells us much, but in this context it is also paradoxical that there is a pervasive sense that before very long there won't be any scientists because there will be nothing for them to do. Here too, I fail to understand the logic. It seems just as likely that we know almost nothing, that our 'triumphs' are merely a small hill projecting from a vast ocean of ignorance.

Unseen worlds

We should not feel embarrassed by calling upon metaphysical arguments – even a nihilist must do so. Moreover, is it necessary to remind ourselves that material instruments can only inform us about the material world, but if mind is indeed different – impinging on the material world, but not of it – then a decidedly different perspective opens up? I can see no reason why there should not be worlds invisible as well as visible. And there are plenty of indications. Think of out-of-body experiences, where clinically dead people see things they cannot. Or to take just one of innumerable such cases, the one of Harold Owen sitting in his cabin on a ship off the African coast in 1918. His brother Wilfred, soldier and poet, joins him. Harold understood at once what had happened. Now if you choose to be a materialist, it cannot be too strongly emphasized that you *must* categorically reject all such stories. For your material (*sic*) well-being they simply *must* be false, and under no circumstances at all are you allowed what otherwise appear to be perfectly sane witnesses on the witness stand. If, for a moment, you even grant the possibility of out of body experiences or that the recently killed Wilfred visited his brother, then your entire materialistic world-picture is in danger of crumbling around you.

But why should one choose Christianity, even if one accepts the transcendental world? The village atheists derive much merriment in pointing out that there are umpteen religions and the one you are born into is most likely the one that will also arrange your last rites. True enough – but self-evidently, there were no Christians before Sunday, 9 April 33 AD (or 5 April 30 AD, if you plump for the only other realistic date for the resurrection [Brown, 1998, pp. 1350–1378]), and just as a bunch of scared women and deeply sceptical men were persuaded, so can you be if you so choose. This is not to make the ridiculous claim that all non-Christian religions lack insights and wisdom – very much the reverse. But one needs to opt for one that is coherent, has historical veracity and offers more than a lifetime's pilgrimage. Even if one is born to one religion, there is nothing to stop you investigating and weighing the alternatives (at least in principle).

For many, when first meeting the Christian faith, the apostle to the sceptics, C. S. Lewis, remains the initial port of call. It was his literary, poetic, philological and intellectual skills that told him that the Gospels not only rang true, but are true. The aforementioned Brosius might, at some point, care to investigate Lewis' life to discover his 'infantilism and indoctrination'. In my journey, it was (and remains) the strong meat offered by Dorothy L. Sayers, and that other apostle of sanity, G. K. Chesterton, which was (and is) instrumental. Dip into Chesterton's *What's Wrong with the World*, or consume *Orthodoxy* and the *Everlasting Man*. If the scales still remain firmly attached to your eyes, find another doctor. But there are many, many others: Peter Kreeft, Ben Witherington, Tom Wright, Stanley Jaki, Austin Farrer, Gerald O'Collins, Charles Williams, Martin Hengel – all offer sustenance and hope in a parched world. Collectively, and in many different ways, these authors speak to a common theme. With respect to the Gospels, they are deeply doubtful of the hermeneutic of suspicion, the pervasive distrust of the text, the insistence that the narratives have evolved and been edited beyond almost all recognition. In reality the evidence points in the opposite direction. Of course one keeps one's critical faculties, but several lines of evidence suggest that the Gospel reports possess veracity and that what happened actually happened: in the reliability of oral tradition, of internal consistencies, and perhaps most intriguingly, small points in the narrative that can too easily escape notice.

Think, for example, of John's account of the miracle at Cana. Jesus' mother would not have told the servants to follow his instructions unless she already knew his powers were a bit out of the ordinary. And why is this miracle not mentioned in the synoptic Gospels? The village atheist will insist that this is because it is a fairy tale, but one can take the view that John was interested in narrating what had not been reported previously. So too it is quite likely that the raising of Lazarus could only be safely reported after he had died, a second time. People were after his blood, literally; in post-resurrection Palestine such witnesses were dangerous.

The central fact is that if Jesus was (and is) who he clearly said he was (and in passing we can notice that Dawkins' (2006) view that he might have been 'honestly mistaken' reveals depths of naivety that are difficult to plumb), then for many the reality (so to speak) of the Gospels still seems unattainable. So dry can be the analyses, so thick the layers of piety, so scoffing the opposition (epitomized by the Bloomsbury trick of ending a debate by finally holding one's head in one's hand and shaking it slowly from side to side) that it takes more than an average effort to project yourself back to AD 33. Forget the libel of the first Christians being credulous peasants and hysterical women; these were hard-nosed individuals far more familiar with the realities of life than most of us. Death, disease, foreign occupation and manifest injustice were all around; these people had neither the time nor inclination to engage in New Age fantasies. What was happening was simply incredible; you hardly have to read between the lines.

All this crystallized in the resurrection. In those few years of Jesus' ministry and its aftermath, not only can a reliable history be reconstructed, but again it is the indirect evidence that oddly enough is the more compelling. We know the resurrection was proclaimed from the earliest days, simply, forcibly and unequivocally, with no ifs and buts. Paul was almost certainly converted within five years of the resurrection, and he insists the central dogma was not his invention, but crucially (so to speak) handed down to him. If we believe the chum of Caesar, the Jewish historian Josephus, in due course James, the brother of Jesus, was murdered by orders of the Sanhedrin. Now that is a bit of a strange fate for a most pious Jew. Except, of course, after Jesus was executed by the Romans, James suddenly changed his mind about his brother, and Paul mentions that he saw (and almost certainly talked to) the resurrected Christ. Disillusioned people who have seen their estranged brother die in the most degrading circumstances are not in the habit of suddenly entertaining a *volte-face*. So too in the list of resurrection appearances Paul mentions 500 people; rather a lot, one might think. But that is the point; to organize such a gathering would require both logistics and secrecy; there were people in Jerusalem who were already rattled by the stories doing the rounds. Of course, like the conversion of James and later his murder, this report by Paul might be a fairy story, but to me its matter of fact description has the ring of truth (see Wenham, 1984).

All these accounts also insist that in some way the resurrected body was material, although in other ways it was completely baffling. But if we think again of worlds visible and invisible, of realities orthogonal to our mundane world, then perhaps there is a glimpse of why the witnesses constantly struggled to articulate what in their eyes, and ours, should be impossible. The scientistic agenda will, of course, have none of this. As we have already seen, for them, to be a Christian one requires the idiocy of children and the whips of indoctrination. But both scientistic belief and Christianity have their metaphysics. Both paradoxically claim there will be a truly glorious future. For those of a scientistic bent, the vision lacks self-doubt: superstition banished, freedom restored, rationality triumphant. Strange, is it not, how repeatedly those hopes wither, how radical evil reasserts its malign grip with each passing generation and with the advances of science the temptations of enforcement, discipline, control, manipulation and monopolization are the more easily achieved? 'All most regrettable,' they murmur, 'but at least we scientists remain pure and detached from the sordid behaviour of our masters. Let us, in freedom and optimism, continue to probe the great secrets of nature.' Let us do so indeed, but unless we take careful heed we will certainly find that at best, like Gollum, those supposed secrets are ultimately worthless and have lost all meaning. And at worst we may find we have opened the door to loathsome worlds from which there is no return.

ACKNOWLEDGMENT

I warmly thank Vivien Brown for typing various versions of this manuscript.

CHAPTER 16

A Christian in Science
Calvin B. DeWitt

Calvin DeWitt is Professor of Environmental Studies at the
Nelson Institute of the University of Wisconsin-Madison, and
the founding Director of the Au Sable Institute of Environmental
Studies. He has been a pioneer and inspiration of Christian
environmentalism in North America for many years. He
has written or edited many seminal works, including *The
Environment and the Christian* (1991), *Missionary Earthkeeping*
(1992, with Ghillean Prance), *The Just Stewardship of Land
and Creation* (1996), and *Earth-wise: A Biblical Approach to
Environmental Issues* (2007).

Science and faith have formed a whole from my youth,
constituting a matrix that has given me the gift of a full life. In
the first part of this essay, I open a window to this joyful matrix of
'faith-full science', which has led to a world-and-life view that has
grown as my understanding of the world and word has matured.
My faith and my love for investigation have insistently motivated
me to discover new things. I fervently believe that this joy would
not have been possible if my science had been separated from
my faith, or if one had replaced the other. This gives me an
expectancy as I write this essay – one that anticipates gaining
new insights as I work to open new windows of discovery.

Within academia today, there is very little that explicitly
encourages one to keep faith and science together. Indeed, there
is very little that encourages keeping any body of knowledge
together as a unified and coherent whole. The spirit of
reductionism is everywhere, and this separates, divides, and sub-
divides most everything in our life, work, and world. Knowledge
is partitioned by academic specialization that channels each

of us along academic valleys that break into the ever smaller tributaries of disciplines, sub-disciplines and highly specific areas of expertise. Even before biology is separated from physics, the humanities are separated from the sciences, universities are separated into colleges, secular is separated from sacred, and science separated from faith. What can one do about this? We need a kind of 'defragmentation' to get things back together in ways that will help us live more rightly; that is the second part of this essay. But first, we may ask, What is a person of faith to do, particularly when we are in love with the pursuit of science as our vocation?

It seems to me helpful to engage the name of the British organization, Christians in Science, as my starting-point. I belong in that category, and very likely you also do, or you are interested in how people so designated think about science and faith. So I am mainly writing from one Christian in science to another Christian in science. What can I write that would be helpful along these lines?

Busy, productive, happy

I am a professor at the University of Wisconsin-Madison and Director of its Nelson Institute, an interdisciplinary institute named after Gaylord Nelson, a US Senator and Wisconsin Governor who organized the first Earth Day in America in 1970 – the same year that the institute was founded. The wider academic community in Madison includes colleagues in InterVarsity Christian Fellowship who take a great deal of interest in the university and its professors and students. One of these people is Dr Terry Morrison, who has left his work in chemistry to work with IVCF in ministry to faculty. A short while ago Terry asked me to speak to a breakfast meeting of Christian faculty on: 'How I Learned to be Busy, Productive and Happy: Time Management for the Christian Academic.' I agreed to do this, but his request made me ask myself, 'Am I really *that* productive?' I took a look at myself and what I accomplished over the course of a day, a year, or decade. I decided that I am in fact productive – as well as busy and happy! But the funny thing was finding out that this was news to me. I simply had not thought of myself in this way before. I was also challenged to ask, why me? There are many other academics at my university – including Christians – who are just as productive as I. And some – including professors who attended my talk – are so exemplary that I often hold them up as models to my graduate students. So, who am I to say anything about this topic?

I took time over the next couple of weeks to look at my own life and work; I compiled a list of words and phrases I believed somehow to be related to my assigned topic. I jotted these down as we drove to church, participated in the service, listened to the sermon, drove home again, and enjoyed some sabbath rest. I did not count this as work, since Sunday is a day of rest for me!

I typed these words and phrases into my computer and then organized and re-organized them into various topics and headings, moving the most important items to the top of the list. A few days later, I hesitantly told my wife what Terry had asked me to do. Very much to my surprise, she immediately volunteered her answer to the question Terry had asked me to address in my talk. Remarkably, it was identical to the one I had put at the top of my list: '*Passion*,' said Ruth!

Passion, science, faith

Ruth and I had agreed – with no debate at all! As Terry had helped me learn that I was productive, Ruth confirmed for me that the root of my productivity was passion. So far, so good… But how can I find a way to make this relevant to you, O Reader? Let me tell you my father's advice to me in my youth: 'Do what you love to do,' he said. 'Then you will do it very well; and eventually someone will even pay you for it!' He was, of course, paraphrasing Matthew 6:33, 'Seek ye first the Kingdom of God, and all these other things will be added unto you.' But he was doing this in a way that would lead me, heuristically, to discover and act upon the passion of my life. Let me describe, through what may seem a peculiar list, how this passion is worked out in my work and life.

- 1. Does it seem odd that I simply cannot wait to get back to my computer, to the library, to my books, to my marsh, to my desert study site, to the prairie remnant – with such passion that I often feel like a wound-up jack-in-the-box, ready to pounce upon my research, just where I had left off, or just where I felt inspired to take a new or fresh look?

- 2. Does it seem an odd thing that, when I discover something new, my heart leaps in my chest with such a doxological thrill that I feel like singing, running, telling, praising, psalming?

- 3. Does it seem an odd thing that upon finding something new, I cannot help but tell others what I have found, enlisting them into the pleasure of investigation and discovery?

- 4. Does it seem an odd thing that I cannot wait to get into the lecture hall to engage my students in my discoveries, and that I am sad to have the lecture period come to an end?

- 5. Does it seem an odd thing that I am sad at the end of the day when my eyes no longer will stay open as, in a drying and raw state, they strive to maintain the connection between me and the text that is flowing in front of me?

For me, of course, these are not odd things. Quite the contrary. These are the things that express and fuel my passion. My passion has as its principal by-products: being busy, productive and happy.

How did I discover my passion – for science, for faith, for life?

- 1. By the care and keeping of animals in my backyard zoo and basement lab room from early childhood and on into grade school, high school, and then college – accompanied by the love, tolerance, and encouragement of my mother who unceasingly cleaned up after my parakeets in the dining-room and my cockatiel in the kitchen and unflinchingly did her washing next to cages of animals that had to be brought inside over the winter; and with the love, tolerance, and encouragement of my father who provided an example of craftsmanship that I attempted to reflect in my own work and whose singing psalms and hymns during the course of his work was a continuing inspiration.

- 2. By doing all of this caring, keeping, and study of the creatures in my backyard – with family and neighbours being intrigued with what I was caring for, what I was keeping, and what I was discovering. Everyone, it seemed, was interested in what I was doing and visits by playmates and neighbours were frequent, each visit providing the opportunity to tell, learn, and teach.

- 3. By discussing the findings of the day with my father nearly every evening. My father and I would sit at the kitchen table, pour out some ginger ale, and he would have me tell my discoveries of the day – in classroom and lab, in the backyard zoo or basement aquarium and aviary.

What I believe is this:

- 1. Discoveries can be a result of passionate love and work with the creatures we can observe, study, care for, and keep.

- 2. Discoveries can and will generate wonder and delight,

making it necessary that they are shared with others, and hence provide the conditions for learning how to teach effectively.

- 3. Sharing of discoveries must involve sufficient truth and detail as to convey them successfully to children, youth, and adults around you.

- 4. Teaching discoveries with passion, truth, and detail, leads to questions and ideas that are inspiring to further discovery.

All of this, taken together, means that here there is an inspiring reciprocity between discovery and teaching: discovery leads to telling and effective teaching; telling and effective teaching generate excitement in other individuals and the wider community; and this excitement spurs me and others with similar passion to further discovery. I find that there is something absolutely wonderful about finding out new things; about the creatures around us; about their relationships with each other and the physical world. It is not only that there are people to tell and people who respond; there are the creatures themselves with which and with whom we interact – some oblivious, some responding reflexively, some responding reciprocally. Communion is not too strong a word to use here – applied to the human community, applied to the creatures being studied, maintained, and nurtured. Discovery, awe, and wonder derive from communion with the community of living beings that join us in the orbit of our knowledge and life.

Ten pointers on passion and productivity

In October 2004, I was invited to speak at a University of Wisconsin Orientation Seminar for incoming graduate students. It was a delightful opportunity to encourage and inspire up-and-coming scholars, researchers, and scientists. I spun out accounts of discovery and wove these into life stories and vocations. In doing this, I unintentionally produced a series of summarizing statements in my talk. The students and faculty present told me later that I had given them ten 'pointers':

- 1. *Plunge in!* Move immediately into your subject, fully, enthusiastically, with full commitment.

- 2. *Inspire!* Engage others in the excitement of your quest, and breathe into your work vibrancy and vigorous life.

- 3. *Profess!* Go beyond training and instructing in the things you discover to professing who you are, why you are doing your work, and why you are so deeply committed to it. And profess with empathy and compassion; envision your students as being your own precious sons and daughters, parents, or brothers and sisters.

- 4. *Celebrate!* The discoveries you make, from the literature or from the creatures you study, should be acknowledged with exclamation, announcement, and joy.

- 5. *Be classic!* Make sure that at least some investigations are so thorough, comprehensive, and original that the published work has a high probability of being recognized as a classic contribution.

- 6. *Dig deeply!* The subject, in reality and in its representation in the literature should be researched as thoroughly as possible, using all the means available for discovery.

- 7. *Be diligent and persistent even in adversity!* Obstacles and hurdles that get in the way must be overcome by thought, persistence, diligence, and wisdom.

- 8. *Be ethical!* Ask, 'What ought to be?' What is discovered should be placed into the broad context not only of how the world works, but in the context of ethical integrity.

- 9. *Put work into practice!* What is discovered should be put into practice or should be so presented that others will put it into practice.

- 10. *Always be on vocation!* Work pursued with love and passion will make vocation appear as a kind of continuous 'vacation' pervaded by joy.

Time and idea management

Back to Terry and his assigned topic: what about time management, and how does this relate to Christians in science? You perhaps may have guessed what I would say: let most of the timing of when and where your product will be produced emerge as a *by-product* of your passion. I do not mean by this that you should not take care to accomplish the work with timeliness and discipline. Here are a few of the many things that I have found to be important, that relate to time management and its relative, productivity:

- 1. Create and nurture an inspiring environment within which to be productive with joy.

- 2. Make sure that your discovery and development continue to produce something every day.

- 3. Pay attention to good craftsmanship; work to get things in right relationship.

- 4. Resist diversion and interruption of work and idea development; keep on the ideas developmental track.

- 5. Organize everything, continuously; order and reorder things as you work to get everything into its right place.

- 6. And keep all the ten pointers I have given above constantly in mind and together!

With these six points as a basis for time and idea management, add a seventh: Maintain eye contact with the people with whom you are discussing or lecturing. This will give you the feedback necessary to restate and paraphrase what you have said in order to achieve understanding in the people with whom you are communicating, thereby moving toward better comprehension. This also provides the benefit of finding new and often better ways to express yourself. It also provides new insights into the work you are doing and new ways to express it in writing.

Three more points:

- 8. Go beyond seeking and teaching knowledge to seeking and teaching understanding. What this means is that you should show how your work coheres with the rest of knowledge – with the life and dynamics of the rest of the world. In working to help others and yourself gain understanding, be consciously rhetorical. Unfold your talk and discussion in ways that bring your listeners/readers with you – and to conclusions they might otherwise not accept, for lack of understanding.

- 9. Take and make time to write following times of observation, speaking and discussing (even if these times are exhausting!). Capture your thoughts and observations soon or immediately after they have come to you, while you still have them fresh in mind. For example, right after a lecture you have given, look over your notes, rearranging and editing them to reflect what you actually said.

- 10. Use your speaking and discussing, including your after-lecture edited notes, as a primer to writing.

Joy in science and life

Other things that are critically important:

- Enjoy your life, spouse, and family and make it possible for them to enjoy you.

- Monitor and seek contentment, both for you and members of your family.

- Give your entire Saturday and Sunday to your family and household while the children are still 'in the nest'.

- Go to church each Sunday with your spouse and children.

- Take Sunday afternoon adventure rides with your family, including picnicking or eating at interesting and, preferably, inexpensive places.

- Take weekly hikes with your family.

- Attend your children's school programmes and parent–teacher meetings.

- Have all breakfasts and supper times, and all three meals on Saturdays and Sundays, with your family, with singing and prayer at each. Make the Sunday noon meal special, including reading of Scripture at the table.

- Sing together as much as possible; help each member to learn to play an instrument.

- Enjoy Friday evenings 'out' with your spouse.

- Go grocery shopping with your spouse about once a month.

- Take care of your own person, including your teeth, health, appearance.

- Deal with everyone with compassion and empathy.

- Apply Christian values to all disciplines and walks of life.

- Know what you believe about yourself, the world, and God.

- Seek the fruits of the Spirit: love, joy, peace, patience, kindness, generosity, faithfulness, gentleness, and self-control.

- Practise hospitality and availability.

- Be gracious and diplomatic.

- Practise discipline.

- Acknowledge God's grace always.

And finally:

- Challenge injustice.

- Challenge neglectful scholarship.

- Challenge obscurant scholarship.

- Challenge and resist the 'dumbing down' of things in your world of work and living – and much like one might sing in beautiful four-part harmony in song, promote four-part harmony at work.

- harmony' in all aspects of life and community

- Serve with grace; but be unswerving in serving.

- Be a student always.

Faith-full science in academia

The observation that there is so little that encourages anyone to keep faith and science together or to keep all of knowledge together, imposes an obligation on every Christian in science (never mind scientists who make no Christian profession). While we may not have much of an idea how to help, every scientist has a duty and mission to contribute to the larger academic community. In particular we can support and join any efforts being made that seek to address the fragmentation of disciplines and the inroads of secularization.[1] Not only is this important for living our lives whole, it also is important because over-specialization can pose serious problems for engaging responsibly with our world, with its high degree of interconnectedness.

The word 'discipline' changed its meaning in the mid-nineteenth century. It began to refer to *disciplinary specialization*, or what we might also call *disciplinary specialism*. Two historians (Jon H. Roberts of Boston University and James Turner of Notre Dame University) put it this way: 'The decisive distinction of the new specialization, separating it from older forms of specialization, was not narrowness of range but acknowledgment of disciplinary isolation.' The new specialization declared 'that knowledge does not form a whole but, on the contrary, properly divides itself into distinct compartments, and that unique methodological principles and scholarly traditions govern life within each of these boxes', and it is this 'new specialization, differing from older expertise in the degree to which it fragmented knowledge into disconnected portions' that came 'to dominate academic knowledge in the United States during the twentieth century' (Roberts & Turner, 2000: 86–87). Of great importance for us is to know that such isolation should not occur in the natural sciences, because it is vitally necessary to operate from the belief of the coherency of the natural world

For Christians in science, another finding by these historians is particularly important, that 'the bite of the new specialization' is seen in 'the growing tendency of university professors who believed in God, as most did, to keep their religious beliefs in one box and their academic ones in another... Hence the new specialization worked, along with other forces, to exclude religious belief as an intellectual tool within the university' (Roberts & Turner, 2000: 88). They conclude that 'if imported from laboratory into lecture hall, specialization could prove toxic to a coherent education.' They then ask, 'If one field of knowledge had no essential connection with another, how could the curriculum hold together? How could students gain a comprehensive view of the world into which they were about to launch themselves?' (Roberts & Turner, 2000: 89).

What does this mean for us? We must not only 'learn how to be busy, productive and happy' as scientists and academics, we must also serve the college and university, the research laboratory and research institute, vocationally. We must join in the work of the institution as a whole and help shape its development toward integrity and wholeness. As Christians in science, there are a number of things that we can do for the institution within which we do our science:

- 1. We can serve as professing professors who model leadership in keeping science, ethics, and praxis together as an integrative framework in our life and work. In classrooms, laboratories, and committee rooms we can model the meaning of vocation.

- 2. We can build deliberate 'integrative sessions' into our courses – and even between courses – to bring disciplines together to address specific situations, places, and problems. For example, these could engage students and colleagues at a landfill site, a sewage treatment facility, a power plant, an ecologically sustainable house, and more.

- 3. We can conduct field trips that go well beyond observation to beholding, and beyond beholding to reflection. What these trips teach us can be recorded in reflective articles, written by professor and student alike, for subsequent voluntary out-loud reading.

- 4. We can work deliberately in classroom, laboratory and field – and in our committee meeting-rooms – to encourage and lead our students and colleagues to develop awareness, to move from awareness to appreciation, and to move from appreciation to stewardship.

- 5. We can help foster the development of interdisciplinary curricula and institutes whose principal mission is to address fragmentation of the disciplines in our college or university.

- 6. We can work with our colleagues to place our various contributions to building scientific knowledge into global biospheric and social contexts, and to develop systems that uncover scientific distortions and misrepresentations.

- 7. We can make our students and colleagues aware of the 'Fifth Mark of Mission'[2]: 'To strive to safeguard the integrity of creation and sustain and renew the life of the earth' as an illustration of what religious institutions are contributing to the appropriate use of science.

- 8. We can provide continuing opportunity for discussing any and all things with our students and colleagues, by having something like regular 'coffee hours' after lectures – at a convenient and comfortable place in a relaxed atmosphere of friendliness and hospitality.

- 9. We can review with our students whatever is apparently indestructible and timeless. These often are messages left by earlier professors and students that were considered to be so important that they should span the generations and provide greater context within which we do the work of our life.

- 10. We can read and ponder Wayne C. Booth's definition of religion as 'the passion, or the desire, both to live right – not just to live but to live *right* –and to *spread* right living…' with reference to the way the world works. And we can ask whether there are secular alternatives to this definition.

- 11. We can reflect and act upon the meaning of publishing not only in our professional journals, but also in our lives and landscapes – including an examination of the various ways that human actions in the world express themselves in our lives and communities.

- 12. We can advocate 'cluster hiring initiatives'. At my university, the Chancellor welcomes short (three-page) 'pre-proposals' on any theme that could fit the needs of the university by developing interdisciplinary 'webs' that span departments, schools, and colleges and which could be supported by hiring a 'cluster' of three to five faculty, usually from different places. For any such 'pre-proposals' the Chancellor then asks for full documentation. Successful proposals result in hiring a full group.

- 13. We can serve on college and university committees that have purpose or potential for integrating across the disciplines. Such service often comes from programmes that have 'Outreach' as their interest – contributing knowledge from the university to the wider society.

- 14. We can help campus Christian ministries by providing them with ideas on how to assist the university in better serving the need for integrative thought and action. New College Madison is an example, particularly its invitation of leading academics with integrative worldviews to speak on campus.

- 15. We can make the college and university a matter of congregational prayer in our churches.

From one Christian in science to another

How can one's faith and science, held together over the course of a lifetime, benefit others? I really am not sure of the answer to this question, but what I have done here is to open a window on my own life. I am hoping that by looking in through this window, you will see a life that is doxological. I do hope it also is logical... but most important is that it be doxo-logical!

There is a doxology that breaks forth from vocation that is motivated by my faith and love – including a love of investigation, for discovering new things. Joy clearly can be the companion of one's vocation – and that joy is complete when science and faith are held together as a whole. Keeping science and faith together fosters a world-and-life view that grows into an edifying and supportive matrix that nurtures the gift of life, helping to make it full. For me, this matrix is one of science and faith; it also is a matrix of story, song, and exposition that was fostered and continues to be developed by communion with the community of Christians, including others in science, in Geneva Campus Church, which I attend.

Some years ago, I contributed a chapter to a volume on *Christianity and Ecology* dealing with my appreciation of the hippopotamus and herpetology: 'Behemoth and Batrachians in the Eye of God'. In it, I reflected on the Book of Job, and then described the cultural matrix that has grown with me through life:

It promulgated a system of ethics, yet continuously reformed this system as knowledge from the Word and the world increased and was clarified. [This is expressed in a phrase I learnt in my youth, *Ecclesia reformata semper reformanda est*: 'the reformed church must always be reforming'.] It sought to bring goodness and integrity to human life, yet did not pursue happiness or other by-products of goodness and integrity for their own sakes. It sought wholeness and care for creation, yet was not afraid to take from creation what was needed to sustain human life and achieve contentment as this was biblically defined in 1 Timothy 6:6–21.

DEWITT, 2000: 299

I accompanied this with twelve 'distillates' that contribute to its fabric, two of which are particularly meaningful to our topic here of holding faith and science together: 'Creation is a powerful teacher' and 'mindless selection should be constrained in mindful society'. Keeping science and faith together as an integral whole makes both of these statements possible. If we were not able to affirm these two statements, our lives would be impoverished.

I have not changed my mind. I end with a paragraph concluding my paper in *Christianity and Ecology*:

The Scriptures tell us that all creation, every creature, praises God. Every creature reflects back something of the love God pours out through all creation. The heavens and all creatures declare the glory of God. The chief end of each creature, the communities of creatures, and all creation is to glorify God and enjoy God's blessings. The Scriptures further tell us that this praise, testimony, and witness to God leaves no one without excuse for not knowing God's divinity and everlasting power. And the keeper/con-server of creation, mirroring God's love for the world, confesses this love in deed. The keeper/con-server of creation admires and sustains the world in beauty.[3] Praise, testimony, and witness are proclaimed to the world 'loud and clear' by human beings and all other creatures: their publication pours forth over all the earth. God's love for the world is published in life and landscape. And the keepers, the con-servers sing: Praise God from whom all blessings flow! Praise God all creatures here below!

NOTE

1. I address this subject more fully in DeWitt, C.B. 2007. The Professor and the Pupil: Addressing Secularization and Disciplinary Fragmentation in Academia, *Perspectives on Science and Christian Faith* 59(2):119-127.

2. The mission of the church has traditionally been defined in a four-fold way:

a. To proclaim the good news of the Kingdom.

b. To teach, baptize and nurture new believers.

c. To respond to human need by loving service.

d. To seek to transform the injust structures of society.

In 1990, the Anglican Consultative Council added a fifth mark:

e. To safeguard the integrity of creation and sustain and renew the life of the earth.

This 'fifth mark' has been accepted by churches worldwide.

3. 'Our duty is to admire and to sustain the world in beauty, and not to impose on others pains and penalties we could not bear ourselves... We ought to live by those laws that an ideal observer or Creator-God would make (perhaps has made) for the world: to respect the integrity of every creature and not to seize more for ourselves and our immediate kin than would be granted under such a dispensation' (Clark, 1997: 168).

CHAPTER 17

What Do *You* Believe, Doctor?[1]

Francis Collins

Francis Collins has a PhD in chemistry and is a qualified physician. From 1993 to 2008, he was the Director of the Human Genome Research Institute at the National Institutes of Health at Bethesda, Maryland. Before taking up that post, he developed the technique for 'positional cloning' of genes in DNA and led a research team at the University of Michigan which identified the genes responsible for cystic fibrosis, Huntington's Disease, neurofibromatosis, and other diseases. He has been a strong protagonist for the privacy of genetic information and prohibiting insurance discrimination on genetic grounds. He is a member of the National Academy of Sciences of the US and a recipient of the Presidential Medal of Freedom. A fuller discussion of the issues in this chapter is contained in his book *The Language of God* (2006).

I was raised in a home where learning was valued – my father was a drama professor, my mother a playwright and they were wonderful at inspiring interest. But science was not really part of my experience. It only became real to me when, as a sixteen-year-old, I fell into the hands of a wonderful chemistry teacher who taught us the joys of using the tools of science to discover things that you didn't already know. I caught that fever, and I've still got it. I went to university soon afterwards and pretty much took every course in chemistry, physics and mathematics that was available. I was twenty years old when my first scientific paper was published, describing a mathematical approach to a quantum-mechanical problem.

I was not brought up as a Christian. My parents did not denigrate faith, but they considered it neither particularly important or relevant. I was sent to the local Episcopal church to learn music, as that church had a wonderful choirmaster and organist. My father made it pretty clear that I need not pay attention to the sermons: 'You should be there for one reason, and that is to learn the joys of harmony.'

If I had known the word, I guess I would have called myself an agnostic when I got to university. But there I met for the first time people who debated whether God existed or not. There were some strong atheists on my particular dorm who were, I thought, rather effective in their arguments. I decided that I was more in sync with their persuasions than those of others who tried to argue the truth of their particular faith tradition.

After I got my degree, I went to Yale to do a PhD in physical chemistry. My life there revolved around second-order differential equations and quantum mechanics. I moved more and more into a deterministic mindset; it seemed quite natural to assume that there really wasn't anything outside physics, chemistry and mathematics.

I slipped into a much more atheistic worldview, although I think I left the door slightly open to the idea that there might be something outside of what science could teach you – but only slightly. Those who started conversations about spiritual matters would encounter a raised eyebrow from me, and a suggestion that they were trapped in past superstitions that they would do better to abandon.

My decision to go into medicine was an unexpected one, because I had previously had no leanings towards biology. At high school, I took a course in biology that I found quite boring. However, in graduate school I decided I ought to broaden my horizons a little and enrolled in a course on biochemistry and molecular biology. I rapidly realized that I had missed out on some pretty profound things that were happening. Life made sense at the scientific level – the idea that there was this information molecule, called 'DNA', and that that could be the way in which all living forms directed their material processes, was truly exciting. Furthermore, I got the sense that this field was breaking wide open and there were going to be consequences for humans in terms of our ability to understand and perhaps treat disease.

And so medicine began to emerge in my mind as an alternative and very attractive career. It's not that I was disappointed or disillusioned with physical chemistry, but medicine seemed more beckoning. It seemed like a very exciting way to combine what I loved, which was science and research, with an approach to humanity that increasingly seemed important to me. It was a radical change – I was married with a child and I was already getting into some debt – but at that stage of life all things seemed possible.

The first two years of medical school were mostly spent in the classroom and I pretty much sustained my atheistic worldview. I was aware there were believers in my class, and some of them would even try to talk to me about their faith, but I wanted nothing to do with them.

This changed in my third year. I was spending days and oftentimes all night on the hospital wards caring for people with serious illnesses. Questions of life and death became increasingly real. This was no longer reading textbook descriptions about some molecular process; this was talking to Edna Jones or Harold Smith about their particular diseases, which often were threatening to end their lives. It was a real eye-opening experience and a growing-up to the realization that life is short and precious, with real people facing terrible challenges every day.

Many of these people impressed me by the way their faith was their rock of support. They talked quite openly about the fact that it brought them a sense of peace and that they were not fearful of what was coming. When I tried to put myself in their position, I thought I would probably be afraid and maybe even angry. The peace they displayed was impressive. I found it difficult to understand, and that got me a bit curious. I assumed their faith was a psychological crutch, but it clearly was a powerful one.

Then one afternoon, one of my patients, a woman with advanced heart disease, told me about her faith in a very personal way and then looked me straight in the eye and asked, 'You know, I've explained to you about my faith and you haven't said anything. What do *you* believe, Doctor?'

Nobody had ever asked me that question so directly, in such a generous, open spirit, and I found myself acutely uncomfortable. I didn't know how to answer. I stammered something like, 'I don't really know' and left the room, feeling very disquieted – and wondering why.

It did not take me long to pinpoint the problem. I was rather proud of the fact that as a scientist I wouldn't draw a conclusion until I'd looked at the data and tried to draw the best conclusion I could. 'What did I believe?' caused me to recognize that I didn't really have an answer based on a proper examination of the evidence. I was forced to accept that outside a few little dabblings here and there, I'd never really tried to understand what was the foundation upon which believers rest their faith. Clearly there must be something there. I knew people who I respected, including some of my own teachers, who said that their faith was an important rock for them, and they didn't seem to be crazy or the sort of people that would stick to something just because they'd been told it in childhood. Surrounded as I was on a daily basis by life and death, was it actually defensible to carry on without considering this most important question: Is there a God?

So, I determined I'd better do something about that. I had little doubt that I would easily survey all the evidence available and find there wasn't much there. This would do no more than strengthen my existing atheism; but at least I would not feel uncomfortable the next time somebody asked me, 'What do you believe?'

And so began a two-year effort to try to understand what the world religions have to say, and what God must be like if he exists.

I did not have a particularly well-designed search strategy. I started by looking at some of the documents that world religions used as their foundation, including the Bible, and I found them very frustrating and confusing. I had little understanding of what

I was reading. However, down the street from our house lived a Methodist minister who seemed like a reasonable fellow, and so I went and asked him a bunch of probably blasphemous questions. He responded by giving me C. S. Lewis's *Mere Christianity* to read. Within an hour or two of sitting down with it, I realized that my arguments against faith were completely naive; there was much more substance to faith than I had ever dreamed. It was uncanny how Lewis addressed my objections one after another. It was as though this Oxford scholar was inside my head. And I began to realize, 'Gosh, this is territory that others have travelled and there's a lot here that I had never been aware of that is actually pretty compelling.'

It probably took me three or four months to get all the way through that little book because it was so unsettling to see the foundations of my atheistic worldview falling apart page by page and leaving me in a position of potentially having to accept the idea of God's existence. Ultimately that resulted – to my great surprise and with a good deal of resistance on my part – in my becoming a Christian at age twenty-seven.

One of my assumptions had been that faith was the opposite of reason and hence that there could be no evidence to undergird it – it was merely a blind leap in the absence of evidence. It surprised me when I found the definition of faith in Hebrews 11:1: 'Faith is the substance of things hoped for, the *evidence* of things not seen.' It was astounding for me to realize that word 'evidence' was in the very definition of faith in the Bible.

What I began to realize was that faith and reason are, in fact, linked together, but faith has the additional element of revelation. At the same time, I began to appreciate that there were pointers to God's existence in the study of nature, some of which I had spent time on without really thinking about it.

Don't get me wrong: you cannot *prove* God's existence, but you can – and I did – get to the point of finding the evidence for God's existence a lot more plausible than the denial of it. And that was a great surprise to me. The sort of evidence that began to pile up for me were things like the Big Bang, the fact that mathematics actually works to describe the universe (suggesting a designer who's a mathematician), the fine-tuning of the universe, and – particularly significant in my thinking – C. S. Lewis's argument about the moral law, a distinct characteristic of humanity that defies an easy explanation from evolution.

All these ideas unsettled me. I decided I really had to learn what the world's religions say about the nature of God. I figured that people who had thought about this over the centuries were worth paying attention to. But it was encountering the person of Jesus, who was different than all other figures in all other religions – and who also solved the problem for me of feeling increasingly like there was an unbridgeable gulf between me and God – that led me to decide to give my life to Christ.

I did not keep quiet about this – I was a young Christian full of excitement, wanting to share my commitment with everybody. My colleagues were generally supportive, albeit a bit puzzled. A few of them, knowing that I was already on the way towards a professional career in the field of genetics, suggested that if I allowed this new faith in Jesus and an exploration of genetics and evolution to come together, my brain could be in danger of exploding. That never happened. I think that is one of the reasons I wrote my book *The Language of God*, to try to explain why such a fate need not happen to anybody.

Evolution and faith

Obviously, an area that many people see as a battleground between science and faith is the whole question of how the diversity of living things on the planet came to be. The scientific evidence for evolution is now overwhelming – in particular from the study of DNA where we have a record of what has been happening down through hundreds of millions of years. Looking at that evidence, one can come away with no other conclusion than that we are descended from a common ancestor with all living things.

Soon after becoming a believer, I arrived at the perspective called 'theistic evolution' – the notion that God, in his awesome intention to create a universe that would support life, and most especially life in his own image that would seek out fellowship with God, used the process of evolution to achieve those goals. An amazing process, an elegant process, a process that may seem slow and even random to our minds, but for God, who is not limited in space or time, it could be achieved in the blink of an eye and in a way that wasn't random at all.

When you have put that all together, you've achieved what I had hoped to find somewhere: a harmony between science and faith that is completely satisfying. I cannot see any major objections to that synthesis. Many biologists who are believers have arrived at this same conclusion, many of them without realizing that others have travelled that same path.

A problem often raised about evolution is that it requires a vast amount of both suffering and wastage. Ninety-nine per cent of all the species that have ever lived have died out. I don't know that there's an easy answer to that. Certainly it's difficult to deny that death is part of the evolutionary process – if it was not, an ever-increasing number of creatures would enter and remain in the world, resulting in an unsustainable model of life. The ugliness of death, you could say, is in a way part of the freedom that God granted to nature. John Polkinghorne has argued quite compellingly that the evolutionary universe is a creation allowed to make itself, and the consequence of that is a creation that contains both beautiful and wonderful things and some things that we are troubled by.

I don't think the notion that moral consciousness, which we so value in humans as a critical part of who we are, applies in other parts of the plant and animal kingdom, and (although this may sound harsh and unfeeling) that may mean that some of the acts that we perceive as being morally unacceptable when applied to humans may be not so in other parts of the natural world.

Another complication is that Christians not infrequently pick out only the beautiful bits of the natural world. I think it has to be emphasized that God's purposes are not served by assuming that everything is always rosy. Indeed, if we lived in a world that lacked any evidence of suffering, including our own experience every day, would we learn very much about who we are and who God is? Is not suffering – and even death – an important part of the way the universe is put together to help us focus on the fact that we're here for only a brief moment, and that the little time we have here ought not to be spent just on 'having a good time'?

God the designer and the Intelligent Design Movement

Though I find it by far the most compelling synthesis, theistic evolution is not the only option proposed to integrate observations about nature with belief in God. Creation science, as most prominently put forward by the late Henry Morris and the Institute for Creation Research, proposes a scheme by which observations of our planet could still be consistent with an age of only 6,000 years. Nearly all mainstream scientists reject this approach as hopelessly inconsistent with vast reams of rigorously consistent data that demonstrate the Earth is actually 4.55 billion years old. A more recent arrival on the scene is Intelligent Design (ID) theory. Some advocates of ID such as Michael Behe accept the old age of the earth and the principle of descent from a common ancestor (including humans), but argue that evolution is insufficient to account for the elegant complexity of the molecular machines one finds inside the cells of all living organisms. Instead, ID proponents postulate that supernatural interventions must have been necessary to provide the driving force for such 'irreducible complexity'. But there are real dangers here: if one postulates divine intervention to explain subjects that currently science has no answer for, you are in a difficult spot when some of these mysteries *are* explained by natural processes. Most mature believers see God as really much too big to be boxed in like that. If you consider, as I do, that God is the Creator of everything and has a plan that goes far beyond anything our puny minds can grasp, and has used processes to achieve amazing goals without having to step in and do magical and mysterious things along the way, then every new scientific discovery provides an opportunity to appreciate and be in great awe of the nature of that creation, and is certainly not a threat to God's omnipotence.

In this context, I fear the ID movement is not turning out to be a useful approach. It is relevant to recall that the movement came from a small group of believers who were troubled that the increasing dominance of evolution in scientific discourse was spilling over into worldviews and threatening the idea that God is the Author of all; it did not arise out of the scientific community.

It is right to acknowledge that anybody who figures that evolution has solved all its problems isn't paying attention to the rich scientific activity in this realm; but the specific arguments of the ID advocates are showing increasingly severe cracks and have been universally rejected by mainstream biologists. The claim that, for example, nano-machines like the bacterial flagellum (which is the poster child of ID) could not have come about by gradual small changes supported by natural selection, is not really defensible any more. ID falls into the unfortunate category of a 'God of the gaps' theory. It is also, I think, fair to criticize ID for having no real scientific agenda of how to test its theory. It is a scientific dead-end. Unfortunately, to add to the confusion, ID also presents a semantic challenge by the 'brand' its authors have used. Without studying the claims of ID proponents closely, it might be concluded from the name that this is simply a way of saying the universe had an intelligent designer. Theistic evolutionists like myself would agree! We are completely on the side of (lower case) intelligent design. But the current (upper case) ID movement proposes an extremely limited and ultimately doomed version of this broader theme. As the Institute for the Study of Science and Religion has recently stated, ID ends up being both bad science and bad theology.

Unfortunately a major stimulant for ID – and indeed creationism as well – has come from the aggressively atheistic agenda of evolutionists such as Richard Dawkins, Daniel Dennett, Sam Harris, and Christopher Hitchens. The atheist philosopher Michael Ruse – unlikely to be a great defender of belief – famously pointed out to Dawkins and Daniel Dennett that their harsh and rigorous atheism is probably the greatest gift that the ID community has had.

As so often happens in human discourse these days, those who take a fairly extreme view are allowed to monopolize the microphone. Instead of trying to find some way of putting the scientific and spiritual worldviews together in a harmonious fashion, we instead see an increasing degree of polarization of perspectives and an escalation of fundamentalism on both sides. And this variety of atheism is certainly a form of fundamentalism: its proponents seem unable to consider the opposing view in a fashion that allows discourse.

The Human Genome Project

When I was invited in 1993 to become Director of the Human Genome project in succession to Jim Watson, I resisted it at first. I was very happy at the University of Michigan, running a research lab, taking care of patients and teaching medical students. But the idea of leading this unique project, which was only going to happen once in the whole of human history, ultimately became irresistible. I took it on at a time when a lot of the scientific community was still opposed to the effort, and there was great scepticism about whether the technology (which hadn't then really been invented) could live up to the prospect of reading out all 3 billion letters of the human DNA instruction book within fifteen years.

But it was exhilarating, too. It was one of the most interdisciplinary enterprises that has ever happened in biology, because it needed automation experts and chemists and physicists and bioethicists as well as physicians and biologists – everybody had to get together on this. It was a wonderful exercise in the sociology of science in that this could only succeed by an international effort where all of the participants basically agreed to put their shoulders to the same wheel.

And early on we made the decision to give the data away. We agreed that the human genome should be considered as the common inheritance of humanity, and its information content should not be withheld for even twenty-four hours. All of these data were therefore immediately posted in a database where anybody with an internet connection could start working with it. That was a pretty drastic policy, and one that has now spread to many other areas of biomedical research that previously provided much more limited data access.

One of the issues we had to deal with was whether to patent our discoveries. I don't regard this primarily as a moral issue, although some people try to make it so. I think patenting is really a practical, legal issue of what you can and should do with a discovery, in order to provide the most benefit to the public. Therein is the point. Patents were developed as a way of increasing public benefit, by providing an incentive for people who had discovered or invented something to turn that into a useful product, and giving them confidence that the ultimate result of their investment would not be subject to unfair competition. In the 1990s, there was a gold rush to patent genes and this didn't really fit that ethic. Outside of the Human Genome Project's no-patenting policy, people were grabbing any old piece of DNA and saying, 'That one's mine' without any clear idea of what it did or how it might turn into a useful product – and as a result those patents became disincentives for further research, turning the whole thing on its head.

Sadly, we have not really recovered from that. There is a thicket of intellectual-property constraints, probably involving as much as 30 per cent of human genes. This can be quite a problem for some applications like the development of diagnostics and therapeutics in the private sector.

'Playing God'

Hubris is a constant risk for humankind. In the past we have pretty reliably shown ourselves capable of demonstrating that kind of arrogance and I'm sure there are good opportunities to do so again when we deal with our genes. But as a physician I also have to say that the idea that the fear of misuse would slow down the study of genetics and DNA does not appeal in the slightest, because I deal every day with people whose lives are devastated by illnesses that could be benefited by this research. We can already see the fruits of research in some instances, particularly in cancer, where a lot of new developments are based on a very exact understanding of the genome.

But with knowledge comes responsibility to determine what the boundaries ought to be for applications. One of the things I'm proudest of with the Human Genome Project was the decision early on to invest a substantial fraction of the budget into studying the ethical, legal and social implications of the research. That had never really been done before – scientific revolutions in the past had just happened and then one day somebody would say, 'Wait a minute! Why didn't we think about the negative implications this might have?'

But a lot of the negative applications of genomics that people worry about are not really sensible science. People talk about whether we're going to use these discoveries not just to cure disease but to improve ourselves and make ourselves better than God intended. Most of these scenarios are not well grounded, because they assume that genes are deterministic in a way that they really are not. If, for instance, you wanted to come up with a designer baby scenario to optimize things like athletic ability or musical talent or intelligence, you would be pretty disappointed, because all those things are heavily influenced by non-genetic factors like good parenting and education.

The Human Genome Project completed all its original goals in 2003. That set the stage for the opportunity to search through the 3 billion letters of the human genome and find the rare glitches that play a role in heart disease, diabetes, cancer, high blood pressure, mental illness, and a long list of common conditions that have previously been poorly understood and therefore poorly managed. In the last couple of years there have been more than a hundred of these discoveries made, pointing in a very surprising and interesting way towards unsuspected pathways involved in disease. Our understanding of most common diseases is undergoing a complete revolution as a result.

The clinical applications from this research will not come overnight but in time they will enable us to practise disease prevention in a much more effective, individualized way. We will in principle be able to identify for each person what their most significant risks of illness are and thus help them to focus on lifestyle and diet and medical surveillance – in other words, on staying well.

In the longer term – maybe ten or fifteen years if we work hard and have adequate research support – these same discoveries will lead us to designer treatments much more precisely targeted to fundamental molecular mechanisms for disease. As a physician, I can tell you it's fairly rare to be able to treat a disease and be absolutely sure that the treatment you're offering is optimal; genetics and the study of the genome give us a new window into developing rational treatments that are likely to be much more effective and less toxic. I'm enormously excited about that.

At the same time, we mustn't duck some tricky practical questions. For example, the increasingly widespread application of pre-implantation genetic diagnosis (PGD) allows a couple using in-vitro fertilization to choose which fertilized eggs to re-implant. This procedure was initially used for rare, early-onset lethal childhood conditions like Tay-Sachs Disease, but increasingly is being considered for use in other situations where the threat is not nearly so great – and even for sex selection.

Whether PGD will be at all useful for common problems like diabetes or heart disease is highly doubtful. Hereditary predisposition to a disease like diabetes (for instance) appears to be mediated by more than a dozen different genes, most of which have a small effect. The chance of optimizing for all those with any given set of five or six embryos is statistically extremely remote. Notwithstanding, PGD will probably continue to have expanded use in single-gene disorders, where there is a high likelihood that one particular diagnostic test will make a very strong prediction about the outcome.

Another deep concern for some people comes from the historical misuse of genetics by racists and racialists. The lessons from the horrific applications of human eugenics – including forced sterilizations and ultimately the Holocaust – in the first half of the twentieth century should never be forgotten. And science can actually help here, as it provides no support for prejudicial claims that sharp boundaries can be drawn around population groups. Yet, it is clear that some culturally or geographically defined populations suffer a disproportionate rate of illnesses, such as diabetes in American Indians and prostate cancer in African-Americans. While those health disparities are likely to have complex origins, and genetics may play a negligible role in many of them, identifying the causes and seeking remedies is currently a very high research priority. We currently have a project underway called '1000 Genomes', to determine the DNA sequence of a thousand people from twelve different populations around the world. The motivation is to provide the database of genetic variation to understand why it is that some diseases occur more frequently in some groups than others. Of course, there is a risk that people may use that information in other ways. When data are there, people with other agendas will try to twist them.

In truth, genetics should be actually a strong antidote against racial prejudice. More than 99 per cent of each person's DNA is identical to that of any other person wherever you look in the world. We are all one family, descended from a common set of recent ancestors. Our science shows us just how similar we are, more similar to each other than most other species on this planet. And we need to keep reminding people of that.

Being a scientist and a Christian

Does the effort to find solutions for these ethical dilemmas regularly pit Christians against non-Christians? Actually, that is not usually the case. In fact, one can argue that this is compelling evidence that the moral law, the knowledge of right and wrong, is a free gift to all humanity, whether or not all of us recognize its source. In my experience, believers and non-believers faced with ethical dilemmas often apply that same moral law, and come to similar conclusions. For me as a believer, however, I find it highly meaningful and reassuring to know God as the source of that ethical foundation.

It has been an enormous privilege to have the chance as a scientist to see God's hand at work in the things we're discovering. And one of the things that I've found most gratifying, especially since the publication of my book, has been the chance to talk to others who are struggling with how to put this together – particularly young people, seeking answers to the question of whether God exists or not. I've recently spoken on the topic of science and faith at Stanford University and some 2,300 students turned up to discuss it. At Berkeley the night before, there were 1,600; at MIT a few months earlier, there were 1,500 students. This is clearly an issue that is coming to the forefront, particularly on university campuses. That gives me hope for the future. My prayer is that we would collectively learn to put aside the unproductive and shrill battles that currently occupy most of the conversation about science and faith, and to instead seek a harmonious way to understand the truth that is written in both of God's books – the Book of God's words (the Bible) and the Book of God's works (nature).

NOTE

1. This chapter is based on an interview with Denis Alexander published in *Third Way* in June 2008.

CHAPTER 18

A Scientist in God's World[1]
Donald MacKay

Professor Donald MacKay, PhD, DSc, FIPhys, FKC. Born 1922, died 1987. Educated at Wick High School, St Andrews University and King's College London. Professor of Communication, University of Keele (1960–82). Foreign Member, Royal Netherlands Academy of Arts and Science (1983). Herman von Helmholtz Prize for Distinguished Research in the Cognitive Neurosciences (1985). Edington Lecturer, University of Cambridge (1967). Foerster Lecturer, University of California Berkeley (1973). Gifford Lecturer, University of Glasgow (1986).

Fog

There is today, it seems, a fog of confusion around the issue of science and faith quite as dense as that which enveloped the unfortunate Darwin a century ago. My plan to pierce this cloud is the converse of the more traditional pattern of defensive apologetics. While wholesale fog dispersal is beyond our means, I hope it may not be too ambitious to try to clear the air around some of the main points at issue. What I shall argue is not just that Christian belief is compatible with the methods and findings of science, but that the two belong together as naturally as fruit and root. So instead of starting with the scientific world picture as a given thing, solidly established on unchallengeable foundations and then later asking what room is left for particular religious claims, it will serve our purpose better to ask first what it is that Christians believe our Creator has told us about the nature of our world: about its fundamental dependence (and *our* dependence) upon his creative power, and about the purpose for which he has brought us into being. If you have the patience to follow me, I believe we shall see the habit of mind we call 'scientific' emerging as something not incidental to Christian obedience, but rather naturally expressing it. I hope to show that any sense of 'irreconcilable contradiction' between the suppositions of Christian faith and those of science is in fact an illusion whose causes are understandable, but whose basis can be seen to be false whether or not one accepts the truth of biblical Christianity.

Dynamic stability

'I believe in one God, Maker of heaven and earth.' So says the ancient creed of the Christian church. The claim of biblical theism is that the world in which we find ourselves is not eternally self-sufficient: it has a Maker, on whom it depends not just for some initial impulse long ago, but for its daily continuance now. This is strange language to modern ears. The world we know seems very stable, reasonably law-abiding (in the non-human domain at least), and not at all obviously in need of any divine power to keep it going. Over the past 200 years and more we have become accustomed to thinking of it as a mechanism, intricate perhaps beyond the grasp of human understanding, but still something self-running and self-contained. Thinking in these terms, we might see some point in bringing in God as the original Creator of the universe; but we might find it particularly hard to visualize any sense in which a universe, once created, could continue to depend on its Creator for its existence.

Without pretending to fathom the mysterious depths of these biblical claims, I believe we can get some feeling for their meaning from the imagery of modern physics. Ask a physicist to describe what he finds as he probes deeper and deeper into the fine structure of our solid world, and he will tell you a story of an increasingly *dynamic* character. Instead of a frozen stillness, he discovers a buzz of activity that seems to intensify with increase of magnification. The molecules he pictures as the stuff of the chair you are sitting on – and of the body sitting in it – are all believed to be in violent motion, vibrating millions of times in a second, or even careering about in apparent disarray, with an energy depending on the temperature. Each of the atoms composing those molecules is thought of as a theatre of even more dramatic activity, likened by Niels Bohr to the whirling of tiny planets around a central sun, but nowadays pictured as the vibrations of a cloud whose shape and density determine the probability of various kinds of discrete events called light-emission, electron-absorption, and the like. According to modem physics, it is to such elementary *events* – myriads of them, continually recurring – that we owe all our experience of the solid world of objects. Even the fundamental particles postulated by theoretical physicists as the building-bricks of our world are thought of as spending their time in snapping from one to another of a variety of different states, or even in continually exchanging identities. For our present purpose it does not matter for how long physics is likely to go on using these particular images. Their relevance here is merely to illustrate a key concept that I think may help us to grasp what the biblical writers mean when they say that the stable existence of our world depends on the creative activity of God. We can call it *dynamic stability*. In our everyday experience chairs, tables, rocks are typically stable objects. There they are. Nothing may seem to be happening to them or in them for most of their existence; yet the modern physicist is quite content to describe such stable objects as a concurrence of unimaginably complex and dramatic sub-microscopic events, without any suggestion that he is contradicting the facts of experience. All he claims is that their stability is not static but dynamic. The quiet solidity of physical objects, he would say, reflects the coherence of uncountable myriads of *events* at the atomic or subatomic level, each of which by itself might seem almost unrelated to its neighbours in space or time.

For another and rather different illustration of dynamic stability, ask a television engineer to explain the patterns of light and shade that form the image on the face of a TV set, say when we are watching the Trooping of the Colour.[2] All that is happening on the screen, he will assure us, is but a succession of isolated sparks of light produced by electron-impact; yet because of the regularities in the *programme* of signals controlling the intensity of the beam of electrons, these sparks fall into a coherent pattern, forming stable images of the objects we are watching, whether the scene is one of violent change or of perfect calm, or indeed whether it continues in being at all; all depends entirely on the modulating *programme*. Any stability the picture has is a dynamic or contingent stability, conditional on the maintenance in being and the coherence of the succession of event-giving signals.

Perhaps a still better example for our purpose would be the kind of 'television tennis game' that modern electronics has made possible, where the players can control the movement of various objects appearing on a TV screen by means of the knobs and switches on a 'black box' in their own living-room. Here again, the 'ball' and the 'bat' are dynamically stable patches of light held in being by a coherent succession of control signals, and moved around the screen by changing the timing of these control signals. But in this case what we are watching is not a representation of the real world as seen through some distant television camera. It is an artificially created scene, in which every object owes both its existence and its motions directly to the sustaining programme generated by the black box, as modulated by the players. Not only the contents of this synthetic world, but its laws of motion too, have dynamic rather than static stability. They are perfectly stable, for just as long as the generating programme is stable. But at the flick of a switch the contents of the synthetic world can alter completely, different laws of motion can come into operation, or the whole show can disappear without trace.

I need hardly say that none of these examples of dynamic stability is meant as an explanatory *model* of our mysterious dependence on God as portrayed in the Bible. But if we ask the writers of the Bible what makes our world tick – the sort of question that underlies any attempt to build a science of nature – we will find them using remarkably similar language. From the biblical standpoint, all the contents of our world, ourselves included, have to be 'held in being' by the continual exercise of God's sustaining power. In Christ, says Paul, 'all things were created, in heaven and on earth, visible and invisible... all things were created through him and for him. He is before all things, and in him *all things hold together*' (Colossians 1:16–17 RSV). Or, as the writer to the Hebrews puts it: 'In these last days [God] has spoken to us by a Son, whom he appointed the heir of all things, through whom also he created the world. He reflects the glory of God and bears the very stamp of his nature, *upholding the universe by his word of power*' (Hebrews 1:2–3 RSV). For biblical theism, then, it is clear that the continuing existence of our world is not something to be taken for granted. Rather, it hangs moment by moment on the continuance of the upholding word of power of its Creator, as dependent on this as the picture on a TV screen is on the maintaining programme of signals.

The solid contents of our world do not give any hint of unreality or illusion – they are as real as we ourselves, as real as their Creator has conceived them to be. But their stability is nevertheless declared to be a dynamic, contingent stability. It is only in and through the continuing say-so of their and our Creator that they cohere or 'hold together'. He is the giver of being, moment by moment, to all the events in and through which we encounter the world of physical objects, *our own bodies included*. This last point is important. Unlike the detached viewers of a television screen, we know the objects of our world by interacting with them – finding ourselves up against them, obliged to reckon with them in the space of our own agency. But however uncompromisingly realist its tone, the Bible has no room for the idea of matter as something eternally self-sufficient or indestructible. The Psalmist may praise God for the stability of the earth and the reliability of the normal links between events on which our rational expectations are based (Psalms 93:1; 104 *passim*); but the same Book of Psalms speaks of a time when the earth and the heavens will perish and will be changed 'as a vesture' at the will of their Creator (Psalm 102:25–27). In the end, the only solid reality for biblical theism is God and what God holds in being. This one framework offers all the support needed both for the scientific enterprise and for the life of Christian faith.

Science in a created world

In order to make good this claim, I suggest we try to imagine that we had never heard of modern science, and then ask ourselves what would follow if we took seriously the biblical picture of our world as dynamically stable, but dependent for its coherence on the stability of its Author's creative will. As a starter, we would obviously need to recognize and respond appropriately to the 'givenness' of all the twists and turns of our experience. Then we would recognize the regular succession of day and night, winter and summer, and so forth, as tokens of the coherence and stability of the creative purpose of their Giver, in which the biblical writers see evidence of God's personal faithfulness to his creatures (Genesis 8:22; Psalm 104).

But there are two emphases in the Bible that would I think stand out as particularly relevant to our prospects of founding a viable scientific enterprise. First, from the Book of Genesis onward, man is commanded by his Creator to make use of ('subdue') the created order intelligently for his own benefit – not in selfish greed, but in a spirit of gratitude and responsible stewardship (Genesis 1:28–30) and reverent admiration for its Giver (Psalm 111:2). Loving the Lord our God with all our mind must include using our minds in a search for the patterns according to which events in his universe are reliably predictable. The more we know of these, the better the foresight we can exercise as responsible stewards. So for someone with the appropriate talents, to gain knowledge and understanding of the created order is more than an optional human recreation; it is a duty to its Giver, the God of all truth.

So far, so good. But just how should our minds be used to gain knowledge? Medieval scholasticism, following Aristotle, saw the task as essentially one of teasing out the logical consequences of the definitions of the objects in the world. As Michael Foster (1934) put it, starting from the assumption that the essence of a natural object is definable in the same way as a geometrical object, means you will have no more use for empirical evidence in establishing the conclusions of natural science than in establishing the conclusions of Euclidean geometry. This is not to say that sensory experience played no part in ancient science, but that it played a different part: it supplied the *illustration* but not the *evidence* of the conclusions of science.

And here we come up against the second key emphasis in biblical theism. The God of the Bible is no mere craftsman, shaping pre-existing matter into forms definable *a priori* in abstract terms. He is a free and unconditioned *Creator*: the giver of being to a world of his own devising whose nature could neither be defined nor fully deduced by reference to any first principles.

In such a world, knowledge by logical deduction from definitions is out. Only sensory experience can offer a valid basis for natural science. To us this conclusion may seem so obvious as hardly to need stating; but this only shows how complete was the eventual victory of the Hebraic doctrine of God and nature over the scornful opposition of the Graeco-medieval tradition. Biblical theism, by denying that we can lay down in advance what the world ought to be like, offers positive encouragement to the experimental approach to nature that we now take for granted as 'scientific'. The history of the rise of modem science amply illustrates the crucial effect of this doctrine in liberating and inspiring the pioneers of empirical investigation (Hookyaas, 1971).

'Customs of the Creator'

All this means that anyone who takes biblical theism seriously will have a strong incentive to gain systematic knowledge of his world, and to do so by meticulous and unprejudiced observation rather than by working out in advance the way things 'ought' to be. A sovereign Creator is not to be tied by what his human creatures judge to be 'reasonable'. But if we were to stop there, the prospect for our science might seem rather bleak: a matter of endless, patient description, with no hint of explanation other than the inscrutable will of the Creator. With such a God surely *anything* might happen? What hope could there be of our making coherent sense of the pattern of events?

An obvious answer is, 'Well, why not try it, and see?'; but there are also important grounds for optimism in what the Bible itself has to say about the *character* of God. The biblical Creator may be all-powerful, and answerable to none of his creatures; but he is not capricious. He is the God of order, dependability, faithfulness. So our theistic scientist would certainly have an incentive at least to look for, if not to predict, a corresponding orderliness in the pattern of observed events in the created world.

As we all know, this adventure of faith has been rewarded beyond the wildest dreams of those who launched it in the six-teenth and seventeenth centuries. The pattern of natural events has turned out to have a marvellously intelligible structure. The regularities – the 'customs of the Creator' as they were called by the pioneers – are of two kinds. The first and most obvious are those of simple succession or co-occurrence: night follows day, summer follows winter, the sun reaches its zenith simultaneously at points on the same meridian. We would not speak of one of these pairs of events as a *cause* of the other. The second kind of regularity we call *causal*. Crop failure follows drought, intoxication follows over-indulgence in alcohol, thunder follows the discharge of lightning. The challenge to the scientist is to discover what he calls the 'mechanism' underlying these observed correlations. In the case of thunder, for example, he will talk of electrical discharge producing heat; heat producing sudden expansion of the air; sud-den expansion producing a shock wave; and so on. Each link in that chain represents a more general type of correlation observed often enough to be taken for granted. If we are not content to take these correlations for granted, more detailed 'mechanisms' can be sketched which exhibit each as the resultant of a still finer chain-mesh of cause-and-effect. Ultimately, the scientist's aim is to find a set of general principles so comprehensive that all such causal sequences can be recognized as instances or combinations of a few basic kinds of regularity. Such basic principles, established by long enough precedent under sufficiently testing conditions, tend to be called 'laws of nature'; an event is said to be 'explained' scientifically if we can show that it conforms to *the general precedent* expressed in such 'laws'. In effect, to explain something scientifically means to show that it *ought not to have surprised* anyone who knew the initial conditions and the general customs of the Creator.

In these terms a scientific *theory* of a phenomenon is an attempt to link together expectations based on accepted general precedent, in such a way that (if the theory is sufficiently 'deterministic') all future instances of the phenomenon can be recognized (at least in principle) as what *ought to have been expected* by a sufficiently well-informed observer. 'Nothing else could have happened', we sometimes say; but what we mean – or what we are strictly justified in meaning – is only that nothing else could have been expected on the basis of precedent. In *our explanatory model* of the situation, only one thing could have happened in those circumstances; but in the end it is for reality to call the tune.

In this sense, although scientific laws do not make things happen, they do more that just describe the way things happen. They also *prescribe* the expectations that would be rational on the basis of precedent. To develop such a theory of the connections between events is, from a biblical standpoint, an act of stewardship that should help men to serve their Creator more effectively. To neglect to do so would be to fail in our religious duty.

Two questions

Starting from a basis in the biblical doctrine of God and nature, we have reached a point at which the whole enterprise of experimental science emerges as an expression of Christian responsibility, with no hint of tension between the two. But to go further there are two questions that you may feel inclined to raise.

First, does not the idea of *looking for a precedent* for a particular created event in terms of earlier created events presuppose that the Creator is bound in some way by precedent? How does this square with the idea that he is free and sovereign? The biblical answer is that the Creator has freely undertaken the creation of 'a cosmos, not a chaos'. He is certainly under no *obligation* to maintain precedent; but he encourages us to believe that his sustaining activity actually has both structure and purpose, some of it intelligible enough to be grasped by even our finite minds. The biblical data leave entirely open to investigation the nature and extent of this intelligible structure. There may be fundamental limits to our ability to predict the future on the basis of precedent; and Christianity need have no more stakes in deterministic than in indeterministic theories of the physical world. But in any case a God who was *bound* to conform to observed precedent in all circumstances would not be the sovereign Creator spoken of in the Bible.

A second question is likely to be pressed by those who see science as undermining Christian faith today. Whatever its status in theory, they might say, is not scientific explanation in practice an *alternative* to a religious understanding of events? For many of our contemporaries the answer to this is 'yes'. Indeed, if the biblical theistic picture is correct, the scientific game of linking events into 'causal chains' can (and indeed should) proceed without bringing in 'God' as one of the links in the chain. For the theist, God comes in as the Giver of all the events, not just as a special kind of link between some of them. It is technically possible to practise science in complete forgetfulness of the One who, according to the Bible, alone gives being to the data, and grounds for the expectations based on them. As Reijer Hookyaas (1960) has put it, even from a biblical standpoint there is a 'proper secularisation' of science.

What is completely unjustified, however, is the suggestion that successful scientific explanation rationally warrants *disbelief* in the Creator. This would be as illogical as to suggest that finding a causal connection between the impact of the 'bat' and the motion of the 'ball' in the television tennis game eliminates any need for the black box as the sustainer-in-being of the whole show. Explanations in terms of links *within* a created world are logically not in contradiction with, but are complementary to, explanations in terms of the power and purpose of the Creator of that world. If, moreover, our Creator has a personal purpose in bringing each of us into being, as the Bible declares – a purpose with which our whole eternal destiny is linked – then to ignore this on grounds of our satisfaction with scientific explanations would be irrational and ultimately self-destructive.

Miracle

Our argument so far has been running pretty much one way. There are biblical grounds for expecting the normal pattern of God's sustaining activity to conform to precedent, and in that sense to be scientifically explicable. To discover such explanations does nothing to diminish the direct dependence of the events in question upon God. So far, so good. But the Christian faith also recognizes the category of miracle. How does this fit into the picture we have been developing?

There is a sense in which, if the picture is true, every natural event is a miracle: an act of God so marvellous that, as John Donne put it, 'only the daily doing takes off the admiration'. But in biblical parlance the term stands for an event that departs from the ordinary run in such a way as to communicate God's personal concern with the situation, and his sovereignty in it. This need not always mean a violation of the precedent we call 'natural'. The drying up of the Red Sea to allow the Israelites to cross could be regarded as miraculous in its timing, whether or not the east wind had a 'natural' explanation. On the other hand, the resurrection of Christ is presented as a unique event with no claim whatsoever to fit with natural precedent. The one who had been done to death was none other than the Creator himself; so, as Peter argues, 'it could not be that death should keep him in its grip' (Acts 2:24 NEB). For such an unprecedented event there could be no rational incentive to seek explanations in terms of precedent.

In our day, post-modernism and the swing against science has brought with it so much irrationality and credulity that this aspect of biblical Christianity is in danger of being misperceived. Spoon-benders and occultists delight to mock the staid conventionality of orthodox physics, and there are signs that miracle in the biblical sense is liable to be regarded as in much the same quasi-magical category – even becoming more socially acceptable in some circles as a result. Christians who are tempted to grind apologetic axes on alleged evidence for the 'paranormal' must, however, remember two things. First, if a God who holds in being a dynamically stable world has reason to bring about a unique and unprecedented event, he can do so as easily as you or I could change the pattern of an artificially created sequence on a TV screen, quite regardless of the regularity with which precedent has been observed in the past. It would make no sense to speak of him as 'using hitherto undiscovered laws' to bring it about, since he has merely to say the word, and it is done (Psalm 33:9). To try to make such an event respectable as an instance of a standard class of phenomena called 'paranormal' (which, if only we knew enough, we could bring about ourselves) would be woefully to mistake its character.

Secondly, it is vital to recognize that the biblical concept of miracle is poles apart from the irrational and the incoherent. What is stressed in the Bible is rather the *fittingness* of a miraculous event, as seen by its Creator, given the circumstances and his concern for those involved. So Peter presents the resurrection of Christ not as a mere magician's act designed to awe us by its inexplicability, but as *what was only to be expected*, given the awesome fact of who Christ was. Such a claim would be only side-tracked, and in no way supported, by any suggestion that the event might 'conform to established paranormal precedents'.

This is perhaps the point at which to express some misgivings about the common use of the (non-biblical) term 'supernatural' to refer to the miraculous. If all it means is 'unprecedented', this is harmless enough; but the term has pagan overtones that can cause confusion. The danger is that it lends credence to a thought-model (derived from ancient Greek sources rather than the Bible) in which 'nature' has a self-sustaining power independent of God, and miracles happen when God 'intervenes' by exerting a superior power. For biblical theism, the miraculous is not so much an intervention (since God's sustaining activity is never absent) as a *change of mode* of the divine agency.

Objectivity

To serve as a scientist in God's world is to base one's mandate for the scientific enterprise on the biblical view of our world and its dependence on God. Contrary to common assumptions, there is nothing but encouragement to build up experimentally based knowledge into a theoretically integrated explanatory framework in which the *concept* of God, for excellent theological reasons, has no explicit use. The key is to recognize that, for the believer, the *agency* of God is the ground of being of the whole subject-matter. In all this, we have found no trace of 'irreconcilable contradiction'.

I would like to point out one further consequence of recognizing the biblical God as the Creator of space–time. Philosophers of science understandably argue as to how objective our scientific knowledge can claim to be. Relativity theory has cast doubt on the idea that one simple description of the universe can be completely valid for all observers. Quantum theory in turn challenges the distinction between the observer and the observed. Psychology and sociology have each their own reasons for voicing similar doubts. In face of all this, it has proved tempting to some thinkers to abandon the concept of objectivity altogether. If universal knowledge valid for all observers is unattainable, they say, should we not admit that there are as many truths as there are knowers?[3]

In the context of biblical theism such reasoning lacks cogency. Let it be admitted, at least for the sake of argument, that what I would be correct to believe about the world must differ in some particulars from what you would be correct to believe. Still, if the flood of experienced events that you and I each encounter day by day owe their being to one and the same Creator, *he* at least is in a position to know what each of us would be correct to believe, and mistaken to disbelieve, about our world. This, for the Creator, is a matter of objective fact. If he has placed you and me in different relationships to a particular situation, the *differences* between what each of us would be correct to believe about it will be equally for him a question of objective fact. True, our scientist in God's world may have no access to the Creator's-eye view of his situation; but because he knows that he is under judgment by that criterion, he is saved from the trap of confusing relativity with a denial of objectivity.

Conclusion

In summary, then, a scientist in God's world who knows and loves the Author of it can rejoice equally in the growth of the explanatory structure of science, and in any surprises that may shake it. For both he returns thanks to the same Giver, recognizing his obligation to do justice both to the normal coherence of the flux of created events, and to its moment-by-moment contingency on the divine fiat. His mind will be open but critical, rational but not rationalistic, realizing that the God of truth is even more concerned than he is that he should not swallow falsehood – but also that he should not disbelieve what is true, however unexpected. He will be careful – especially in his public pronouncements – to distinguish as clearly as possible between data and theoretical extrapolations; chary of baseless speculation; and alert to illegitimate attempts to turn science into scientism. In all this – if he can only be true to it – he may find much of value for the defence of the biblical faith. But the Christian's motive can never be one of apologetic expediency. His one desire must be to do the fullest justice to all the data given him by God, to whom he will be accountable for keeping the record straight.

NOTES
1. Edited version of a Riddell Memorial Lecture given in the University of Newcastle upon Tyne and published in MacKay, 1988. Reproduced with permission from the University.
2. This analogy is developed further by MacKay, 1974, chapter 6.
3. A variety of views of this kind are surveyed and criticized by Roger Trigg, 1973. See also Paul Helm, 1987.

Further Reading

All of us, scientists and non-scientists alike, have to face similar questions about God and faith. Seven of the contributors herein acknowledge their debt to C. S. Lewis, particularly his *Mere Christianity* (most conveniently available in a 1977 reprint from Fount). Other valuable apologetic books are *Basic Christianity* by John Stott (IVP) and *Simply Christian* by Tom Wright (SPCK).

There are a number of general books on the relationship between science and Christianity. Classical works include:

Barbour, I. (1966). *Issues in Science and Religion.* SCM
Coulson, C. A. (1955). *Science and Christian Belief.* Oxford University Press
Henry, C. F. H. (ed.) (1978). *Horizons of Science.* Harper & Row
Ramm, B. (1954). *The Christian View of Science and Scripture.* Eerdmans

Among many more recent treatments are:

Alexander, D. (2001). *Re-Building the Matrix.* Lion
Alexander, D. (2008). *Creation or Evolution. Do We Have to Choose?.* Monarch
Alexander, D. & White, R. S. (2004). *Beyond Belief.* Lion
Berry, R. J. (2003). *God's Book of Works.* T&T Clark
Forster, R. & Marston, P. (1989). *Reason and Faith.* Monarch
Houghton, J. T. (rev. ed., 2007). *The Search for God. Can Science Help?.* Regent College Publishing
Hummel, C. E. (1986). *The Galileo Connection.* IVP (Downer's Grove)
Jeeves, M. A. & Berry, R. J. (1998). *Science, Life and Christian Belief.* Apollos
McGrath, A. E. (1999). *Science & Religion. An Introduction.* Blackwell
Peters, T. & Bennett, G. (2002). *Bridging Science and Religion.* SCM
Polkinghorne, J. C. (1998). *Science & Theology. An Introduction.* SPCK
Poole, M. W. (3rd ed., 2007). *User's Guide to Science and Belief.* Lion
Richardson, W. M. & Wildman, W. J. (eds.) (1996). *Religion and Science. History, Method, Dialogue.* Routledge
Southgate, C. *et al.* (eds.) (2nd ed., 2005). *God, Humanity and the Cosmos.* T&T Clark
Ward, J. F. K. (1996). *God, Chance and Necessity.* Oneworld

Histories of the relationship between science and faith:

Brooke, J. H. & Canter G. (2000). *Reconstructing Nature: The Engagement of Science and Religion.* Oxford University Press

Brooke, J. H. (1991). *Science and Religion. Some Historical Perspectives.* Cambridge University Press

Harrison, P. (1998). *The Bible, Protestantism and the Rise of Natural Science.* Cambridge University Press

Hookyaas, R. (1972). *Religion and the Rise of Modern Science.* Scottish Academic Press

Russell, C. A. (1985). *Cross-Currents. Interactions between Science and Faith.* IVP

Of making of books there is no end: there are many other studies of particular topics, many of them concerned with the ethical implications of scientific advances – evolution, environment, determinism, energy, medical dilemmas (particularly the nature of life). But the above list is a starting-point for anyone wanting to read further.

References

Aleksander, I. (2002). 'Understanding information, bit by bit: Shannon's equations'. In *It Must be Beautiful: Great Equations of Modern Science*: 213–30. Farmelo, G. (ed.). London: Granta Books.

Alexander, D. R. (2001). *Rebuilding the Matrix*. Oxford: Lion.

Alexander, D. R. & White, R. S. (2004). *Beyond Belief: Science, Faith and Ethical Challenges*. Oxford: Lion.

Argot, C. (2004). 'Evolution of South American mammalian predators (Borhyaenoidea): anatomical and palaeobiological implications'. *Zoological Journal of the Linnean Society*, 140: 487–521.

Barbour, I. G. (1966). *Issues in Science and Religion*. London: SCM.

Barfield, O. (1952). *Poetic diction: A study in meaning*. London: Faber & Faber.

Behe, M. (1996). *Darwin's Black Box*. New York: Free Press.

Benjamin, S. C. *et al.* (2006). 'Towards a fullerene-based quantum computer'. *Journal of Physics-Condensed Matter*, 18: S867–83.

Blalock, J. E. (1994). 'The syntax of immune-neuroendocrine communication'. *Immunology Today*, 15: 504–11.

Bonhoeffer, D. (1971). *Letters and Papers from Prison*. Enlarged Edition. London: SCM.

Brooke, J. H. (2001). 'The Wilberforce-Huxley debate: why did it happen?' *Science & Christian Belief*, 13: 127–41.

Brosius, J. (2005). 'Disparity, adaptation, exaptation, bookkeeping, and contingency at the genome level'. *Paleobiology*, 31 (Supplement to part 2): 1–16.

Brown, R. E. (1998). *The Death of the Messiah: From Gethsemane to the Grave*. New York: Doubleday.

Byl, J. (2004). *The Divine Challenge: on Matter, Mind, Math and Meaning*. Edinburgh: Banner of Truth Trust.

Carmeliet, P. & Tessier-Lavigne, M. (2005). 'Common mechanisms of nerve and blood vessel wiring'. *Nature*, 436: 193–200.

Carpenter, K. E & Springer, V. G. (2005). 'The center of the center of marine shorefish biodiversity: the Philippine Islands'. *Environmental Biology of Fishes*, 72: 467–80.

Clark, S. R. L. (1997). *Animals and their Moral Standing*. London: Routledge.

Clark, S. R. L. (1998). *God, Religion and Reality*. London: SPCK.

Clayton, P. & Schall, J. (eds.) (2007). *Practicing Science, Living Faith: Interviews with 12 Leading Scientists*. New York: Columbia University Press.

Climate Institute (2006). *Common Belief: Australia's Faith Communities on Climate Change*. Sydney: the Climate Institute.

Collar, N. J. & Stuart, S. N. (1985). *Threatened Birds of Africa and Related Islands: The ICBP/IUCN Red Data Book*. Series 3, volume 1. Cambridge: International Council for Bird Preservation and International Union for Conservation of Nature and Natural Resources.

Collins, F. (2006). *The Language of God*. New York: Free Press.

Conway Morris, S. (1985). 'The Middle Cambrian metazoan *Wiwaxia corrugata*

(Matthew) from the Burgess Shale and *Ogygopsis* Shale, British Columbia, Canada'. *Philosophical Transactions of the Royal Society of London* B, 307: 507–86.

Conway Morris, S. (1987). 'Cambrian enigmas'. *Geology Today*, 3: 88–92.

Conway Morris, S. (1991). Review in *Times Literary Supplement*, 4628: 6.

Cook-Deegan, R. (1994). *The Gene Wars*. New York: Norton.

Cooper, T. F., De'ath, G., Fabricius, K. E. & Lough, J. M. (2007). 'Declining coral calcification in massive Porites in two nearshore regions of the northern Great Barrier Reef'. *Global Change Biology*, 14: 1–10.

Coulson, C. A. (1958). *Science and the Idea of God*. Cambridge: Cambridge University Press.

Darwin, C. (1859). *The Origin of Species*. John Murray, London

Darwin, F. (1887). *The Life and Letters of Charles Darwin*. Volume 2. London: John Murray.

Dawkins, R. (1976). *The Selfish Gene*. Oxford: Oxford University Press.

Dawkins, R. (1986). *The Blind Watchmaker*. Oxford: Oxford University Press.

Dawkins, R. (2006). *The God Delusion*. New York: Houghton Mifflin.

Deutsch, D. (1985). 'Quantum theory, the Church-Turing Principle and the universal quantum computer'. *Proceedings of the Royal Society of London*, A, 400: 97–117.

DeWitt, C. B. (2000). 'Behemoth and batrachians in the eye of God: responsibility to other kinds in biblical perspective'. In *Christianity and Ecology*: 291–316. Hessel, D. T. & Ruether, R. R. (eds.). Cambridge, MA: Harvard University Press.

Diamond, J. (1995). 'Alone in a crowded universe'. In *Extraterrestrials: Where are They?*: 157–64. Zuckerman, B. & Hart, M. H. (eds.). Cambridge: Cambridge University Press.

Dobzhansky, T. (1973). 'Nothing in biology makes sense except in the light of evolution'. *American Biological Teacher*, 35: 125–29.

Feynman, R. P., Leighton, R. B. & Sands, M. (1993). *The Feynman Lectures on Physics*. Volume 1. Reading, MA: Addison Wesley.

Flieger, V. (2002). *Splintered Light: Logos and Language in Tolkien's World*. Kent, OH: Kent State University Press.

Foster, M. B. (1934). 'The Christian doctrine of creation and the rise of modern natural science'. *Mind*, 43: 446–68.

Gaston, K. and Spicer, J. (1998). *Biodiversity: an Introduction*. Oxford: Wiley-Blackwell.

Gray, P. M., Krause, B., Atema, J., Payne, R., Krumhansl, C. & Baptista, L. (2001). 'The music of nature and the nature of music'. *Science*, 291: 52–54.

Gould, S. J. (1990). *Wonderful Life: The Burgess Shale and the Nature of History*. New York: Norton.

Gould, S. J. (1999). *Rocks of Ages*. New York: Ballantine.

Hambler, C. (2004). *Conservation*. Cambridge: Cambridge University Press.

Haught, J. F. (2004). *Deeper Than Darwin: The Prospect for Religion in the Age of Evolution*. Boulder, CO: Westview Press.

Haynes, R. (1982). *The Society for Psychical Research 1882–1982: A History*. London: Macdonald.

Helm, P. (1987). *Objective Knowledge*. Leicester: IVP.

Hookyaas, R. (1960). *The Christian Approach in Teaching Science*. London: Tyndale

Press.

Hookyaas, R. (1971). *Religion and the Rise of Modern Science.* Edinburgh: Scottish Academic Press.

Hughes, G. W. (1985). *God of Surprises.* London: Darton Longman Todd.

IUCN (2001). *IUCN Red List Categories and Criteria: Version 3.1.* IUCN Species Survival Commission: IUCN, Gland, Switzerland and Cambridge, UK.

Jablonka, E. & Lamb, M. J. (2006). *Evolution in Four Dimensions: Genetic, Epigenetic, Behavioral and Symbolic Variation in the History of Life.* Boston, MA: MIT Press.

Jasanoff, S. (2007). 'Technologies of Humility'. *Nature,* 450: 33.

Jeeves, M. A. (2004). 'How free is free? Reflections on the neuropsychology of thought and action'. *Science & Christian Belief,* 16: 101–22.

Jeeves, M. A. & Berry, R. J. (1998). *Science, Life and Christian Belief.* Leicester: Apollos.

Jones, D. G. (1984). *Brave New People.* Leicester: IVP.

Jones, D. G. (1987). *Manufacturing Humans.* Leicester: IVP.

Jones, D. G. (1999). *Valuing People. Human Value in a World of Medical Technology.* Exeter: Paternoster.

Jones, D. G. (2000, 2009). *Speaking for the Dead. Cadavers in Biology and Medicine.* Aldershot: Ashgate.

Jones, D. G. (2001). *Clones: the Clowns of Technology?* Exeter: Paternoster.

Jones, D. G. (2005). *Designers of the Future.* Oxford: Monarch.

Jones, D. G. (2007). *Bioethics.* Hindmarsh, South Australia: ATF Press.

Kidner, D. (1967). *Genesis,* Tyndale Old Testament Commentaries. London: IVP.

Kuhse, H. & Singer, P. (1985). *Should the Baby Live?* Oxford: Oxford University Press.

Landauer, R. (1996). 'The physical nature of information'. *Physics Letters A,* 217: 188–93.

Lewis, C. S. (1947). *Miracles.* London: Geoffrey Bles.

Lewis, C. S. (1955). *Surprised by Joy: The Shape of my Early Life.* London: Geoffrey Bles.

Lewis, C. S. (1967). *Christian Reflections.* Hooper, W. (ed.). Grand Rapids, MI: Eerdmans.

Lewis, C. S. (1977). *Mere Christianity.* London: Fount (originally published by Geoffrey Bles, 1942).

Lucas, E. (2001). *Can we Believe Genesis Today?* Leicester: IVP.

McGrath, A. E. (1998). *The Foundations of Dialogue in Science and Religion.* Oxford: Blackwell.

McGrath, A. E. (2001–2003). *A Scientific Theology.* 3 volumes. Edinburgh: T&T Clark.

McGrath, A. E. (2005). *Dawkins' God. Genes, Memes and the Meaning of Life.* Oxford: Blackwell.

McGrath, A. E. (2007). *The Dawkins Delusion.* London: SPCK.

McGrath, A. E. (2008). *The Open Secret: a New Vision for Natural Theology.* Oxford: Blackwell.

MacKay, D. M. (1960). *Science and Christian Faith Today.* London: Falcon. (Reprinted in *Real Science, Real Faith*: 196–218. Berry, R. J. (ed.). Crowborough: Monarch).

MacKay, D. M. (1974). *The Clockwork Image.* Leicester: IVP. (Reprinted as a

'Christian Classic', 1997.)

MacKay, D. M. (1988). *The Open Mind*, edited by Tinker, M. Leicester: IVP

Mace, G. M., Collar, N. J., Gaston, K. J., Hilton-Taylor, C., Akçakaya, H. R., Leader-Williams, N., Milner-Gulland, E. J. & Stuart, S. N., 2008. 'Quantification of extinction risk: the background to IUCN's system for classifying threatened species'. *Conservation Biology*, 22: 1424–1442.

Mace, G. M. & Lande, R. (1991). 'Assessing extinction threats: toward a re-evaluation of IUCN threatened species categories'. *Conservation Biology* 5: 148–57.

Medawar, P. (1984). *The Limits of Science*. Oxford: Oxford University Press.

Midgley, M. (1992). *Science as Salvation*. London: Routledge.

Miller, K. (1999). *Finding Darwin's God. A Scientist's Search for Common Ground Between God and Evolution*. New York: HarperCollins.

Moore, A. (1889). 'The Christian doctrine of God'. In *Lux Mundi*: 57–109. Gore, C. (ed.). London: John Murray.

Moore, G. (1996). *Believing in God. A Philosophical Essay*. Edinburgh: T&T Clark.

Morison, F. (1930). *Who Moved the Stone?* London: Faber & Faber.

Murphy, R. E. (1992). *Ecclesiastes. Word Bible Commentary, 23A*: lxix. Dallas, TX: Word Books.

Myers, D. (2008). *A Friendly Letter to Skeptics and Atheists*. San Francisco: Jossey Bass/Wiley.

Myers, D. & Jeeves, M. A. (2002). *Psychology Through the Eyes of Faith*, 2nd ed. San Francisco: HarperOne.

Myers, D. & Scanzoni, L. D. (2007). *What God Has Joined Together. The Christian Case for Gay Marriage*. San Francisco: Harper.

Noble, D. (2006). *The Music of Life*. Oxford: Oxford University Press.

Norton, B. (2005). *Sustainability*. Chicago: Chicago University Press.

Oldroyd, D. (2005). 'Evolution, paleontology and metaphysics'. In *Darwinism and Philosophy*: 30–57. Hösle, V. & Illies, C. (eds.). Notre Dame, IN: University of Notre Dame Press.

Peacocke, A. R. (2004). *Evolution: the Disguised Friend of Faith?* West Conshohocken, PA: Templeton Foundation Press.

Pippard, A. B. (1987). 'The Cavendish Laboratory'. *European Journal of Physics*, 8: 231–35.

Polkinghorne, J. (1996). *Scientists as Theologians*. London: SPCK.

Polkinghorne, J. (1998a). *Belief in God in an Age of Science*. New Haven: Yale University Press.

Polkinghorne, J. (1998b). *Science and Theology: An Introduction*. London: SPCK.

Ridley, M. (1985). *The Problems of Evolution*. Oxford: Oxford University Press.

Roberts, J. H. & Turner, J. (2000). *The Sacred and the Secular University*. Princeton, NJ: Princeton University Press.

Ruse, M. (2001). *Can a Darwinian be a Christian?* Cambridge: Cambridge University Press.

Ruse, M. (2004). *Darwin and Design: Does Evolution Have a Purpose?* Cambridge, MA: Harvard University Press.

Russell, C. (1991). 'Surprised by science'. In *Real Science, Real Faith*: 11–21. Berry, R. J. (ed.). Crowborough: Monarch.

Salvetat, J-P. *et al.* (1999). 'Elastic and shear moduli of single-walled carbon nanotube ropes'. *Physical Review Letters*, 82: 944–47.

Simpson, G. G. (1964). 'The nonprevalence of humanoids'. *Science*, 143: 769–75.

Sober, E. & Wilson, D. S. (1999). *Unto Others: Evolution and Psychology of Unselfish Behavior.* Cambridge MA: Harvard University Press.

Spencer, N. & White, R. (2007). *Christianity, Climate Change and Sustainable Living.* London: SPCK.

Steane, A. M. (1996). 'Error connecting codes in quantum theory'. *Physical Review Letters*, 77: 793–97.

Stott, J. R. W. (1978). *Christian Counter-Culture: the Message of the Sermon on the Mount.* Leicester: IVP.

Stuart, S. N. (1986). *Conservation of Cameroon Montane Forests.* Cambridge: International Council for Bird Preservation.

Stuart, S. N., Archibald, G. W., Ball, J., Berry, R. J., Emmerich, S. D., Evans, D. M., Flenley, J. R., Gaston, K. J., Given, D. R., Gosler, A. G., Harris, P., Houghton, J., Lindquist, E. D., Mahan, D. C., Morecroft, M. D., Moyer, D. C., Murdiyarso, D., Musiti, B. W. W., Nicolson, C., Oteng-Yeboah, A., Plumptre, A. J., Prance, G., Ramachandra, V., Sale, J. B., Sheldon, J. K., Simiyu, S., Storey, R., Underhill, L. G., Vickery, J. & Whitten, T. (2005). 'Conservation theology for conservation biologists – a reply to David Orr'. *Conservation Biology*, 19: 1689–92.

Stuart, S. N., Chanson, J. S., Cox, N. A., Young, B. E., Rodrigues, A. S. L., Fischman, D. L. & Waller, R. W. (2004). 'Status and trends of amphibian declines and extinctions worldwide'. *Science*, 306: 1783–86.

Trigg, R. (1973). *Reason and Commitment.* Cambridge: Cambridge University Press.

Turing, A. M. (1937). 'On computable numbers, with an application to the Entschelungsproblem'. *Proceedings of the London Mathematical Society*, series 2, 42: 230–65.

Vanauken, S. (1980). *A Severe Mercy.* New York: HarperCollins.

Ward, K. (1996). *God, Chance and Necessity.* Oxford: Oneworld.

Wenham, J. (1984). *Easter Enigma: Do the Resurrection Stories Contradict One Another?* Exeter: Paternoster Press.

White, R. S. (1999). 'Drummond Hoyle Matthews'. *Biographical Memoirs of Fellows of the Royal Society*, 45: 275–94.

White, R. S. (2007). 'The Age of the Earth', Faraday Paper No. 8, available for download from www.faraday-institute.org

Wiens, R. C. (2002). 'Radiometric dating. A Christian perspective'. Available at www.asa3.org/ASA/resources/Wiens.html; see also the comprehensive website www.answersincreation.org

Wilkinson, D. (2002). *The Message of Creation.* Leicester: IVP.

Wilson, E. O. (2006). *The Creation. An Appeal to Save Life on Earth.* New York: W. W. Norton.

Wright, N. T. (2007a). 'The Faraday Lecture. Can a Scientist Belief in the Resurrection?' Available at
http://www.st-edmunds.cam.ac.uk/faraday/Lectures.php

Wright, N. T. (2007b). *Surprised by Hope.* London: SPCK.

Young, J. Z. (1951). *Doubt and Certainty in Science.* Oxford: Clarendon Press.

Index of Bible References

Index